HEROES OF SPACE

WHO CHANGED THE WORLD

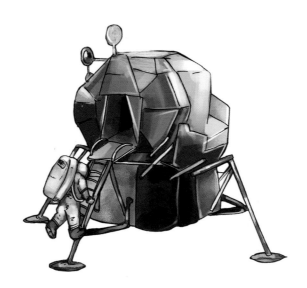

First edition for the United States and Canada published in 2019
by B.E.S. Publishing Co.

All inquiries should be addressed to:
B.E.S. Publishing Co.
250 Wireless Boulevard
Hauppauge, NY 11788
www.bes-publishing.com

ISBN: 978-1-4380-1201-8

Library of Congress Control No.: 2018959970

Conceived, designed, and produced by The Bright Press,
an imprint of The Quarto Group.
The Old Brewery, 6 Blundell Street,
London, N7 9BH, United Kingdom
T (0) 20 7700 6700 F (0) 20 7700 8066
www.QuartoKnows.com

Publisher: Mark Searle
Creative Director: James Evans
Managing Editor: Jacqui Sayers
Editor: Judith Chamberlain
Project Editor: Natalia Price-Cabrera
Art Director: Katherine Radcliffe
Design: Lyndsey Harwood and Geoff Borin

Date of Manufacture: December 2018
Manufactured by: Hung Hing Printing, Shenzhen, China

Printed in China

9 8 7 6 5 4 3 2 1

HEROES OF SPACE

WHO CHANGED THE WORLD

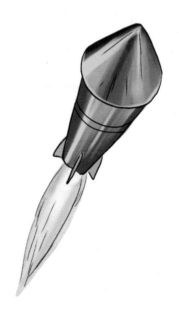

ILLUSTRATED BY CHARLI VINCE
CONSULTANT EDITOR EMILY SOHN

B.E.S.
PUBLISHING

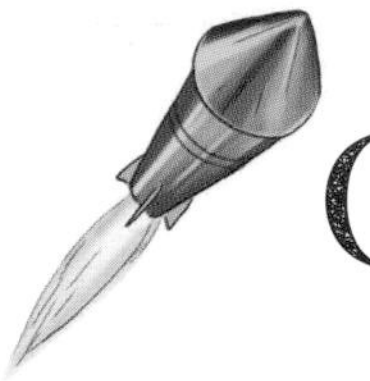

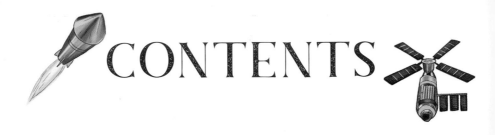

CONTENTS

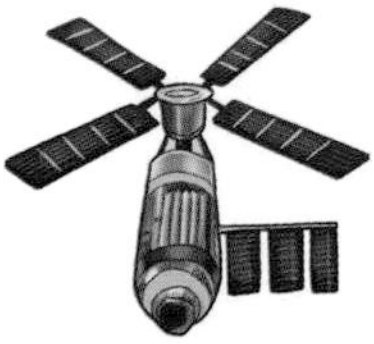

In Galileo's time, people thought that Earth was the center of the universe. This astronomer built powerful telescopes and used them to look into the night sky. There, he found clues about a different kind of universe: one where the planets move around the sun, where Jupiter has moons, and the sun has spots. His discoveries would forever change the way we think about space.

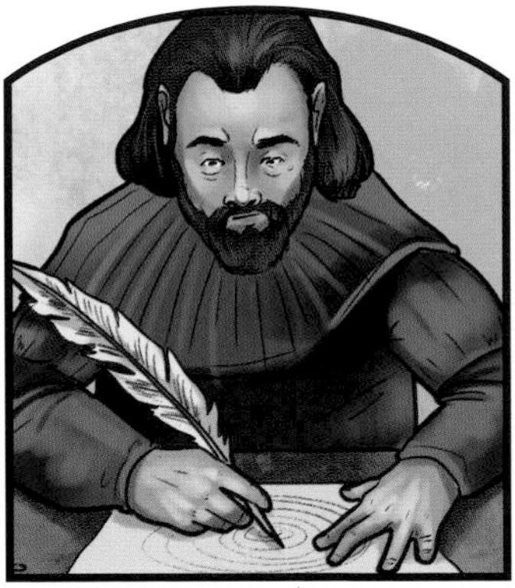

Henrietta figured out, for the first time, how to measure exact distances to the stars. After she died, Edwin used her findings to discover that there are other galaxies in the universe besides our Milky Way. Later, he discovered that the universe is expanding. It was a radical new concept that was only possible thanks to Henrietta and her work.

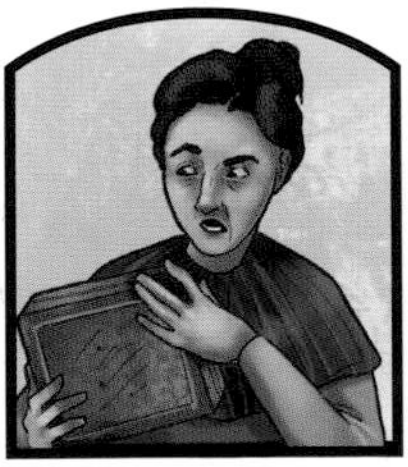

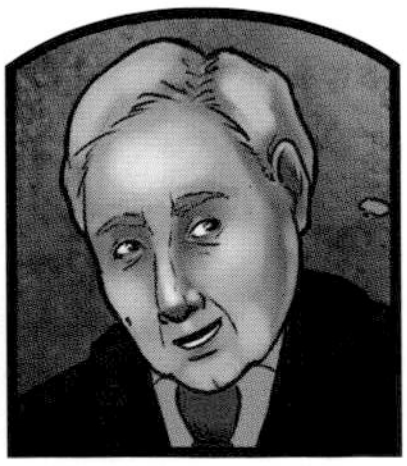

ROBERT H. GODDARD\dotfill30
American (1882–1945)

As a teenager, Robert dreamed of sending spacecraft to the stars. Eventually, he developed liquid-fueled rockets that traveled faster than the speed of sound. He also tested the first rockets to carry scientific instruments. His work paved the way for the development of rockets that would reach outer space. It was a major step into the era of space exploration.

SERGEI KOROLEV\dotfill42
Russian (1907–1966)

Sergei began his career as an airplane designer and later became a rocket designer. His work helped launch the Soviet space program. He contributed to many engineering landmarks, including the first satellite to orbit Earth and the first spacecraft to land on the moon. He also helped send the first dog and first person into orbit around Earth.

ANIMAL ASTRONAUTS\dotfill54

Fruit flies were the first animal astronauts to travel beyond Earth's atmosphere. That was in 1947. In the decades that followed, space travelers included monkeys, dogs, chimpanzees, spiders, fish, and turtles. Many of the first animals died on their journeys. Yet, more successful missions gave space agents the confidence to send humans into space.

YURI GAGARIN
Russian (1934–1968)

After proving himself as a pilot, Yuri was selected to be the first person to travel to space. At age 27, he spent 89 minutes in orbit on *Vostok 1*. He landed safely and became a hero. It was a big first. In the years to come, many astronauts would follow his lead. His flight was the beginning of human space exploration.

VALENTINA TERESHKOVA
Russian (1937–present)

Born into a poor family, Valentina studied hard and became a skydiving champion. Then, she volunteered for the space program. At age 26, she became the first woman to travel to space. Over three days, she orbited Earth 48 times, spending more time in space than anyone had before her. Although she was the first woman in space, she was definitely not the last.

THE APOLLO 11 CREW: NEIL ARMSTRONG, BUZZ ALDRIN & MICHAEL COLLINS
American (1930–2012; 1930–present; 1930–present)

Neil was a Navy pilot. Buzz and Michael flew with the U.S. Air Force. All three became NASA astronauts. In 1969, they traveled to the moon. Neil and Buzz became the first people to stand on its surface. 600 million people watched the moon landing live on TV. It was one small step for man and one giant leap for mankind.

JOHN W. YOUNG & ROBERT L. CRIPPEN
American (1930–2018; 1937–present)

As a NASA astronaut, John was the first person to fly around the moon by himself. And he was the ninth person to walk on the moon. Robert worked as support crew for many NASA missions. In 1981, the duo teamed up to pilot the first space shuttle—the *Columbia.* They orbited Earth 36 times. Through the space shuttle program, NASA would study and observe space for the next 30 years.

KOICHI WAKATA
Japanese (1963–present)

Koichi was five years old when Neil Armstrong and Buzz Aldrin first stepped on the moon. He dreamed of going to space and eventually he did. He became the first Japanese mission specialist, the first Japanese astronaut to help build the International Space Station (ISS), and the first Japanese commander of the ISS. While on the ISS, he circled Earth 3,000 times and collaborated with astronauts from around the world.

GALILEO GALILEI
(1564–1642)
THE IMPRISONED GENIUS

IN 1609, NEWS OF THE INVENTION OF A "SPYGLASS," WHICH MADE DISTANT OBJECTS APPEAR CLOSER, SPREAD THROUGH EUROPE.

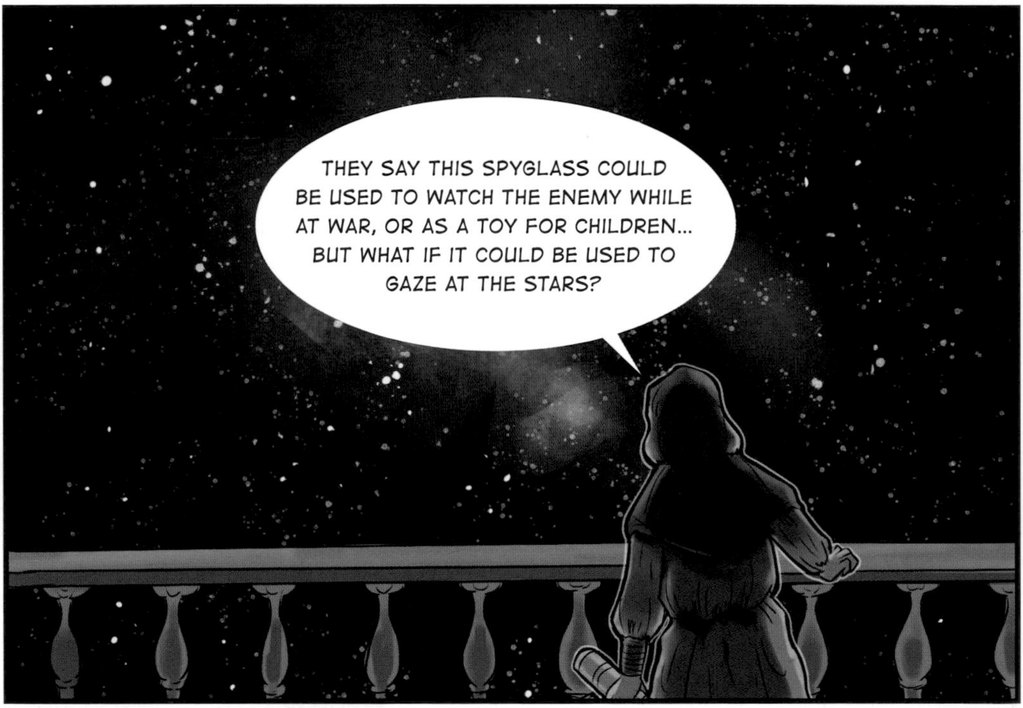
THEY SAY THIS SPYGLASS COULD BE USED TO WATCH THE ENEMY WHILE AT WAR, OR AS A TOY FOR CHILDREN... BUT WHAT IF IT COULD BE USED TO GAZE AT THE STARS?

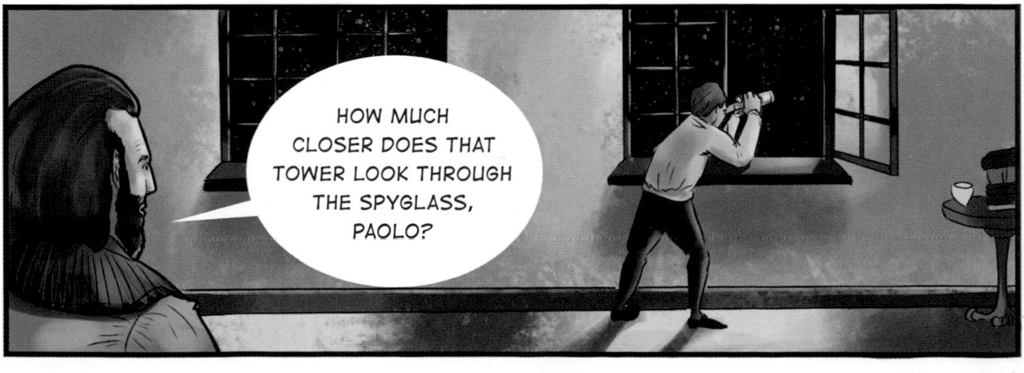
HOW MUCH CLOSER DOES THAT TOWER LOOK THROUGH THE SPYGLASS, PAOLO?

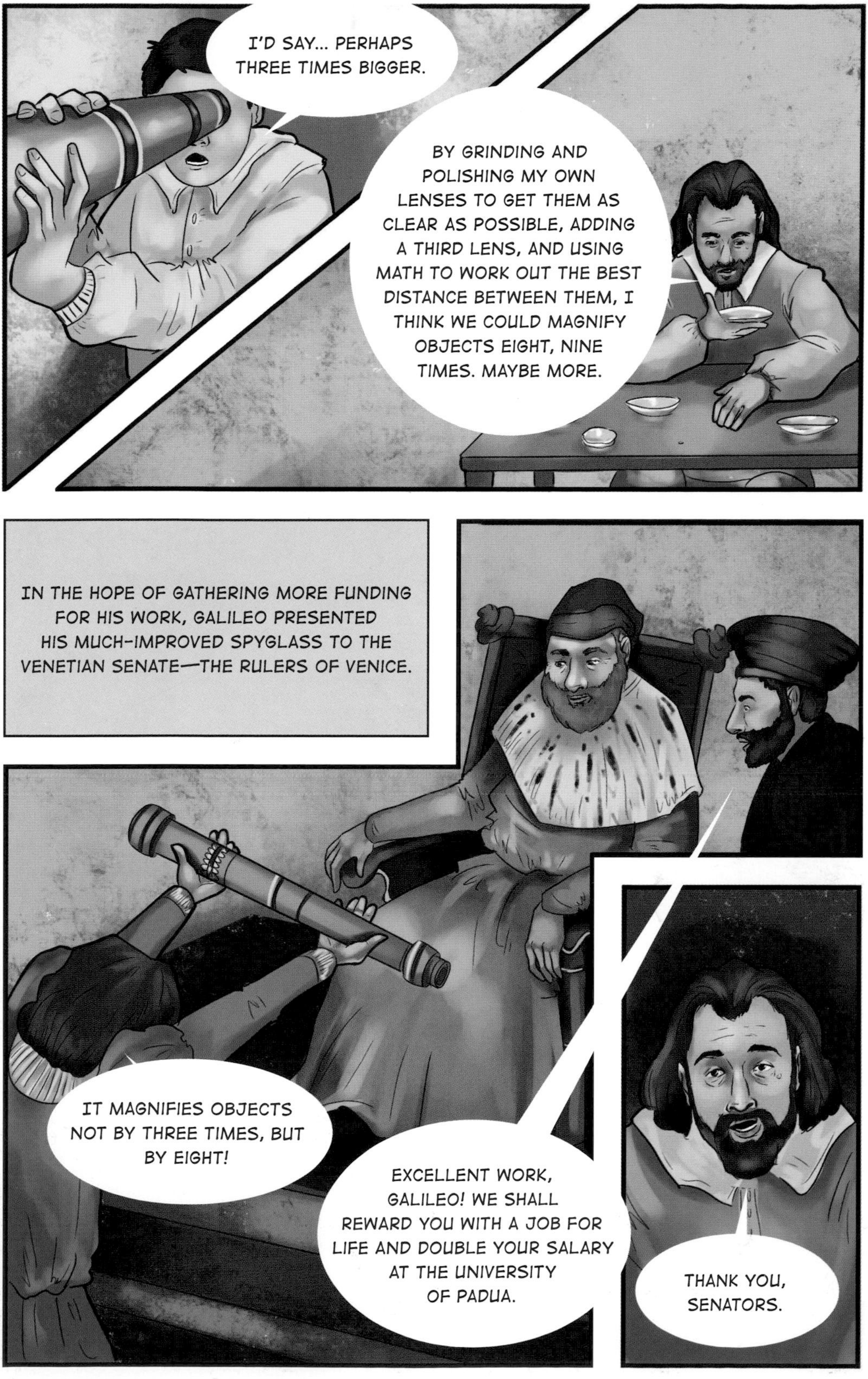
I'D SAY... PERHAPS THREE TIMES BIGGER.
BY GRINDING AND POLISHING MY OWN LENSES TO GET THEM AS CLEAR AS POSSIBLE, ADDING A THIRD LENS, AND USING MATH TO WORK OUT THE BEST DISTANCE BETWEEN THEM, I THINK WE COULD MAGNIFY OBJECTS EIGHT, NINE TIMES. MAYBE MORE.
IN THE HOPE OF GATHERING MORE FUNDING FOR HIS WORK, GALILEO PRESENTED HIS MUCH-IMPROVED SPYGLASS TO THE VENETIAN SENATE—THE RULERS OF VENICE.
IT MAGNIFIES OBJECTS NOT BY THREE TIMES, BUT BY EIGHT!
EXCELLENT WORK, GALILEO! WE SHALL REWARD YOU WITH A JOB FOR LIFE AND DOUBLE YOUR SALARY AT THE UNIVERSITY OF PADUA.
THANK YOU, SENATORS.

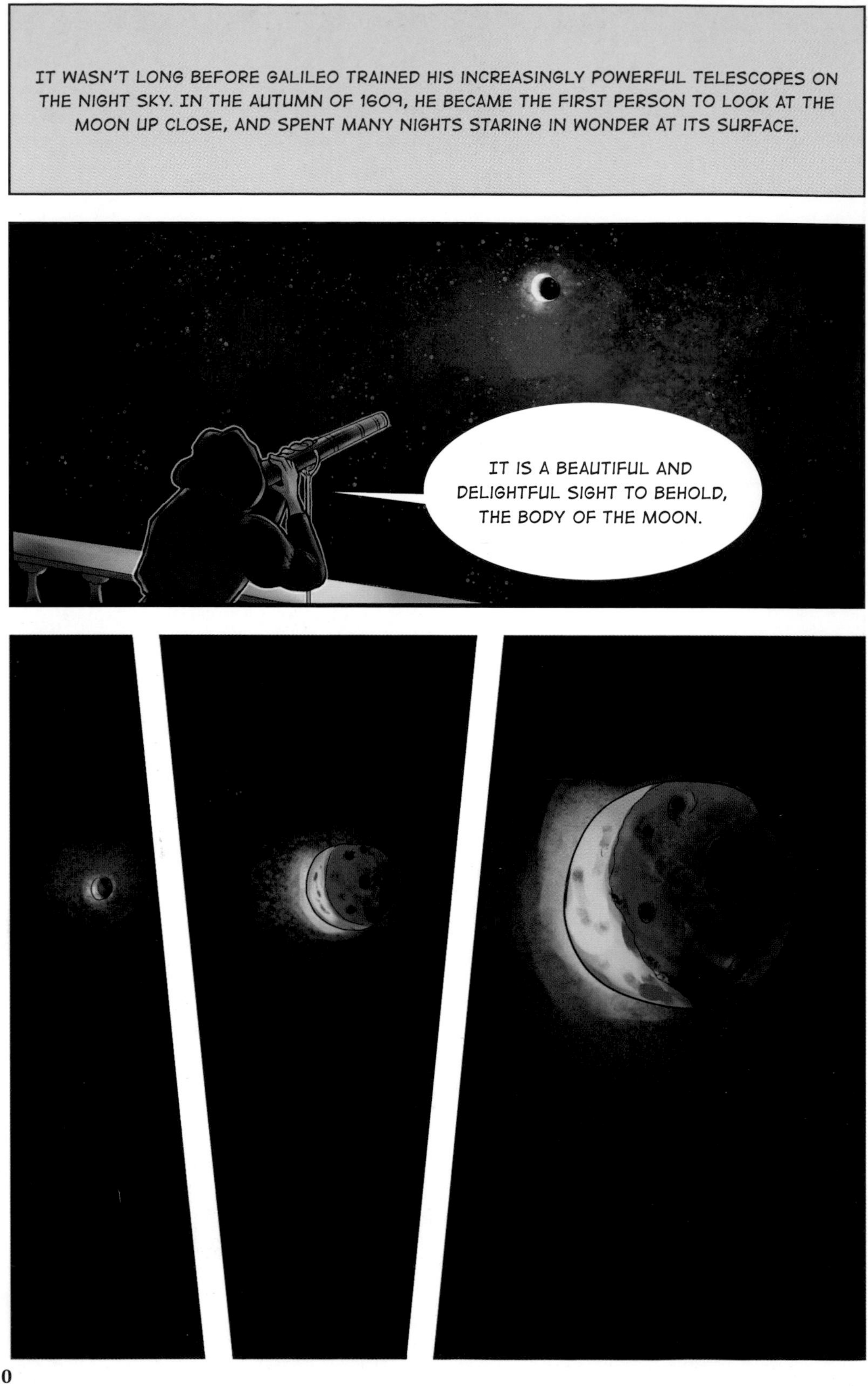
IT WASN'T LONG BEFORE GALILEO TRAINED HIS INCREASINGLY POWERFUL TELESCOPES ON THE NIGHT SKY. IN THE AUTUMN OF 1609, HE BECAME THE FIRST PERSON TO LOOK AT THE MOON UP CLOSE, AND SPENT MANY NIGHTS STARING IN WONDER AT ITS SURFACE.
IT IS A BEAUTIFUL AND DELIGHTFUL SIGHT TO BEHOLD, THE BODY OF THE MOON.

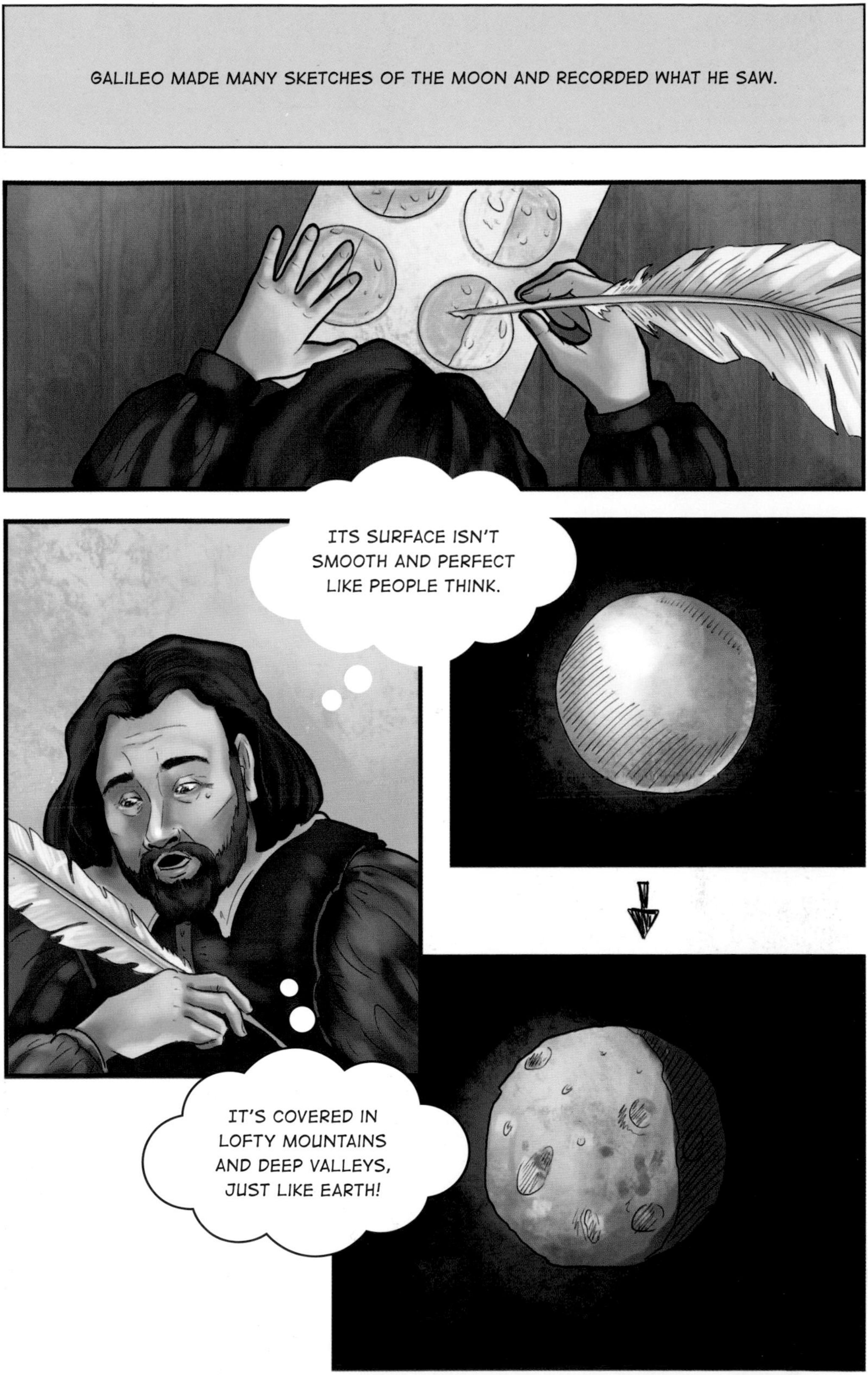
GALILEO MADE MANY SKETCHES OF THE MOON AND RECORDED WHAT HE SAW.
ITS SURFACE ISN'T SMOOTH AND PERFECT LIKE PEOPLE THINK.
IT'S COVERED IN LOFTY MOUNTAINS AND DEEP VALLEYS, JUST LIKE EARTH!

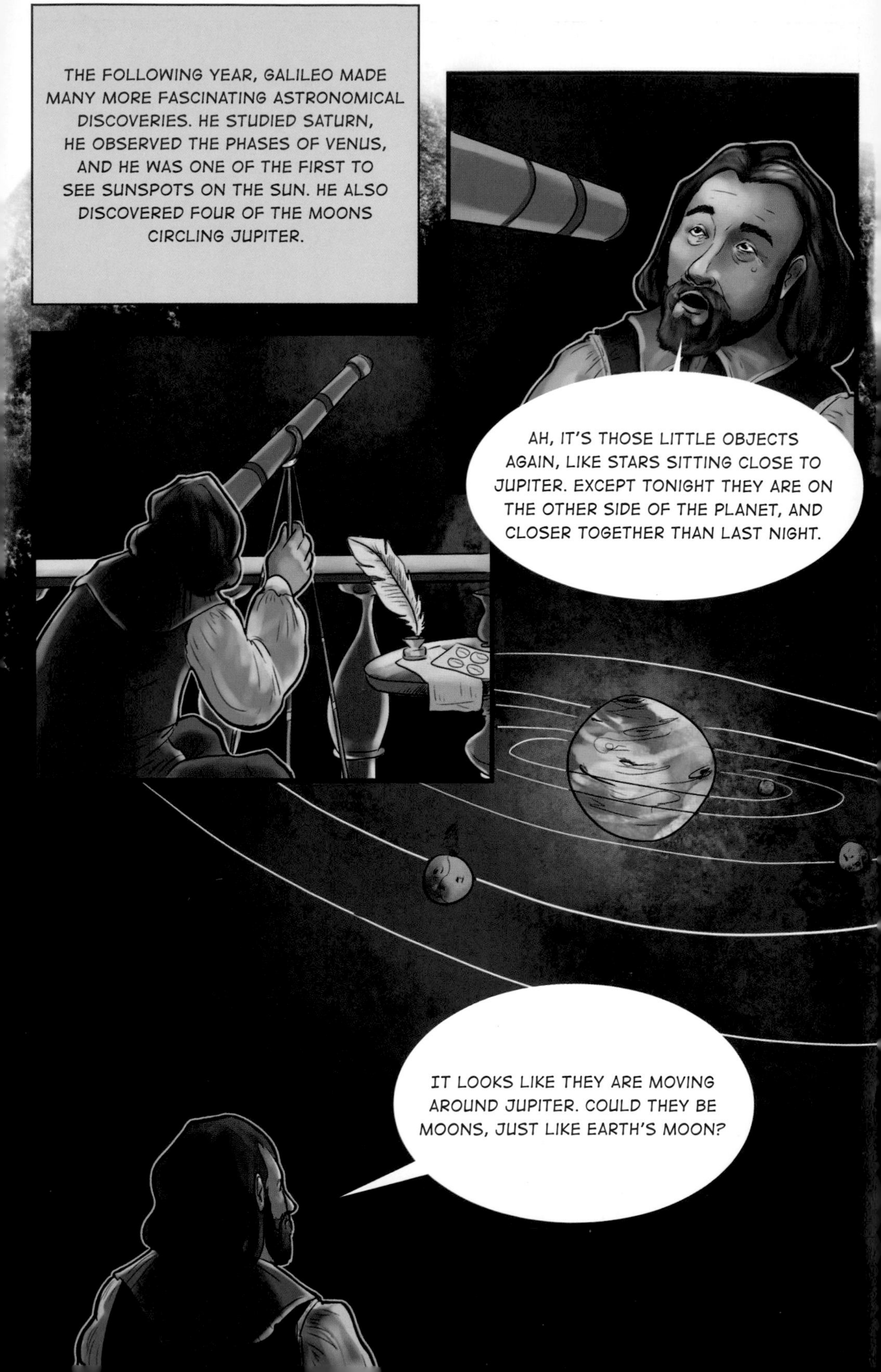
THE FOLLOWING YEAR, GALILEO MADE MANY MORE FASCINATING ASTRONOMICAL DISCOVERIES. HE STUDIED SATURN, HE OBSERVED THE PHASES OF VENUS, AND HE WAS ONE OF THE FIRST TO SEE SUNSPOTS ON THE SUN. HE ALSO DISCOVERED FOUR OF THE MOONS CIRCLING JUPITER.
AH, IT'S THOSE LITTLE OBJECTS AGAIN, LIKE STARS SITTING CLOSE TO JUPITER. EXCEPT TONIGHT THEY ARE ON THE OTHER SIDE OF THE PLANET, AND CLOSER TOGETHER THAN LAST NIGHT.
IT LOOKS LIKE THEY ARE MOVING AROUND JUPITER. COULD THEY BE MOONS, JUST LIKE EARTH'S MOON?

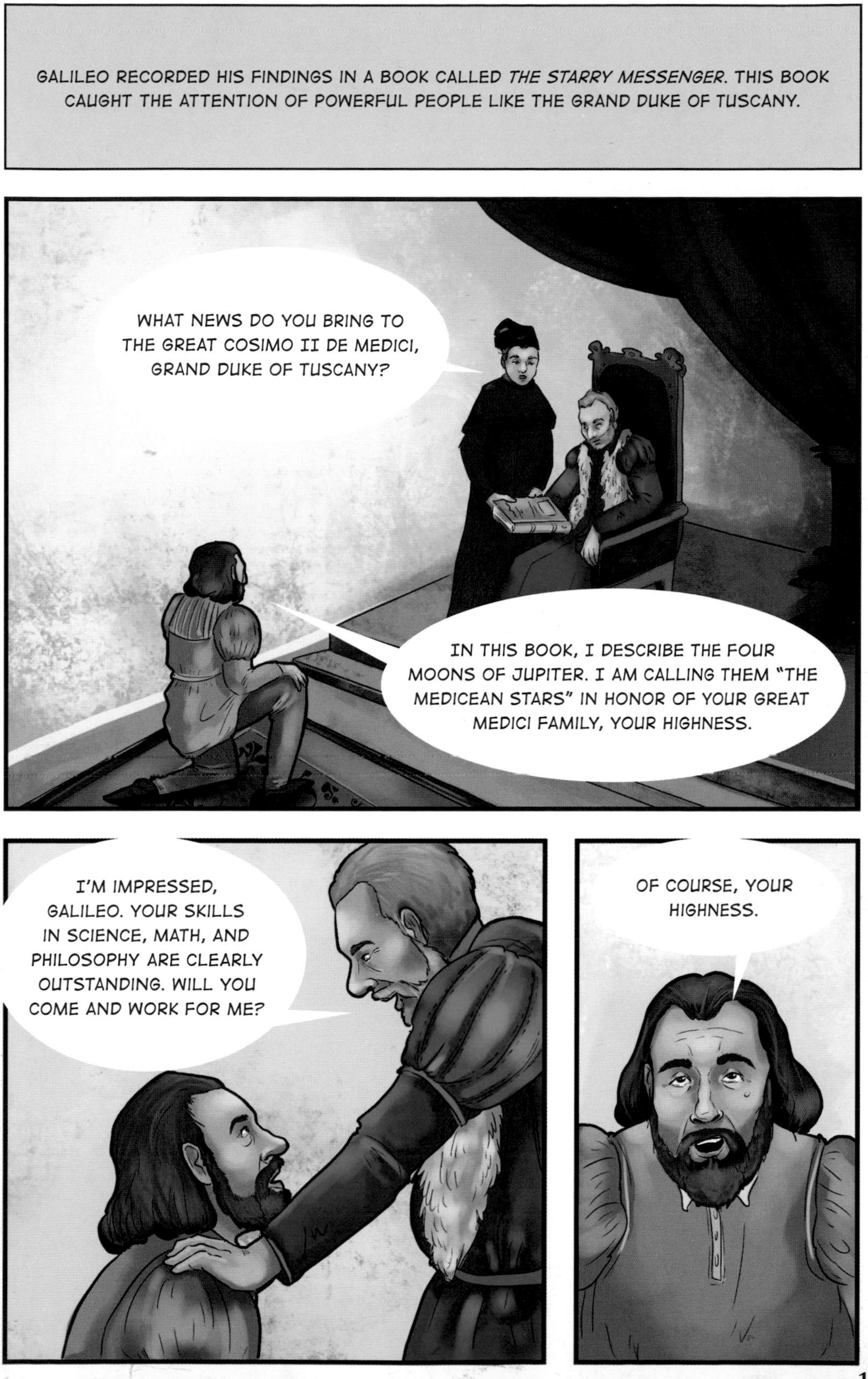
GALILEO RECORDED HIS FINDINGS IN A BOOK CALLED *THE STARRY MESSENGER*. THIS BOOK CAUGHT THE ATTENTION OF POWERFUL PEOPLE LIKE THE GRAND DUKE OF TUSCANY.
WHAT NEWS DO YOU BRING TO THE GREAT COSIMO II DE MEDICI, GRAND DUKE OF TUSCANY?
IN THIS BOOK, I DESCRIBE THE FOUR MOONS OF JUPITER. I AM CALLING THEM "THE MEDICEAN STARS" IN HONOR OF YOUR GREAT MEDICI FAMILY, YOUR HIGHNESS.
I'M IMPRESSED, GALILEO. YOUR SKILLS IN SCIENCE, MATH, AND PHILOSOPHY ARE CLEARLY OUTSTANDING. WILL YOU COME AND WORK FOR ME?
OF COURSE, YOUR HIGHNESS.

THE CATHOLIC CHURCH TAUGHT ITS FOLLOWERS THAT EARTH LAY AT THE CENTER OF THE UNIVERSE, AND THAT THE HEAVENS REVOLVED AROUND IT. BUT GALILEO KEPT SPOTTING NEW THINGS IN THE NIGHT SKY THAT RAISED DOUBTS OVER THE CHURCH'S TEACHINGS.

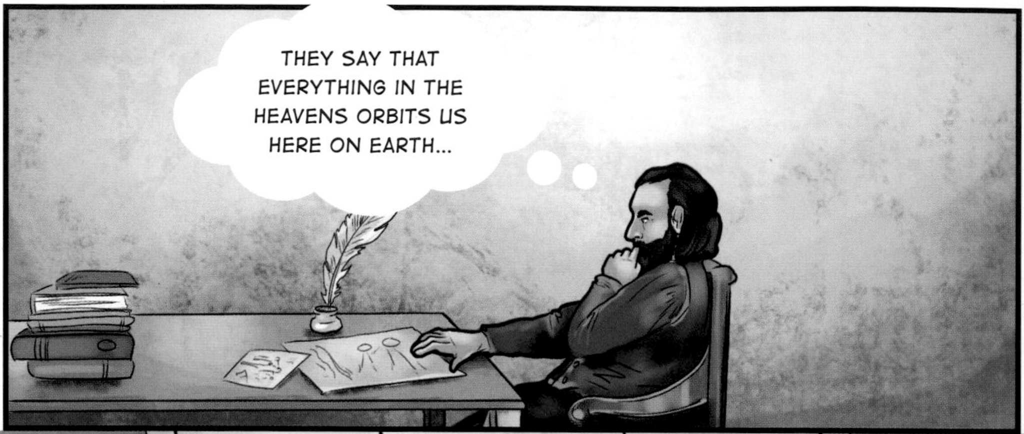
THEY SAY THAT EVERYTHING IN THE HEAVENS ORBITS US HERE ON EARTH...

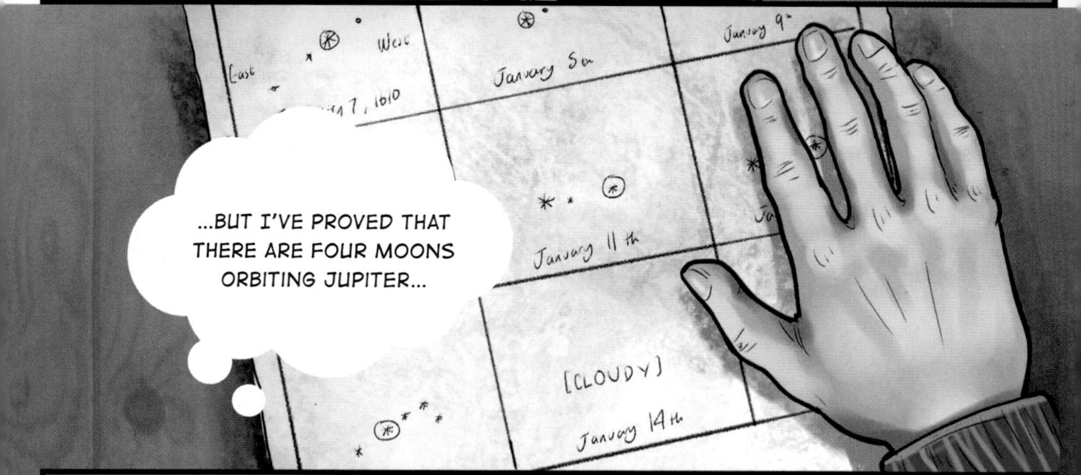
...BUT I'VE PROVED THAT THERE ARE FOUR MOONS ORBITING JUPITER...
January 11th
[CLOUDY]
January 14th

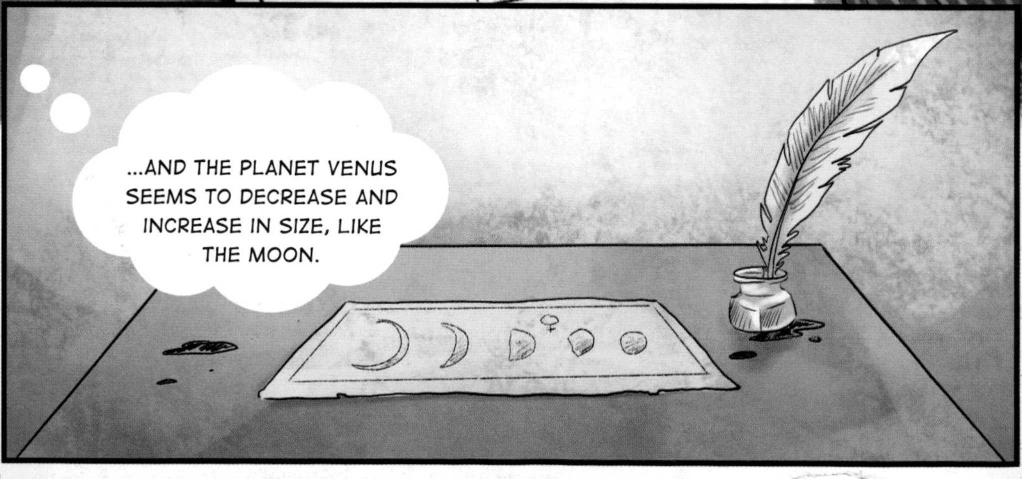
...AND THE PLANET VENUS SEEMS TO DECREASE AND INCREASE IN SIZE, LIKE THE MOON.

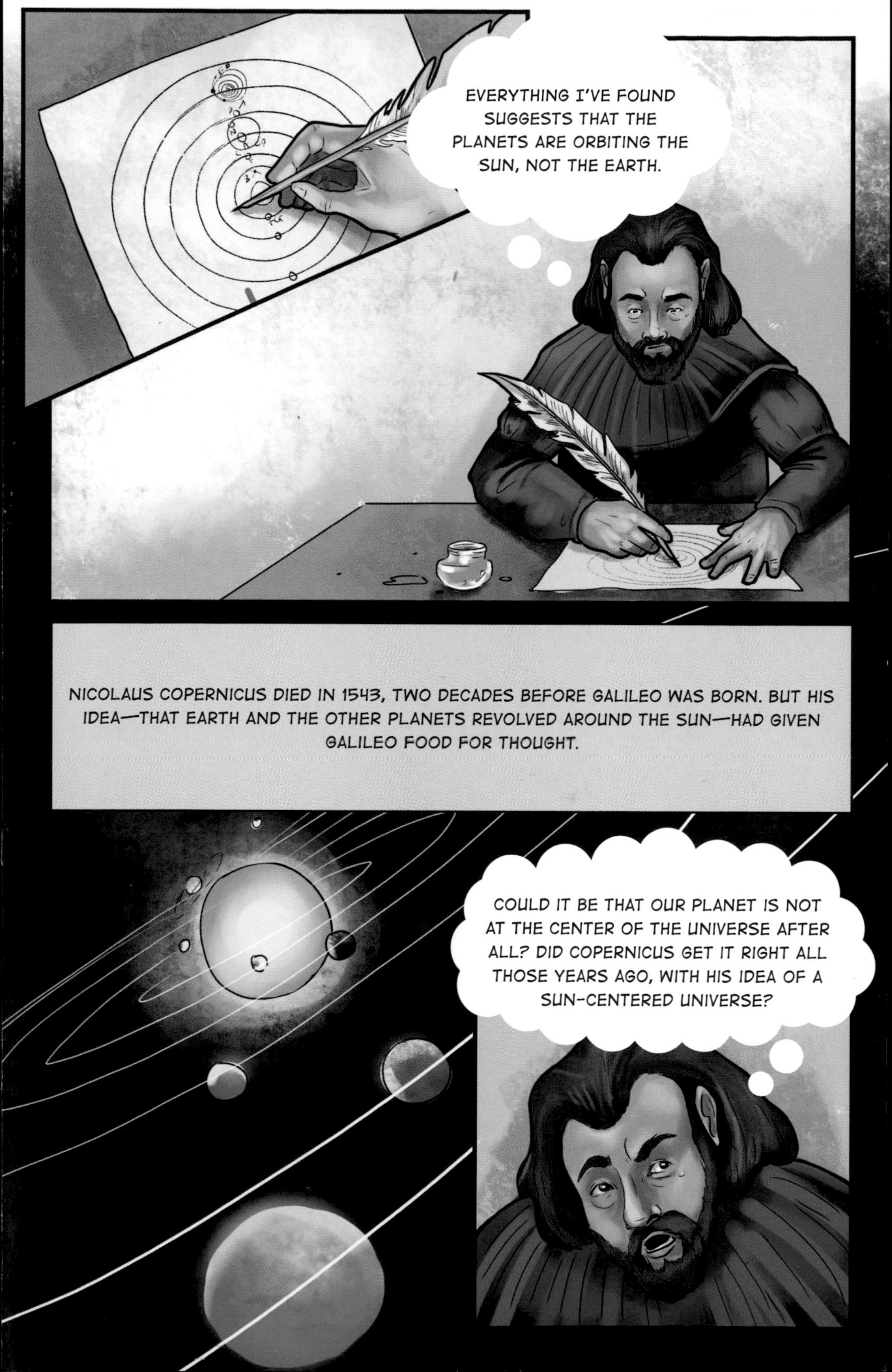
EVERYTHING I'VE FOUND SUGGESTS THAT THE PLANETS ARE ORBITING THE SUN, NOT THE EARTH.
NICOLAUS COPERNICUS DIED IN 1543, TWO DECADES BEFORE GALILEO WAS BORN. BUT HIS IDEA—THAT EARTH AND THE OTHER PLANETS REVOLVED AROUND THE SUN—HAD GIVEN GALILEO FOOD FOR THOUGHT.
COULD IT BE THAT OUR PLANET IS NOT AT THE CENTER OF THE UNIVERSE AFTER ALL? DID COPERNICUS GET IT RIGHT ALL THOSE YEARS AGO, WITH HIS IDEA OF A SUN-CENTERED UNIVERSE?

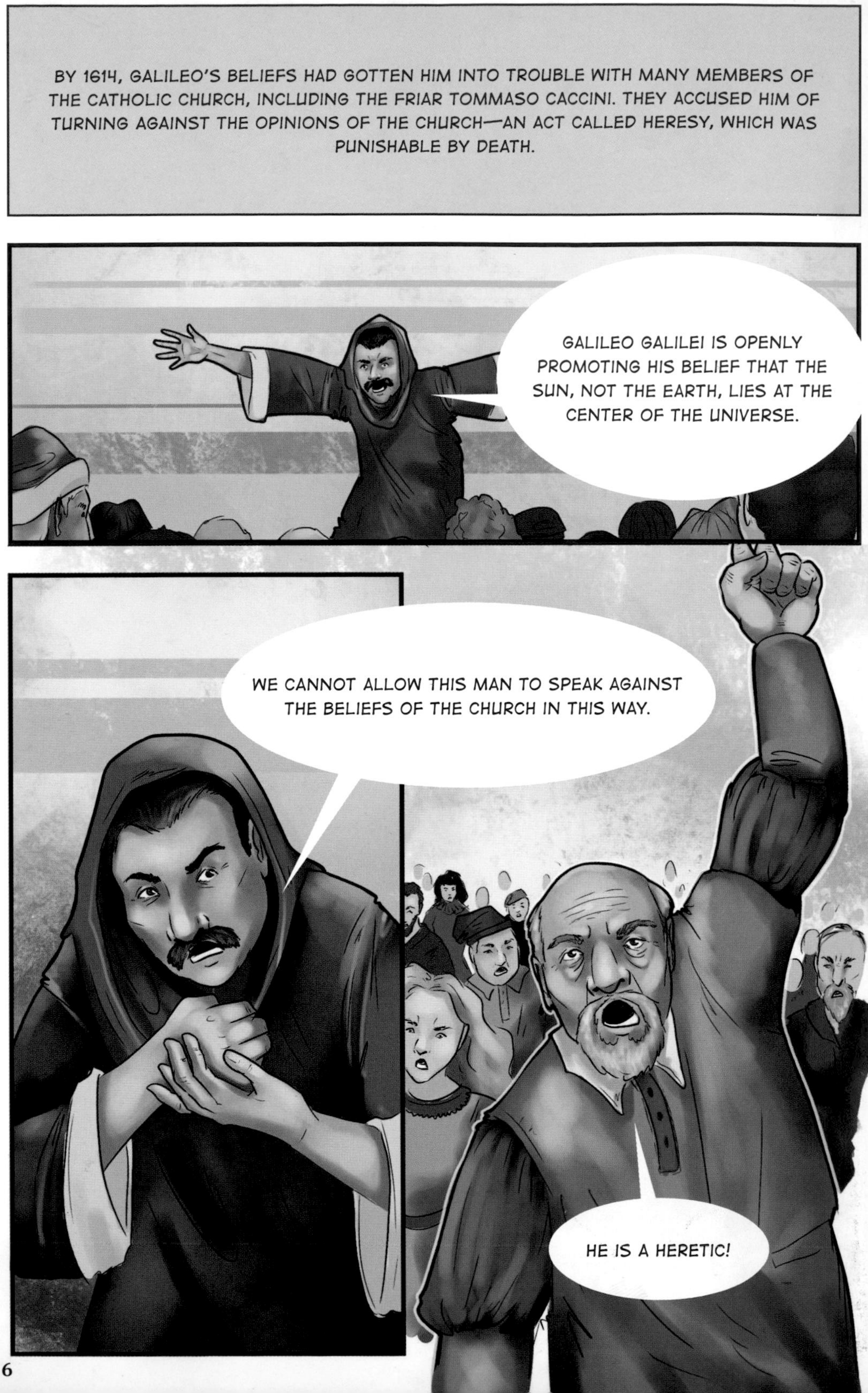
BY 1614, GALILEO'S BELIEFS HAD GOTTEN HIM INTO TROUBLE WITH MANY MEMBERS OF THE CATHOLIC CHURCH, INCLUDING THE FRIAR TOMMASO CACCINI. THEY ACCUSED HIM OF TURNING AGAINST THE OPINIONS OF THE CHURCH—AN ACT CALLED HERESY, WHICH WAS PUNISHABLE BY DEATH.
GALILEO GALILEI IS OPENLY PROMOTING HIS BELIEF THAT THE SUN, NOT THE EARTH, LIES AT THE CENTER OF THE UNIVERSE.
WE CANNOT ALLOW THIS MAN TO SPEAK AGAINST THE BELIEFS OF THE CHURCH IN THIS WAY.
HE IS A HERETIC!

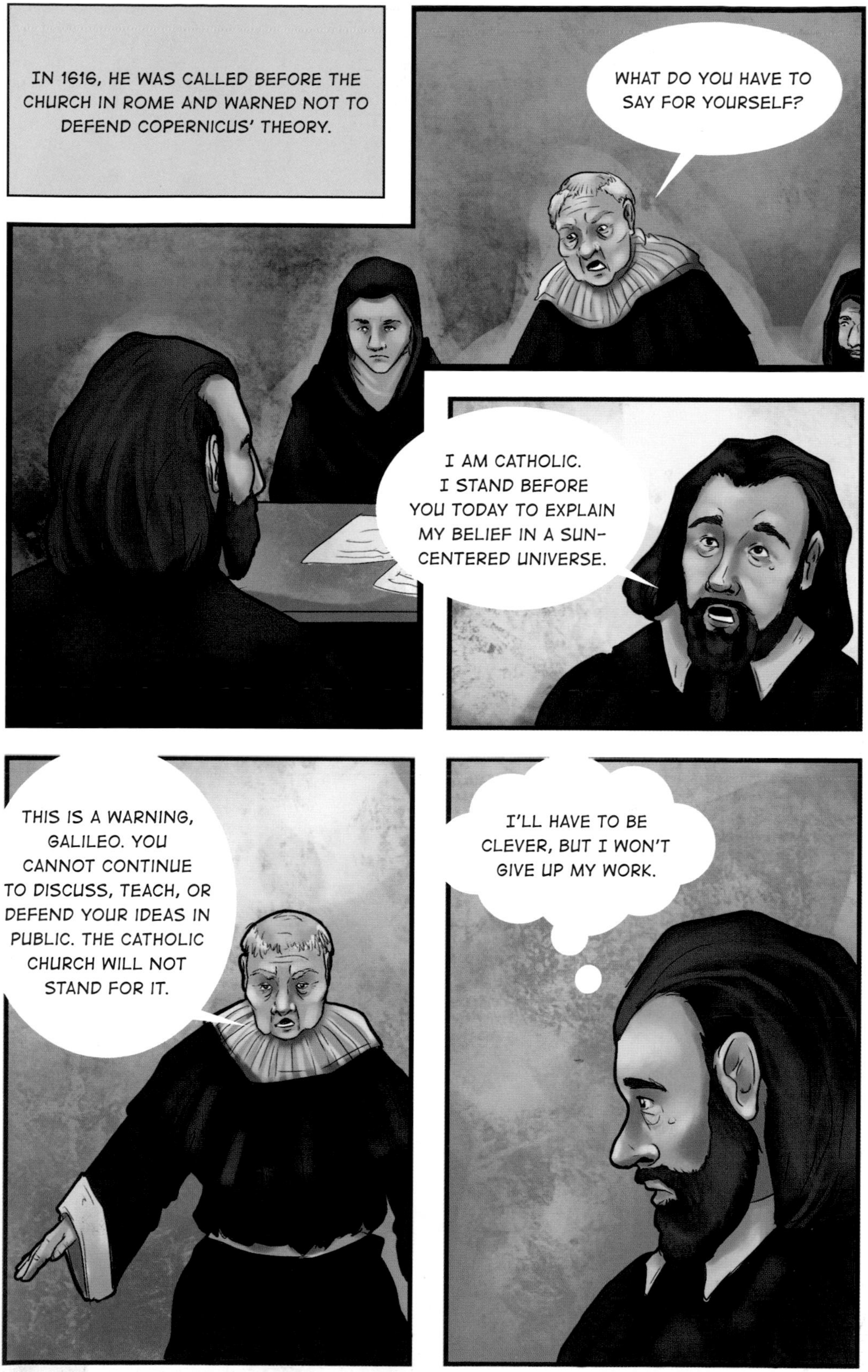
IN 1616, HE WAS CALLED BEFORE THE CHURCH IN ROME AND WARNED NOT TO DEFEND COPERNICUS' THEORY.
WHAT DO YOU HAVE TO SAY FOR YOURSELF?
I AM CATHOLIC. I STAND BEFORE YOU TODAY TO EXPLAIN MY BELIEF IN A SUN-CENTERED UNIVERSE.
THIS IS A WARNING, GALILEO. YOU CANNOT CONTINUE TO DISCUSS, TEACH, OR DEFEND YOUR IDEAS IN PUBLIC. THE CATHOLIC CHURCH WILL NOT STAND FOR IT.
I'LL HAVE TO BE CLEVER, BUT I WON'T GIVE UP MY WORK.

GALILEO, ALTHOUGH A FAITHFUL CATHOLIC, DIDN'T HEED THE CHURCH'S WARNING FOR THAT LONG. IN 1632, HE PUBLISHED A BOOK THAT EXPLAINED HIS BELIEF IN A SUN-CENTERED UNIVERSE. HE WAS SUMMONED TO ROME AND PUT ON TRIAL BY THE INQUISITION—A GROUP OF PEOPLE WHO PUNISHED HERESY AGAINST THE CATHOLIC CHURCH.

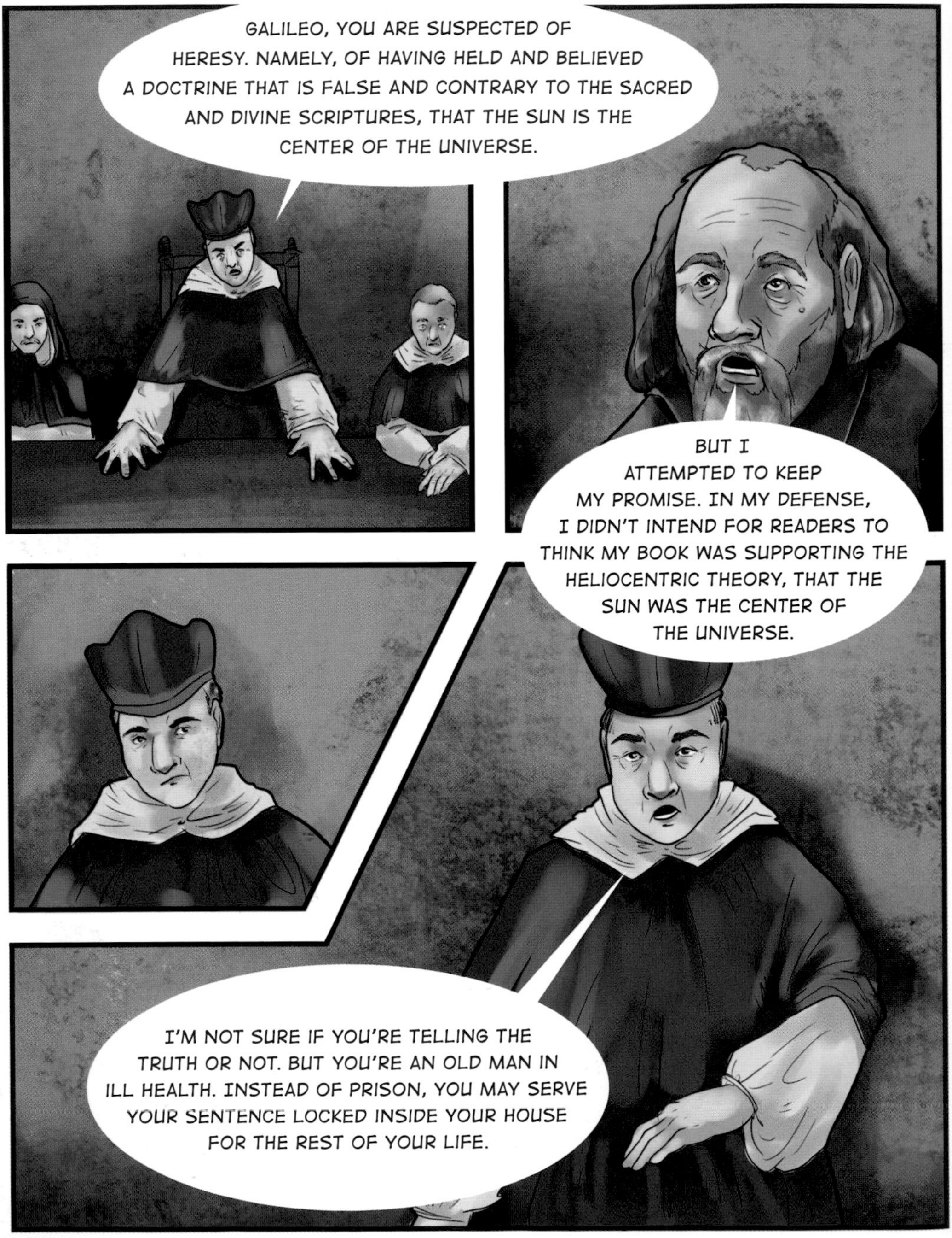
GALILEO, YOU ARE SUSPECTED OF HERESY. NAMELY, OF HAVING HELD AND BELIEVED A DOCTRINE THAT IS FALSE AND CONTRARY TO THE SACRED AND DIVINE SCRIPTURES, THAT THE SUN IS THE CENTER OF THE UNIVERSE.
BUT I ATTEMPTED TO KEEP MY PROMISE. IN MY DEFENSE, I DIDN'T INTEND FOR READERS TO THINK MY BOOK WAS SUPPORTING THE HELIOCENTRIC THEORY, THAT THE SUN WAS THE CENTER OF THE UNIVERSE.
I'M NOT SURE IF YOU'RE TELLING THE TRUTH OR NOT. BUT YOU'RE AN OLD MAN IN ILL HEALTH. INSTEAD OF PRISON, YOU MAY SERVE YOUR SENTENCE LOCKED INSIDE YOUR HOUSE FOR THE REST OF YOUR LIFE.

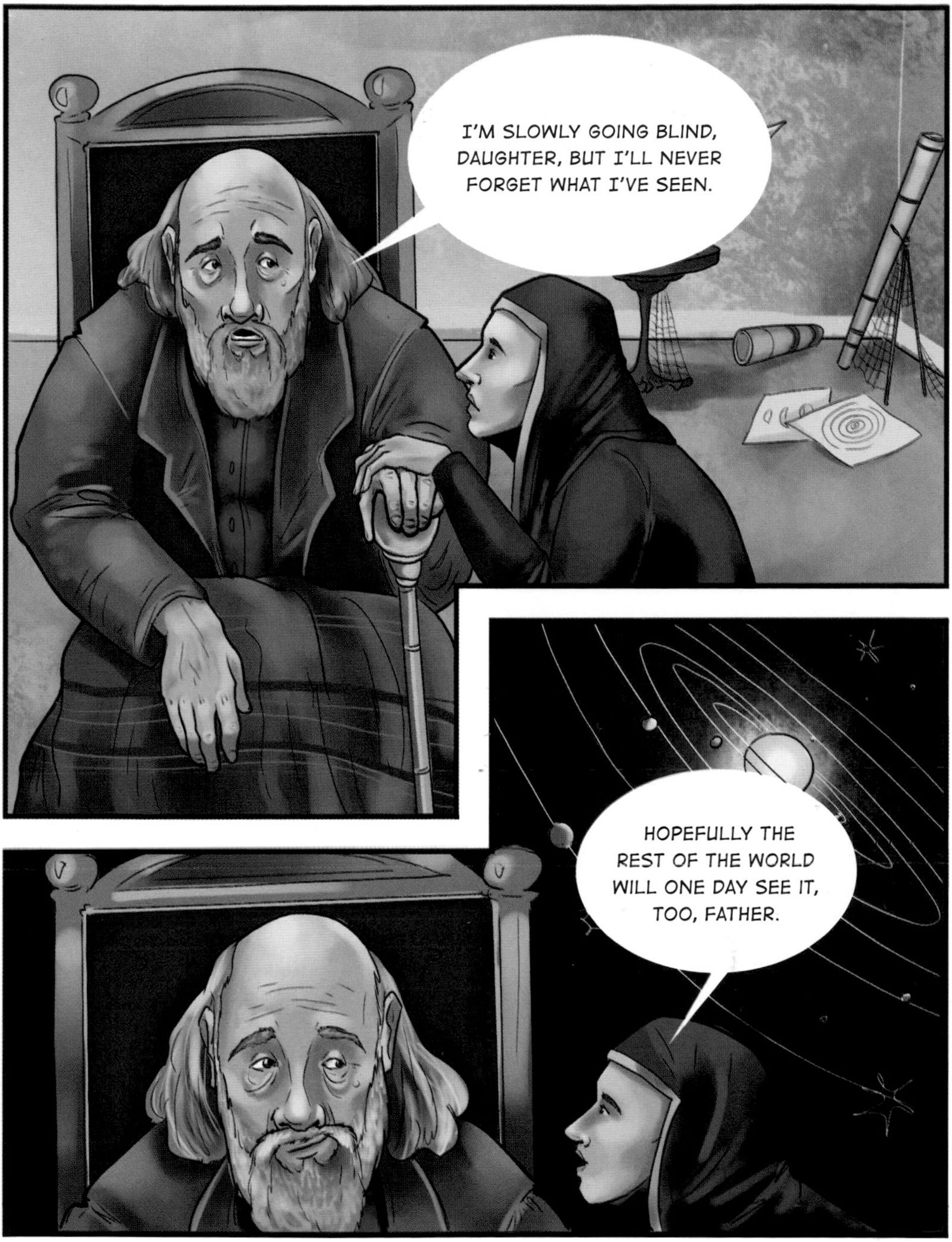
I'M SLOWLY GOING BLIND, DAUGHTER, BUT I'LL NEVER FORGET WHAT I'VE SEEN.
HOPEFULLY THE REST OF THE WORLD WILL ONE DAY SEE IT, TOO, FATHER.

AMAZINGLY, IT WASN'T UNTIL 1992—350 YEARS AFTER HIS DEATH—THAT THE CATHOLIC CHURCH ACKNOWLEDGED GALILEO'S THEORY TO BE CORRECT AND THAT HE HAD BEEN WRONGLY PUNISHED. BY THEN, HIS FINDINGS HAD ALREADY PAVED THE WAY FOR THE EXPLORATION OF SPACE.

HENRIETTA SWAN LEAVITT & EDWIN HUBBLE (1868–1921; 1889–1953) MEASURING THE UNIVERSE

AFTER FINISHING COLLEGE IN 1892, HENRIETTA SWAN LEAVITT SUFFERED A LONG ILLNESS THAT LEFT HER DEAF. SHE KNEW SHE WANTED TO BE AN ASTRONOMER, EVEN THOUGH IT WAS CONSIDERED A MAN'S JOB. IN 1893, SHE WAS OFFERED A JOB BY ASTRONOMER EDWARD PICKERING AT THE HARVARD COLLEGE OBSERVATORY. AT FIRST, IT WAS UNPAID. EVENTUALLY, SHE MADE 30 CENTS PER HOUR, AROUND THE SAME WAGE A SERVANT OF THE TIME WOULD HAVE EARNED.

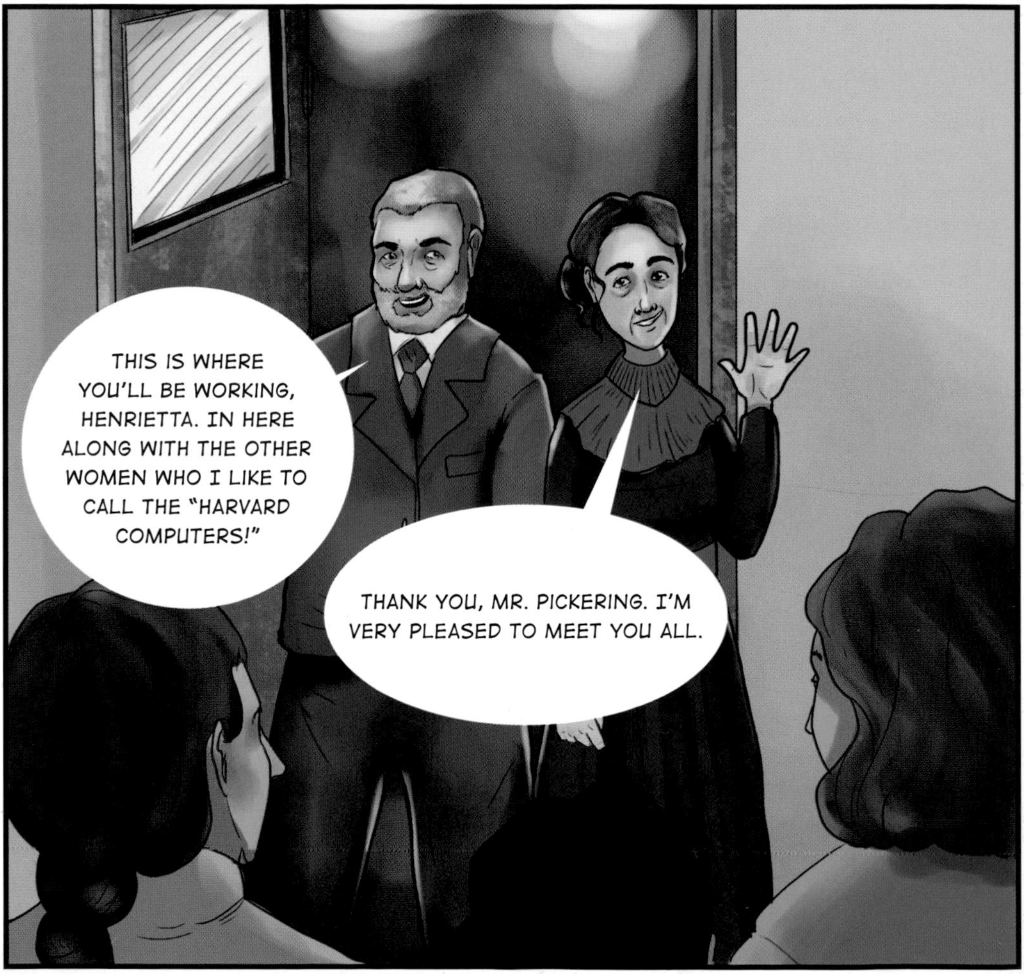

THIS IS WHERE YOU'LL BE WORKING, HENRIETTA. IN HERE ALONG WITH THE OTHER WOMEN WHO I LIKE TO CALL THE "HARVARD COMPUTERS!"
THANK YOU, MR. PICKERING. I'M VERY PLEASED TO MEET YOU ALL.

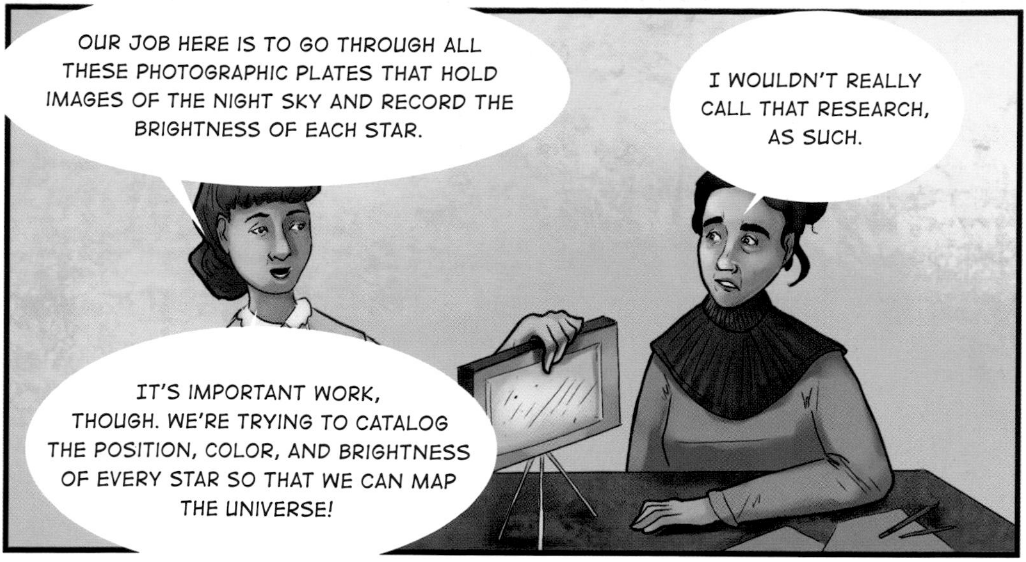
OUR JOB HERE IS TO GO THROUGH ALL THESE PHOTOGRAPHIC PLATES THAT HOLD IMAGES OF THE NIGHT SKY AND RECORD THE BRIGHTNESS OF EACH STAR.
I WOULDN'T REALLY CALL THAT RESEARCH, AS SUCH.
IT'S IMPORTANT WORK, THOUGH. WE'RE TRYING TO CATALOG THE POSITION, COLOR, AND BRIGHTNESS OF EVERY STAR SO THAT WE CAN MAP THE UNIVERSE!

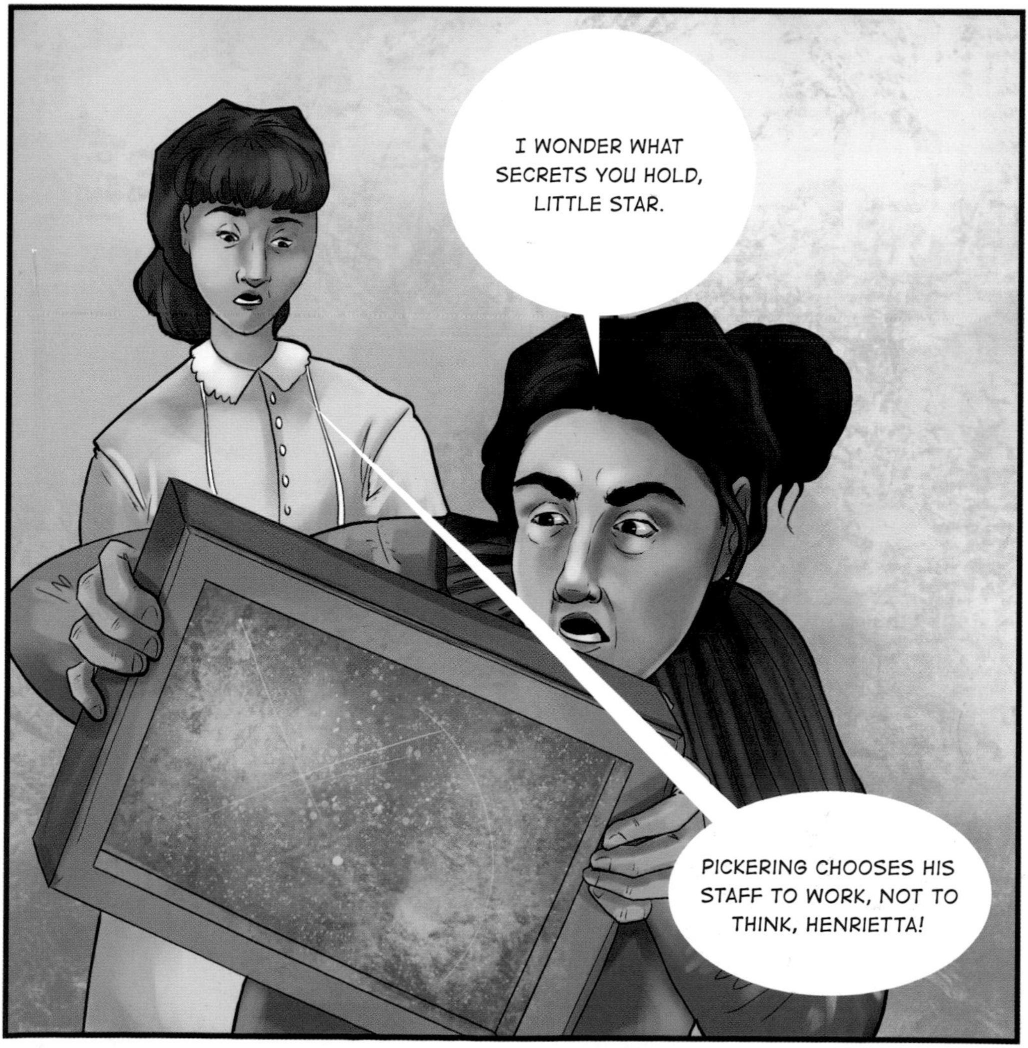
I WONDER WHAT SECRETS YOU HOLD, LITTLE STAR.
PICKERING CHOOSES HIS STAFF TO WORK, NOT TO THINK, HENRIETTA!

HENRIETTA IMPRESSED THE STAFF WITH HER ABILITY AND HARD WORK. SEVERAL YEARS AFTER FIRST STARTING AT THE OBSERVATORY, SHE LEFT TO SPEND A COUPLE OF YEARS TRAVELING AROUND EUROPE, BUT SHE WAS READY TO GET BACK TO STUDYING THE STARS. IN 1902, SHE ASKED EDWARD PICKERING FOR A PERMANENT JOB.

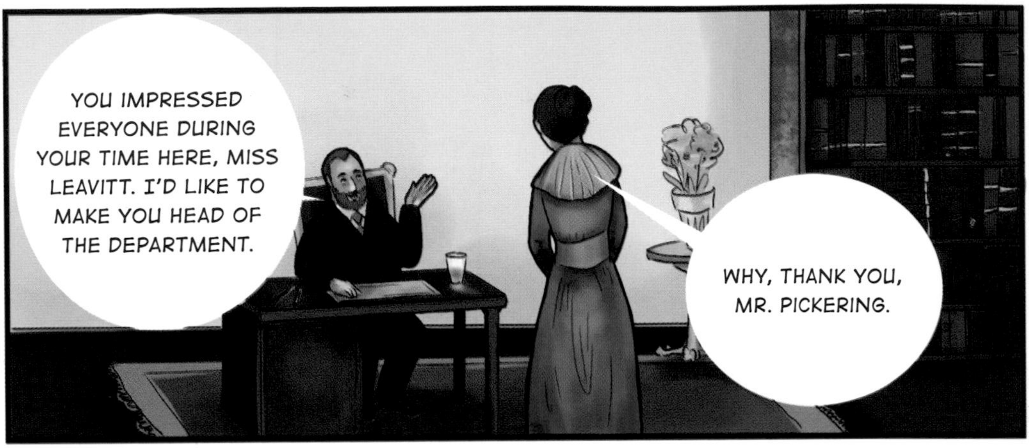
YOU IMPRESSED EVERYONE DURING YOUR TIME HERE, MISS LEAVITT. I'D LIKE TO MAKE YOU HEAD OF THE DEPARTMENT.
WHY, THANK YOU, MR. PICKERING.

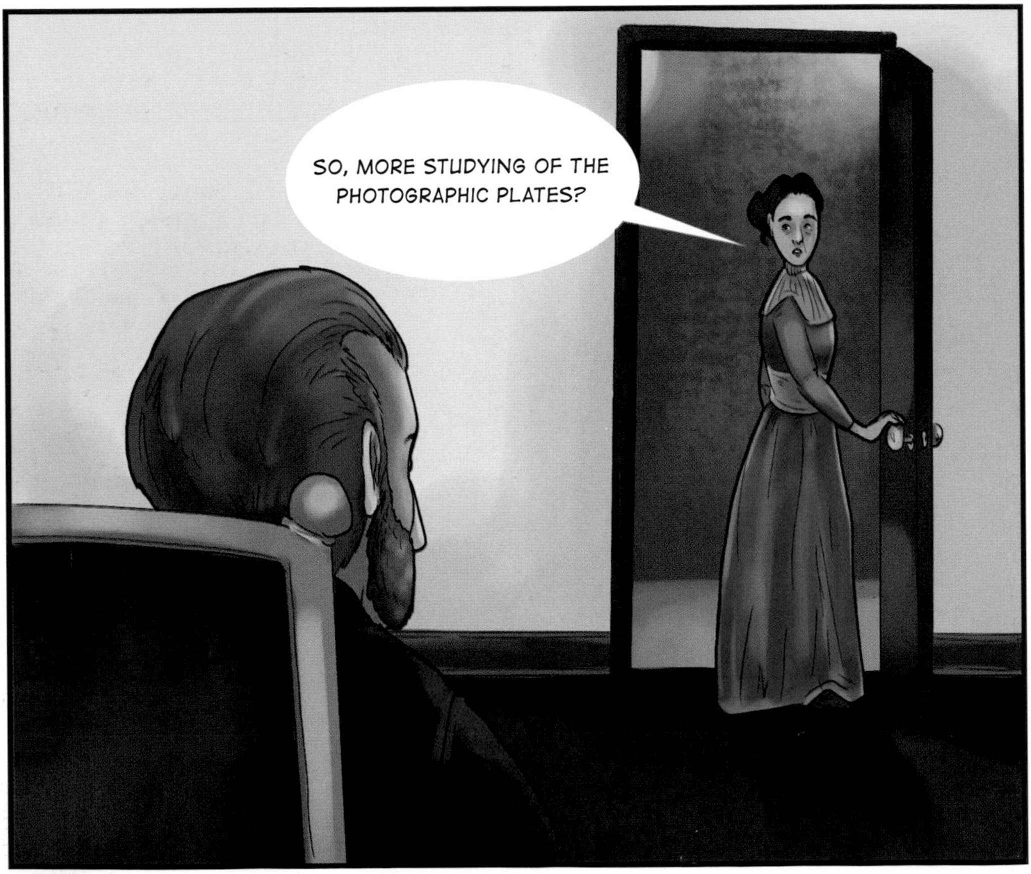
SO, MORE STUDYING OF THE PHOTOGRAPHIC PLATES?

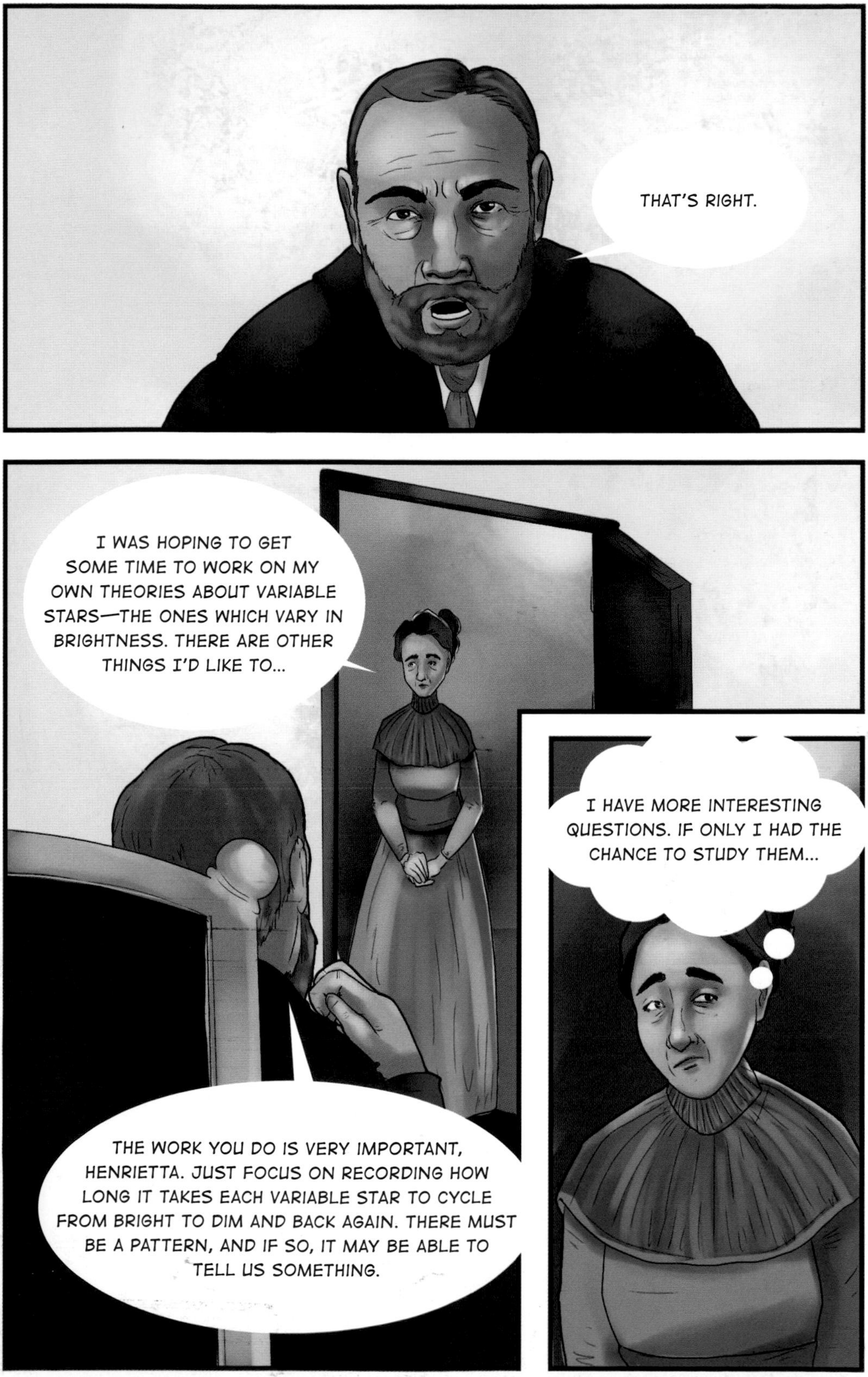
THAT'S RIGHT.
I WAS HOPING TO GET SOME TIME TO WORK ON MY OWN THEORIES ABOUT VARIABLE STARS—THE ONES WHICH VARY IN BRIGHTNESS. THERE ARE OTHER THINGS I'D LIKE TO...
THE WORK YOU DO IS VERY IMPORTANT, HENRIETTA. JUST FOCUS ON RECORDING HOW LONG IT TAKES EACH VARIABLE STAR TO CYCLE FROM BRIGHT TO DIM AND BACK AGAIN. THERE MUST BE A PATTERN, AND IF SO, IT MAY BE ABLE TO TELL US SOMETHING.
I HAVE MORE INTERESTING QUESTIONS. IF ONLY I HAD THE CHANCE TO STUDY THEM...

HENRIETTA'S ROLE WAS TO SEARCH THE PHOTOGRAPHIC PLATES FOR VARIABLE STARS. SHE WENT ON TO DISCOVER 2,400 OF THEM. IN 1912, SHE BECAME ESPECIALLY INTERESTED IN A TYPE OF VARIABLE STAR CALLED A CEPHEID, WHICH PULSED IN PREDICTABLE PATTERNS.

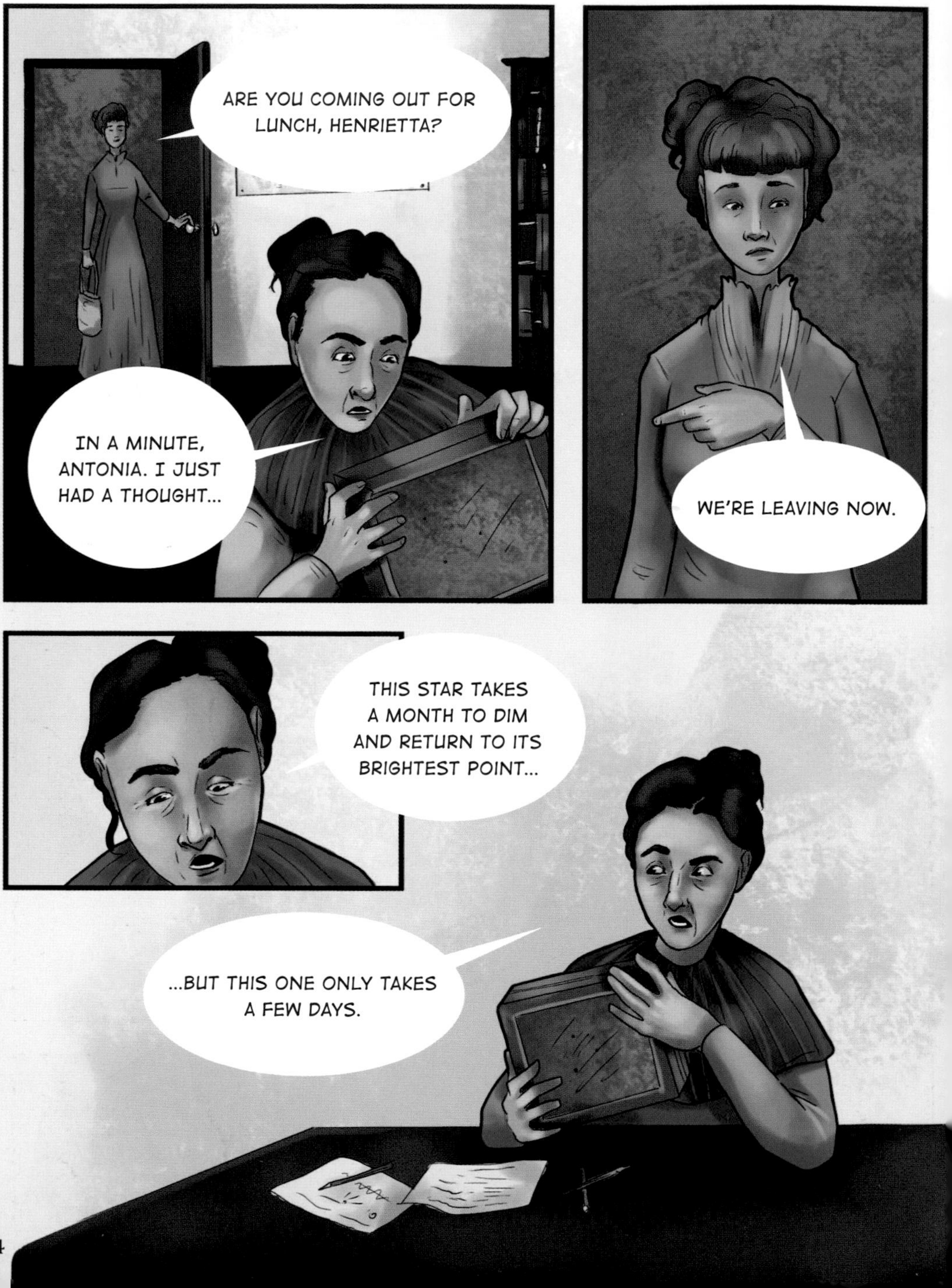
ARE YOU COMING OUT FOR LUNCH, HENRIETTA?
IN A MINUTE, ANTONIA. I JUST HAD A THOUGHT...
WE'RE LEAVING NOW.
THIS STAR TAKES A MONTH TO DIM AND RETURN TO ITS BRIGHTEST POINT...
...BUT THIS ONE ONLY TAKES A FEW DAYS.

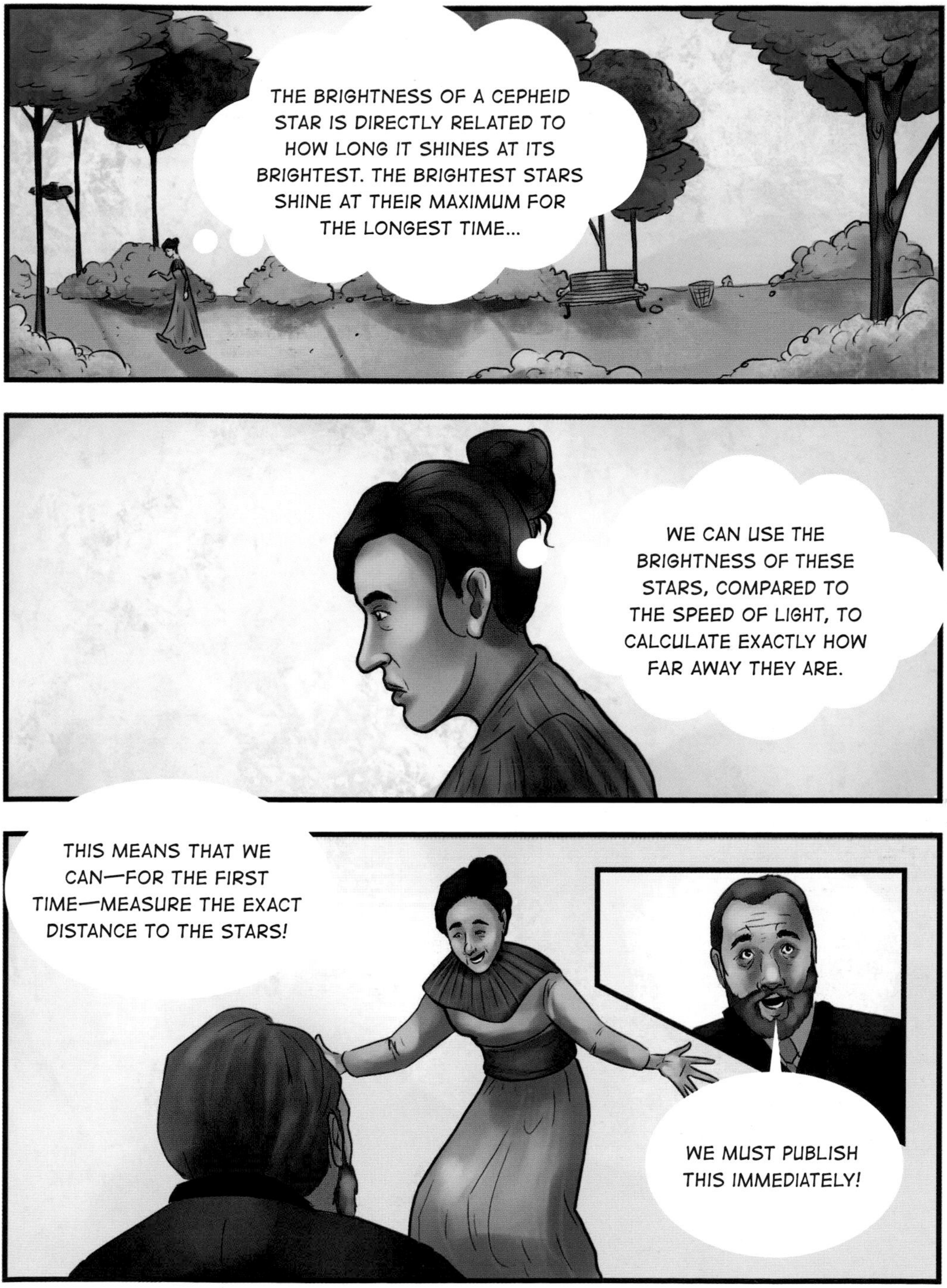
THE BRIGHTNESS OF A CEPHEID STAR IS DIRECTLY RELATED TO HOW LONG IT SHINES AT ITS BRIGHTEST. THE BRIGHTEST STARS SHINE AT THEIR MAXIMUM FOR THE LONGEST TIME...
WE CAN USE THE BRIGHTNESS OF THESE STARS, COMPARED TO THE SPEED OF LIGHT, TO CALCULATE EXACTLY HOW FAR AWAY THEY ARE.
THIS MEANS THAT WE CAN—FOR THE FIRST TIME—MEASURE THE EXACT DISTANCE TO THE STARS!
WE MUST PUBLISH THIS IMMEDIATELY!

HENRIETTA'S WORK APPEARED AS A SCIENTIFIC PAPER IN THE HARVARD COLLEGE OBSERVATORY CIRCULAR IN 1912. IT WAS PUBLISHED UNDER EDWARD PICKERING'S NAME.

IN 1924, A FEW YEARS AFTER HENRIETTA'S DEATH, AMERICAN ASTRONOMER EDWIN HUBBLE AND HIS ASSISTANT MILTON HUMASON WERE STUDYING A SPIRAL CLUSTER OF STARS, KNOWN AS THE ANDROMEDA NEBULA. THEY WORKED OUT THE DISTANCE TO THE NEBULA USING HENRIETTA'S FINDINGS...AND MADE AN EXTRAORDINARY DISCOVERY.

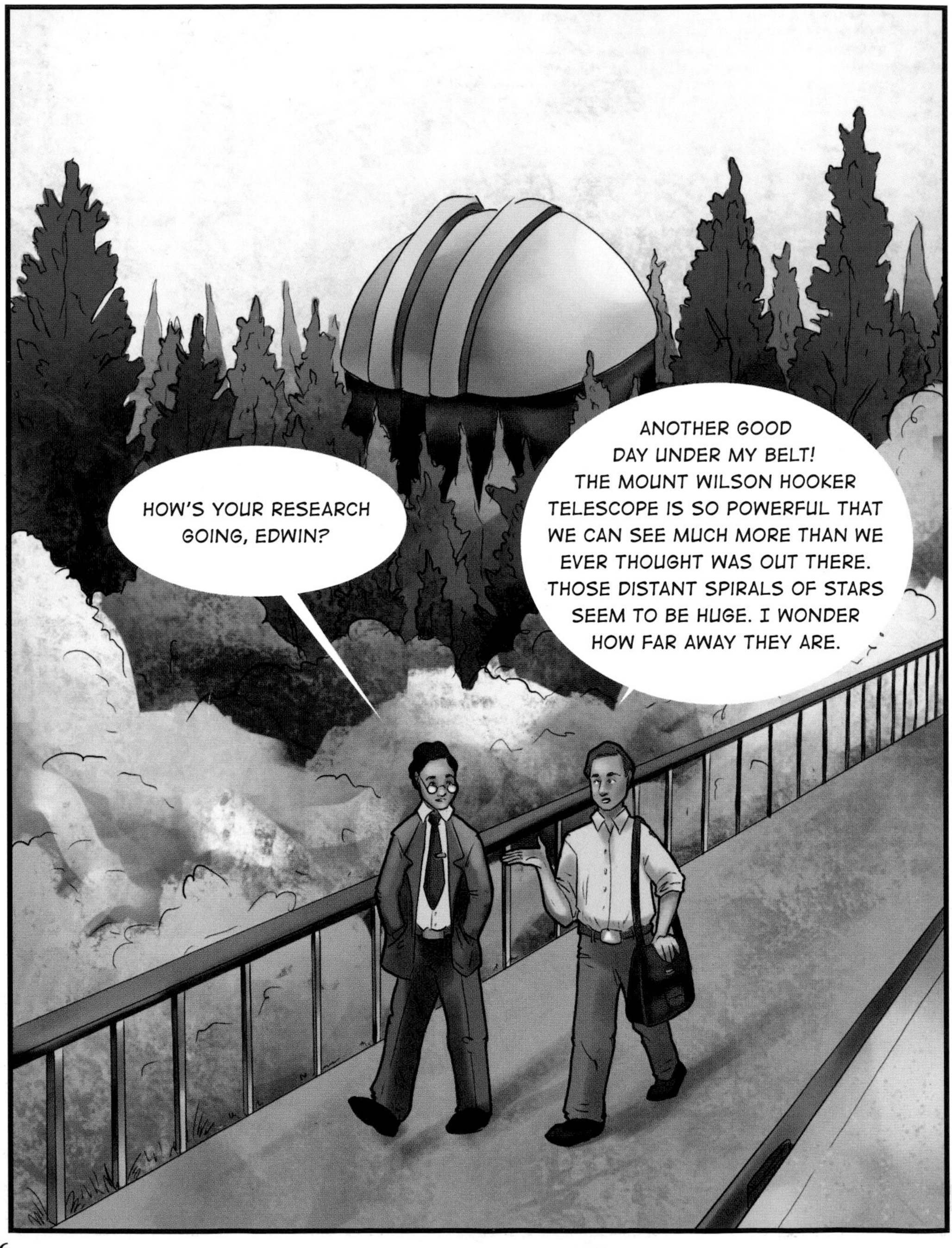
HOW'S YOUR RESEARCH GOING, EDWIN?
ANOTHER GOOD DAY UNDER MY BELT! THE MOUNT WILSON HOOKER TELESCOPE IS SO POWERFUL THAT WE CAN SEE MUCH MORE THAN WE EVER THOUGHT WAS OUT THERE. THOSE DISTANT SPIRALS OF STARS SEEM TO BE HUGE. I WONDER HOW FAR AWAY THEY ARE.

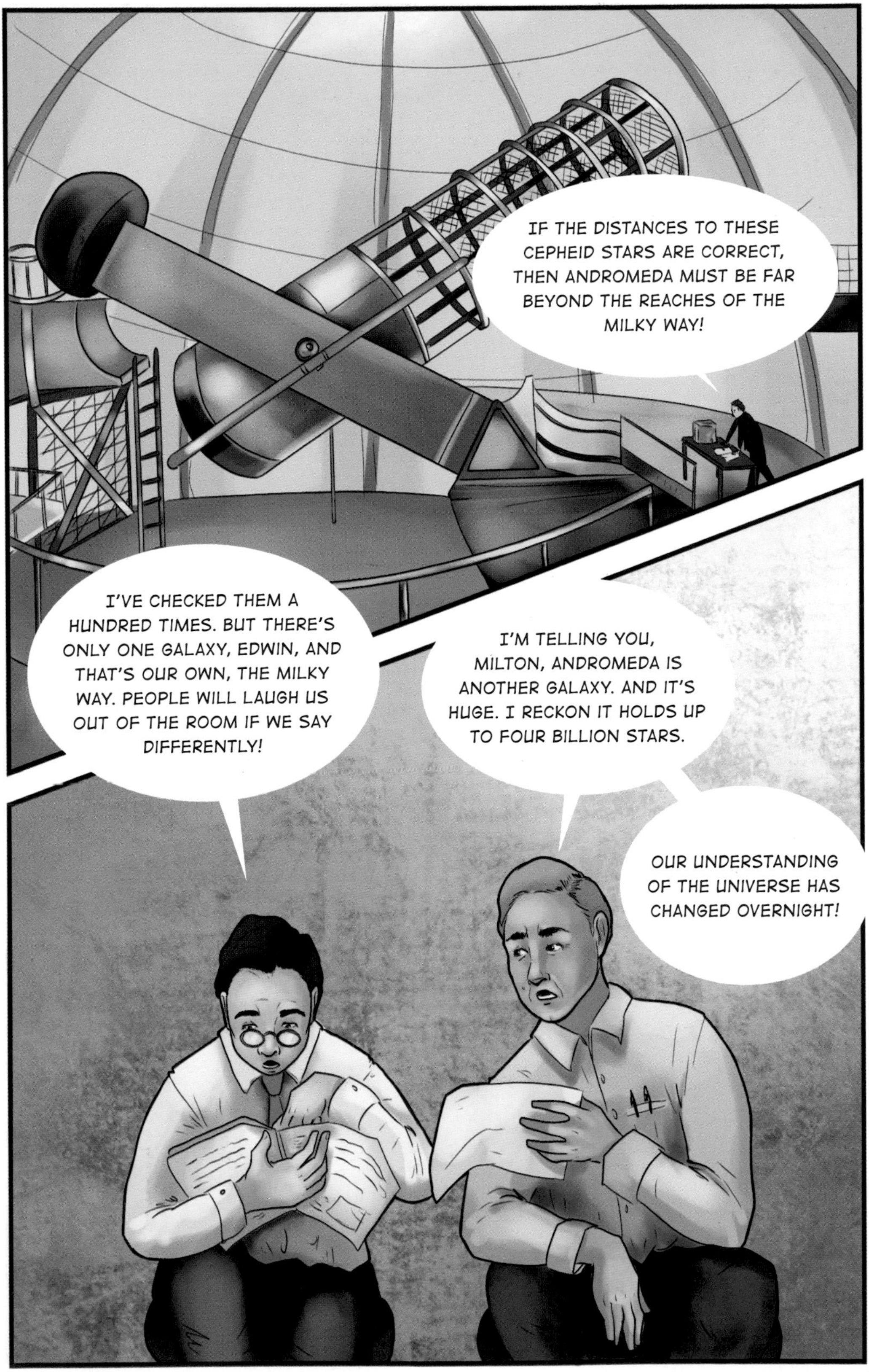
IF THE DISTANCES TO THESE CEPHEID STARS ARE CORRECT, THEN ANDROMEDA MUST BE FAR BEYOND THE REACHES OF THE MILKY WAY!
I'VE CHECKED THEM A HUNDRED TIMES. BUT THERE'S ONLY ONE GALAXY, EDWIN, AND THAT'S OUR OWN, THE MILKY WAY. PEOPLE WILL LAUGH US OUT OF THE ROOM IF WE SAY DIFFERENTLY!
I'M TELLING YOU, MILTON, ANDROMEDA IS ANOTHER GALAXY. AND IT'S HUGE. I RECKON IT HOLDS UP TO FOUR BILLION STARS.
OUR UNDERSTANDING OF THE UNIVERSE HAS CHANGED OVERNIGHT!

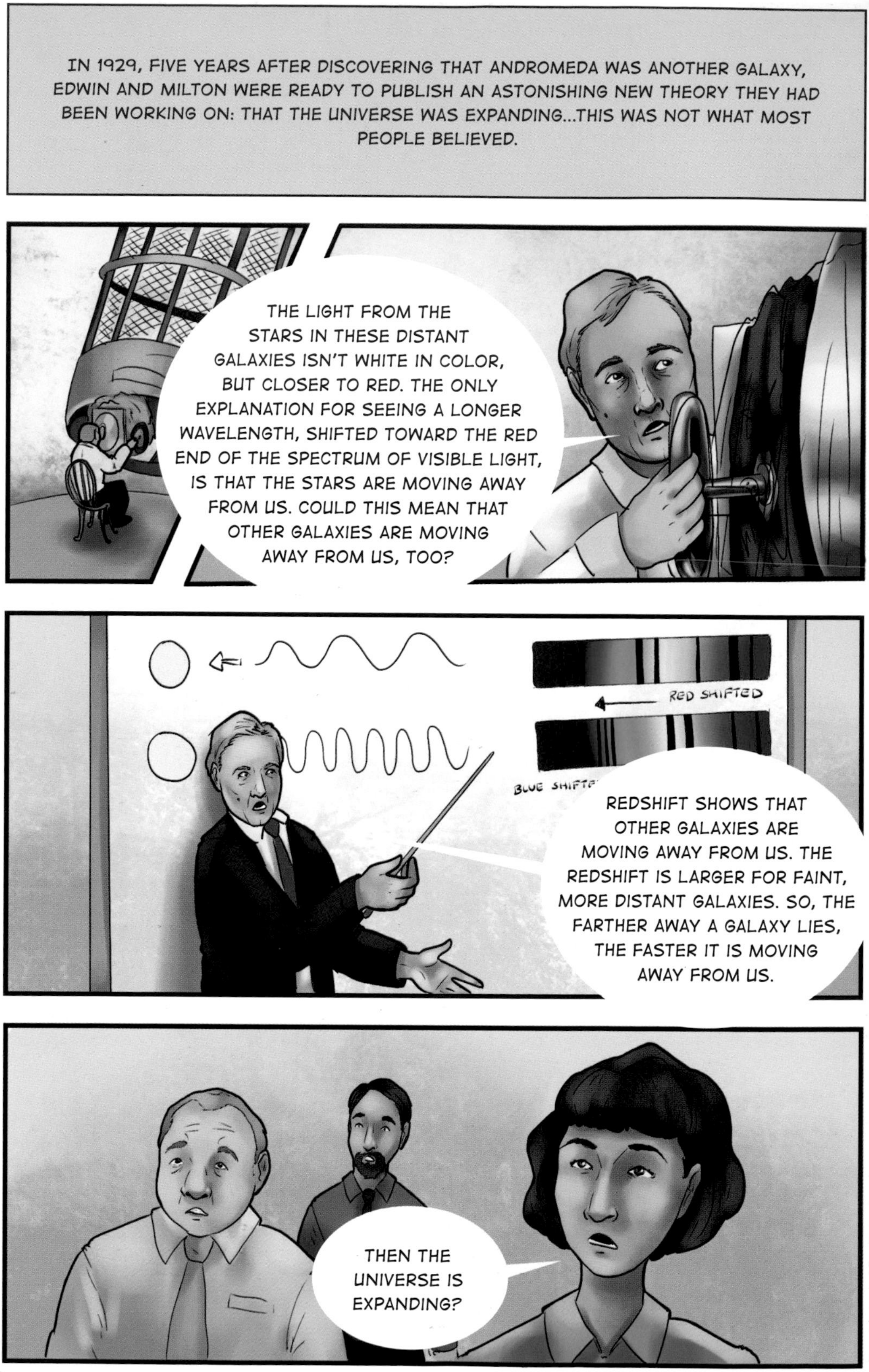
IN 1929, FIVE YEARS AFTER DISCOVERING THAT ANDROMEDA WAS ANOTHER GALAXY, EDWIN AND MILTON WERE READY TO PUBLISH AN ASTONISHING NEW THEORY THEY HAD BEEN WORKING ON: THAT THE UNIVERSE WAS EXPANDING...THIS WAS NOT WHAT MOST PEOPLE BELIEVED.
THE LIGHT FROM THE STARS IN THESE DISTANT GALAXIES ISN'T WHITE IN COLOR, BUT CLOSER TO RED. THE ONLY EXPLANATION FOR SEEING A LONGER WAVELENGTH, SHIFTED TOWARD THE RED END OF THE SPECTRUM OF VISIBLE LIGHT, IS THAT THE STARS ARE MOVING AWAY FROM US. COULD THIS MEAN THAT OTHER GALAXIES ARE MOVING AWAY FROM US, TOO?
RED SHIFTED
REDSHIFT SHOWS THAT OTHER GALAXIES ARE MOVING AWAY FROM US. THE REDSHIFT IS LARGER FOR FAINT, MORE DISTANT GALAXIES. SO, THE FARTHER AWAY A GALAXY LIES, THE FASTER IT IS MOVING AWAY FROM US.
THEN THE UNIVERSE IS EXPANDING?

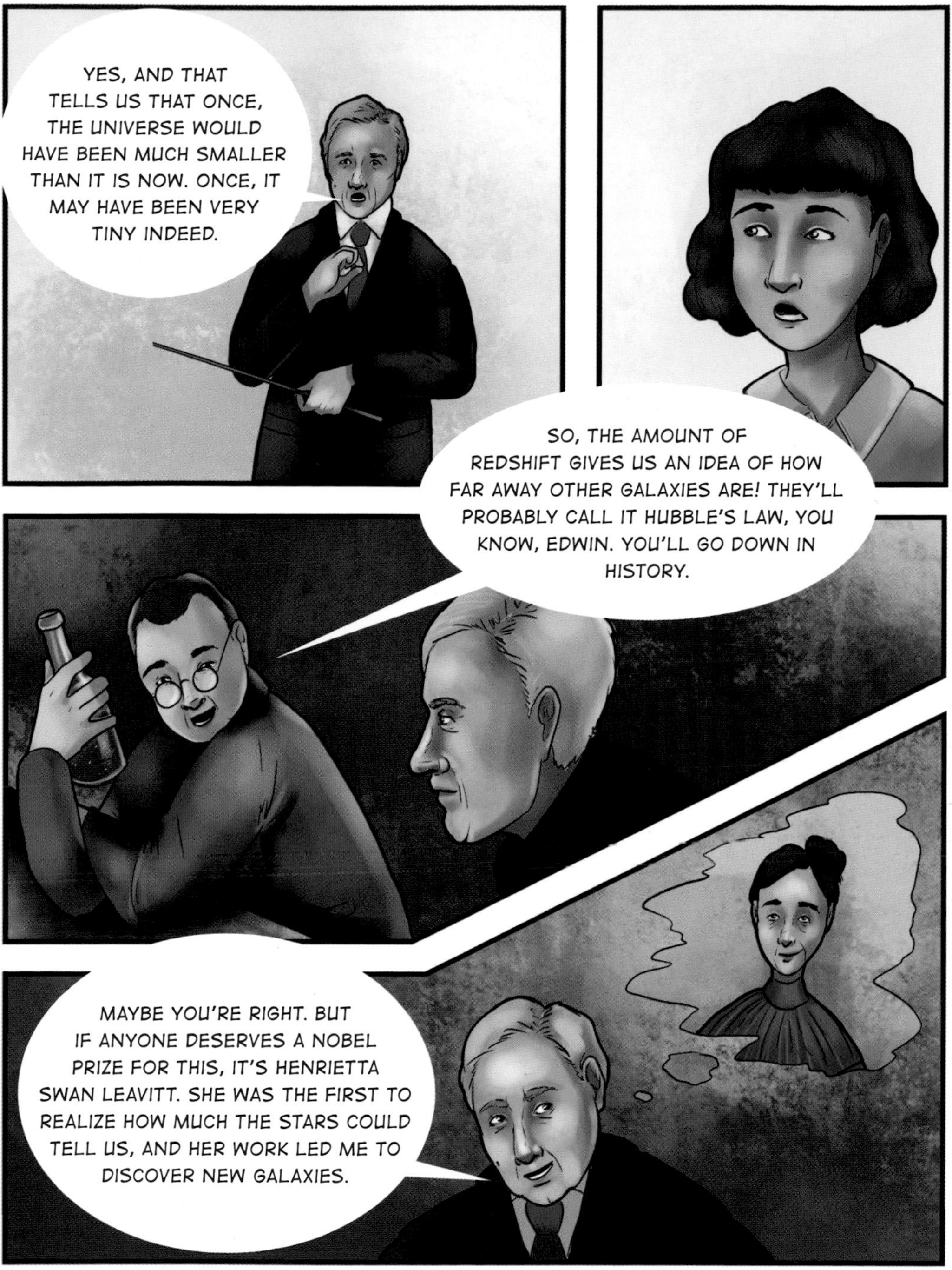
YES, AND THAT TELLS US THAT ONCE, THE UNIVERSE WOULD HAVE BEEN MUCH SMALLER THAN IT IS NOW. ONCE, IT MAY HAVE BEEN VERY TINY INDEED.
SO, THE AMOUNT OF REDSHIFT GIVES US AN IDEA OF HOW FAR AWAY OTHER GALAXIES ARE! THEY'LL PROBABLY CALL IT HUBBLE'S LAW, YOU KNOW, EDWIN. YOU'LL GO DOWN IN HISTORY.
MAYBE YOU'RE RIGHT. BUT IF ANYONE DESERVES A NOBEL PRIZE FOR THIS, IT'S HENRIETTA SWAN LEAVITT. SHE WAS THE FIRST TO REALIZE HOW MUCH THE STARS COULD TELL US, AND HER WORK LED ME TO DISCOVER NEW GALAXIES.

EDWIN AND HENRIETTA'S WORK EXPANDED OUR VIEW OF THE UNIVERSE. THE INNOVATIVE HUBBLE SPACE TELESCOPE—NAMED IN EDWIN'S HONOR AND LAUNCHED IN 1990 ON SPACE SHUTTLE *DISCOVERY* INTO ITS ORBIT ABOVE EARTH'S ATMOSPHERE—CONTINUES TO EXPLORE AND PHOTOGRAPH THE FAR REACHES OF THE COSMOS.

ROBERT H. GODDARD
(1882–1945)
THE ORIGINAL ROCKET MAN

IN 1899, IN WORCESTER, MASSACHUSETTS, ROBERT H. GODDARD, AT AGE 17, FIRST DREAMED OF BUILDING A MACHINE THAT COULD REACH THE STARS.

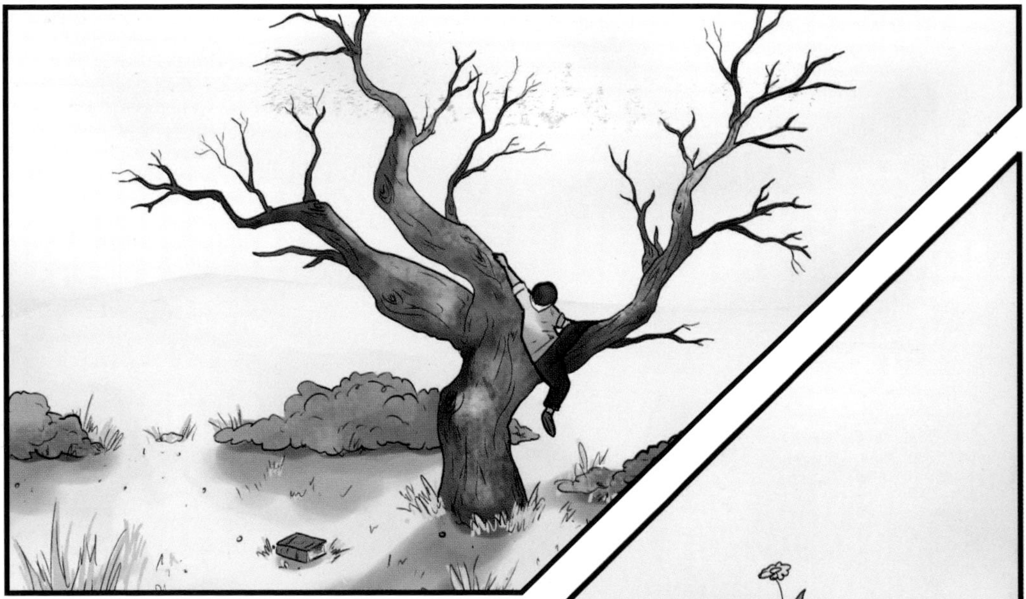

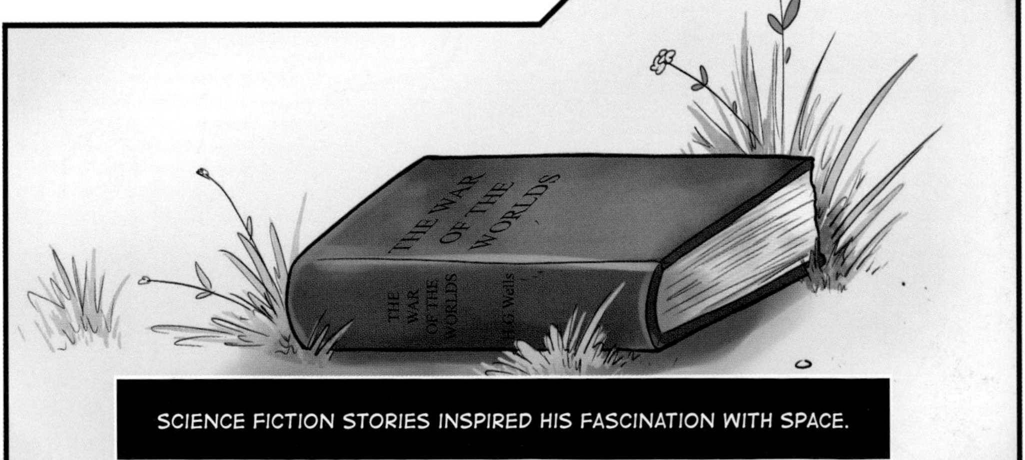
THE WAR OF THE WORLDS
THE WAR OF THE WORLDS
H.G. Wells
SCIENCE FICTION STORIES INSPIRED HIS FASCINATION WITH SPACE.

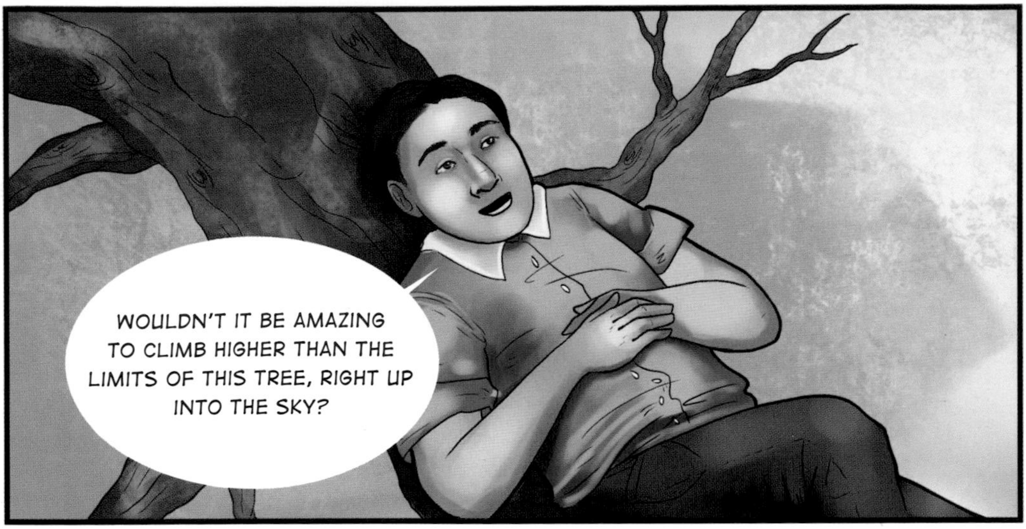
WOULDN'T IT BE AMAZING TO CLIMB HIGHER THAN THE LIMITS OF THIS TREE, RIGHT UP INTO THE SKY?

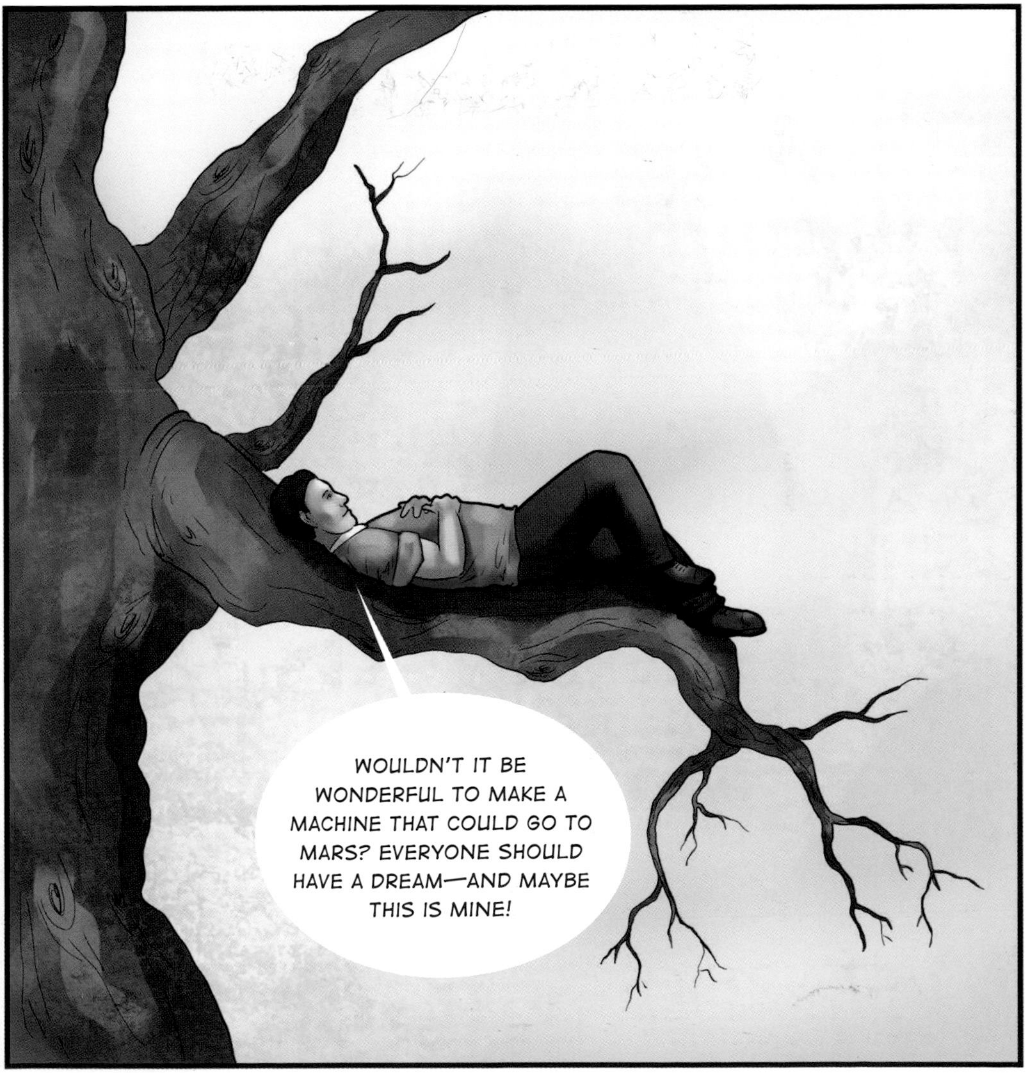
WOULDN'T IT BE WONDERFUL TO MAKE A MACHINE THAT COULD GO TO MARS? EVERYONE SHOULD HAVE A DREAM—AND MAYBE THIS IS MINE!

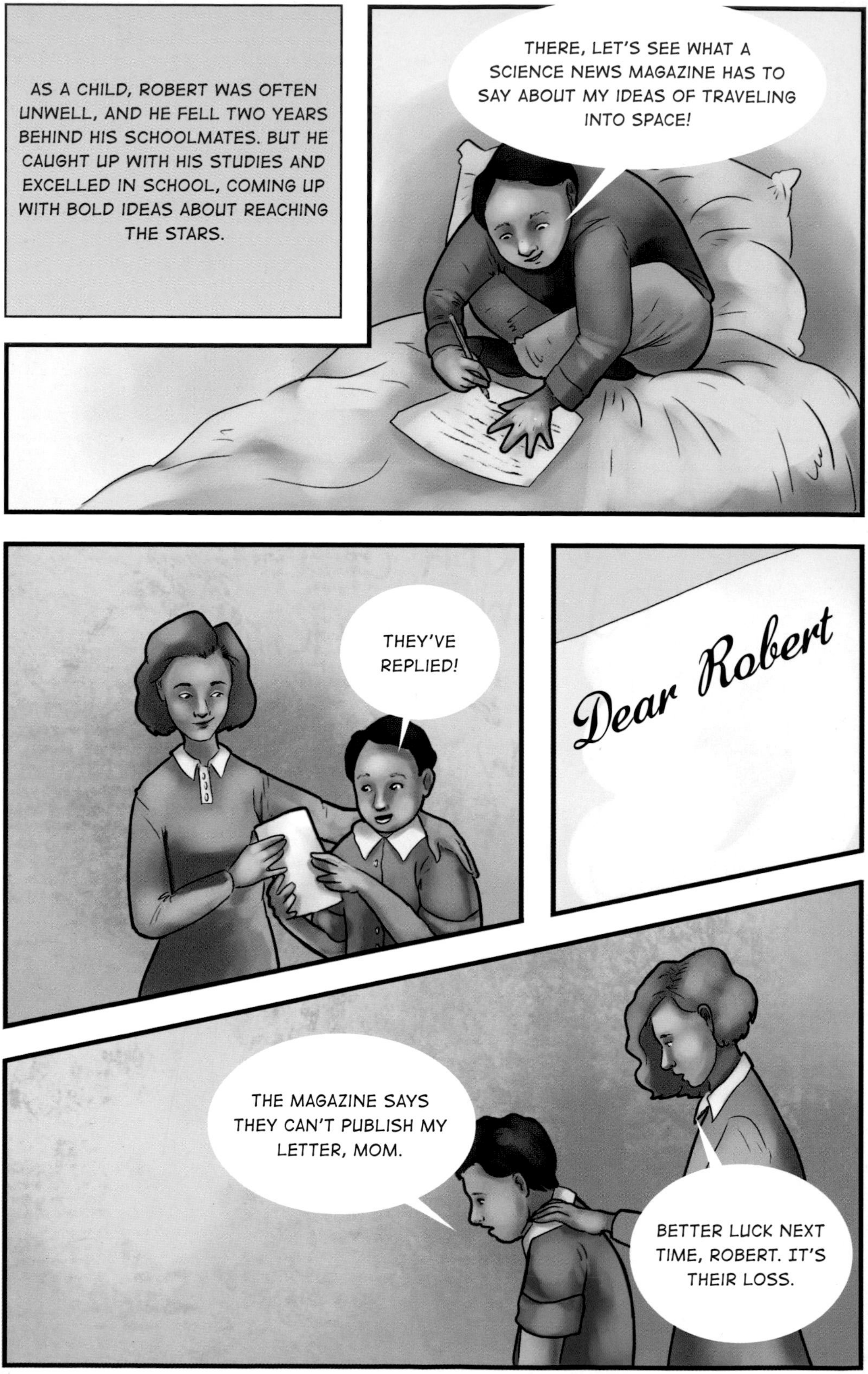
AS A CHILD, ROBERT WAS OFTEN UNWELL, AND HE FELL TWO YEARS BEHIND HIS SCHOOLMATES. BUT HE CAUGHT UP WITH HIS STUDIES AND EXCELLED IN SCHOOL, COMING UP WITH BOLD IDEAS ABOUT REACHING THE STARS.
THERE, LET'S SEE WHAT A SCIENCE NEWS MAGAZINE HAS TO SAY ABOUT MY IDEAS OF TRAVELING INTO SPACE!
THEY'VE REPLIED!
Dear Robert
THE MAGAZINE SAYS THEY CAN'T PUBLISH MY LETTER, MOM.
BETTER LUCK NEXT TIME, ROBERT. IT'S THEIR LOSS.

ROBERT GRADUATED FROM SOUTH HIGH SCHOOL IN WORCESTER, MASSACHUSETTS, AT AGE 21. AS VALEDICTORIAN OF HIS CLASS, HE GAVE A ROUSING FAREWELL SPEECH ABOUT PURSUING DREAMS.

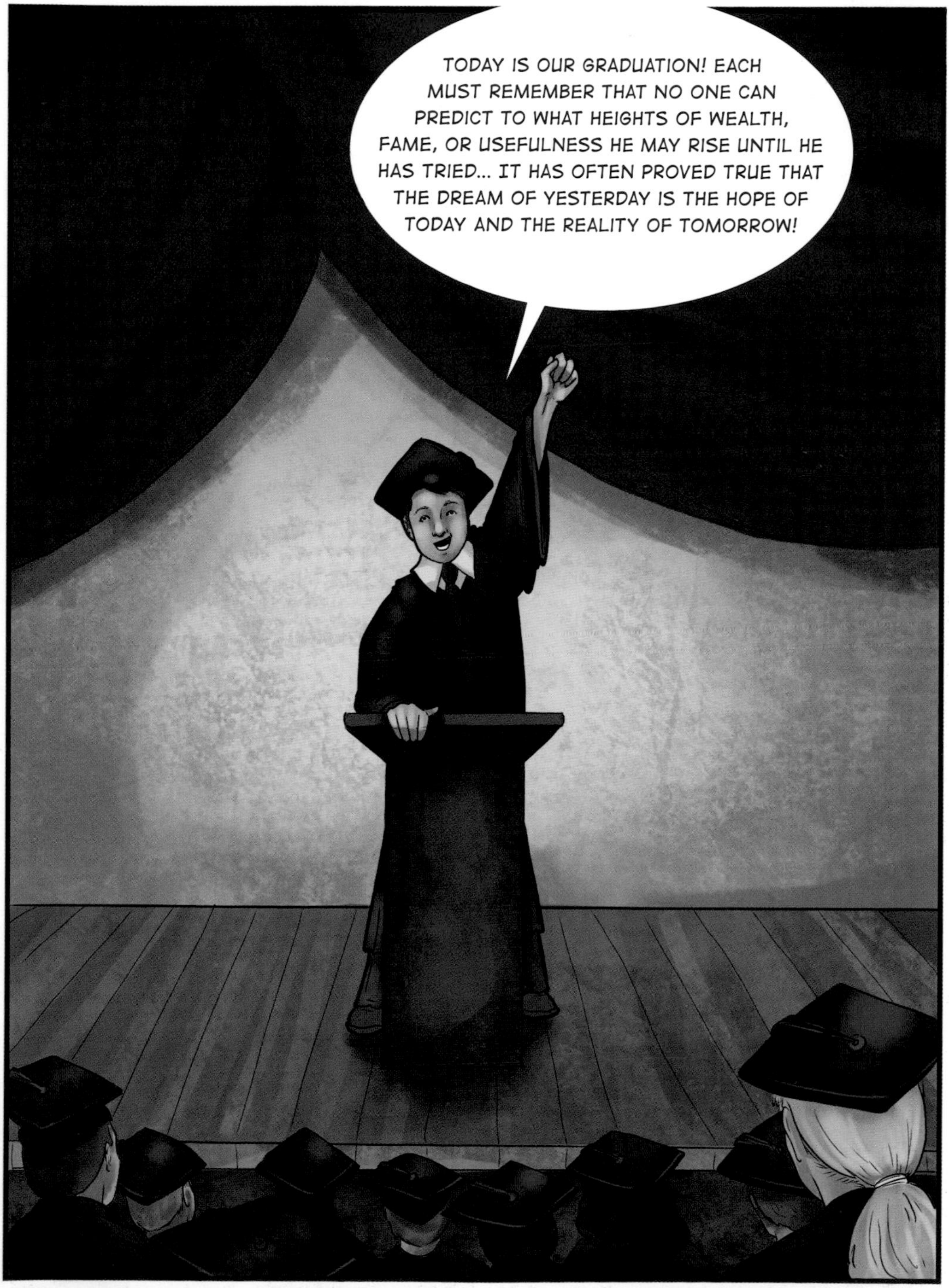
TODAY IS OUR GRADUATION! EACH MUST REMEMBER THAT NO ONE CAN PREDICT TO WHAT HEIGHTS OF WEALTH, FAME, OR USEFULNESS HE MAY RISE UNTIL HE HAS TRIED... IT HAS OFTEN PROVED TRUE THAT THE DREAM OF YESTERDAY IS THE HOPE OF TODAY AND THE REALITY OF TOMORROW!

WHILE STUDYING FOR HIS UNDERGRADUATE DEGREE IN PHYSICS AT WORCESTER POLYTECHNIC INSTITUTE, MASSACHUSETTS, ROBERT STARTED EXPERIMENTING WITH GUNPOWDER-FUELED ROCKETS.

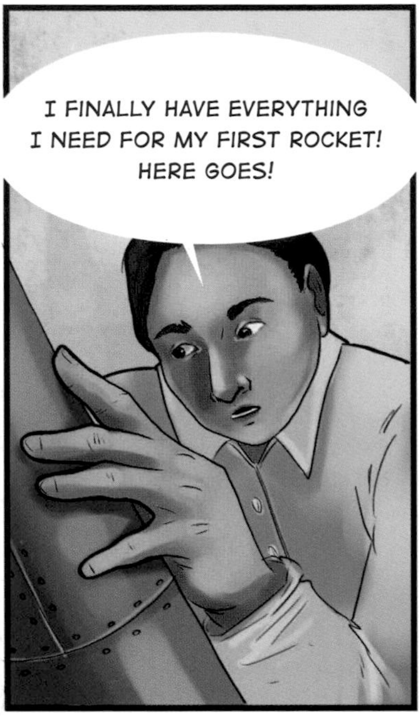
I FINALLY HAVE EVERYTHING I NEED FOR MY FIRST ROCKET! HERE GOES!

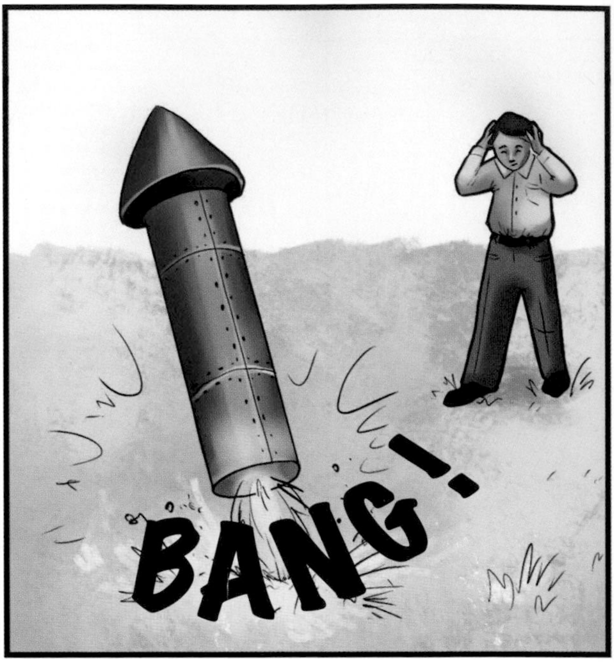
BANG!

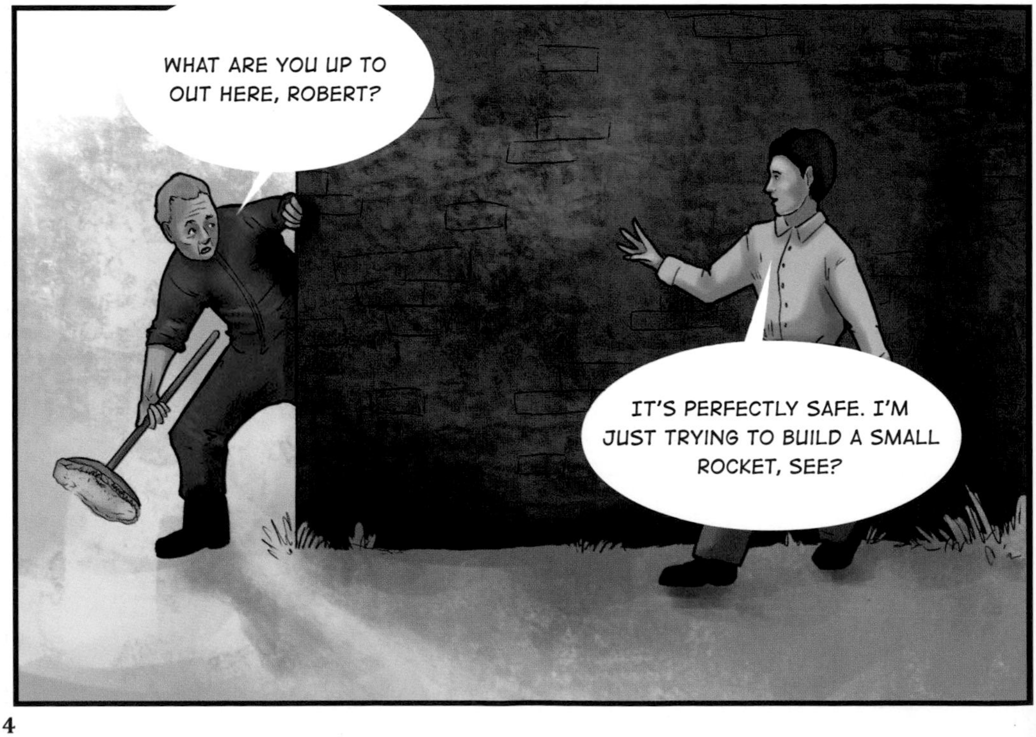
WHAT ARE YOU UP TO OUT HERE, ROBERT?
IT'S PERFECTLY SAFE. I'M JUST TRYING TO BUILD A SMALL ROCKET, SEE?

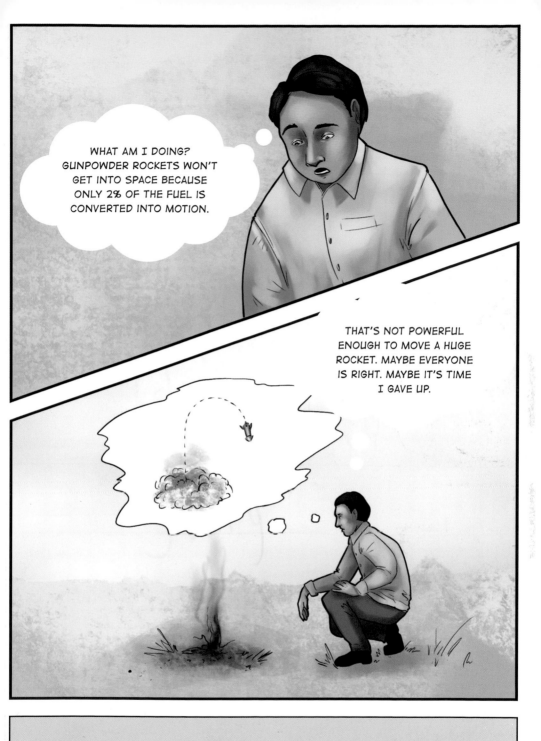

WHAT AM I DOING? GUNPOWDER ROCKETS WON'T GET INTO SPACE BECAUSE ONLY 2% OF THE FUEL IS CONVERTED INTO MOTION.

THAT'S NOT POWERFUL ENOUGH TO MOVE A HUGE ROCKET. MAYBE EVERYONE IS RIGHT. MAYBE IT'S TIME I GAVE UP.

AFTER GRADUATING IN 1908, ROBERT JOINED CLARK UNIVERSITY, MASSACHUSETTS, AS A RESEARCH FELLOW. HE SPENT SEVERAL YEARS TRYING TO IMPROVE HIS ROCKETS, FUNDING HIS EXPERIMENTS FROM HIS PAYCHECK.

BY APPLYING NEW TECHNOLOGIES TO HIS ROCKETS OVER THE YEARS, ROBERT WAS ABLE TO INCREASE THEIR EFFICIENCY GREATLY. IN 1916, ADDING A NEW COMPONENT—A DE LAVAL NOZZLE—TO HIS ROCKETS IMPROVED THEIR EFFICIENCY BY OVER 60%.

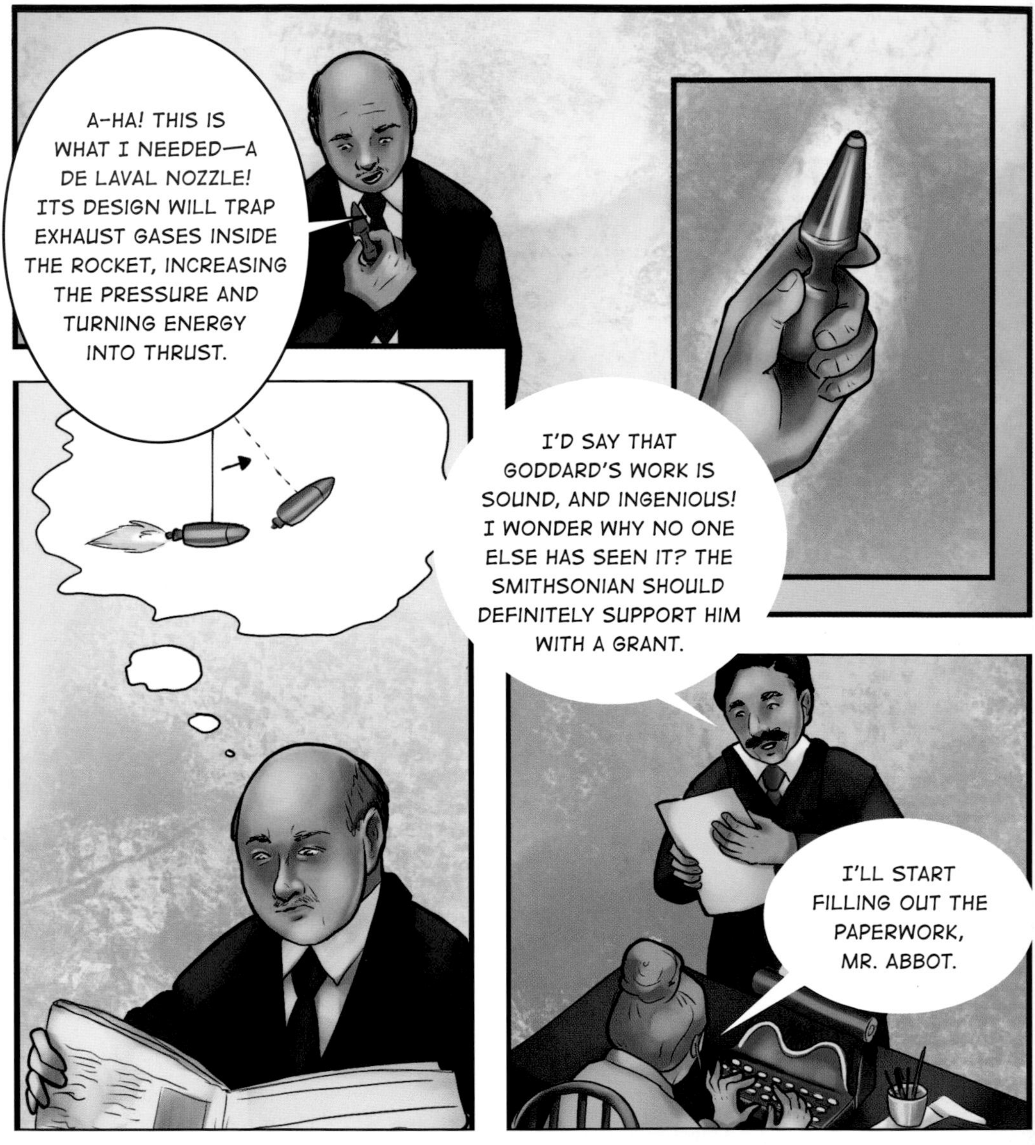
A-HA! THIS IS WHAT I NEEDED—A DE LAVAL NOZZLE! ITS DESIGN WILL TRAP EXHAUST GASES INSIDE THE ROCKET, INCREASING THE PRESSURE AND TURNING ENERGY INTO THRUST.
I'D SAY THAT GODDARD'S WORK IS SOUND, AND INGENIOUS! I WONDER WHY NO ONE ELSE HAS SEEN IT? THE SMITHSONIAN SHOULD DEFINITELY SUPPORT HIM WITH A GRANT.
I'LL START FILLING OUT THE PAPERWORK, MR. ABBOT.

IN 1917, CHARLES GREELEY ABBOT AT THE SMITHSONIAN INSTITUTION APPROVED THE FUNDS ROBERT GODDARD NEEDED TO EXPAND HIS RESEARCH.

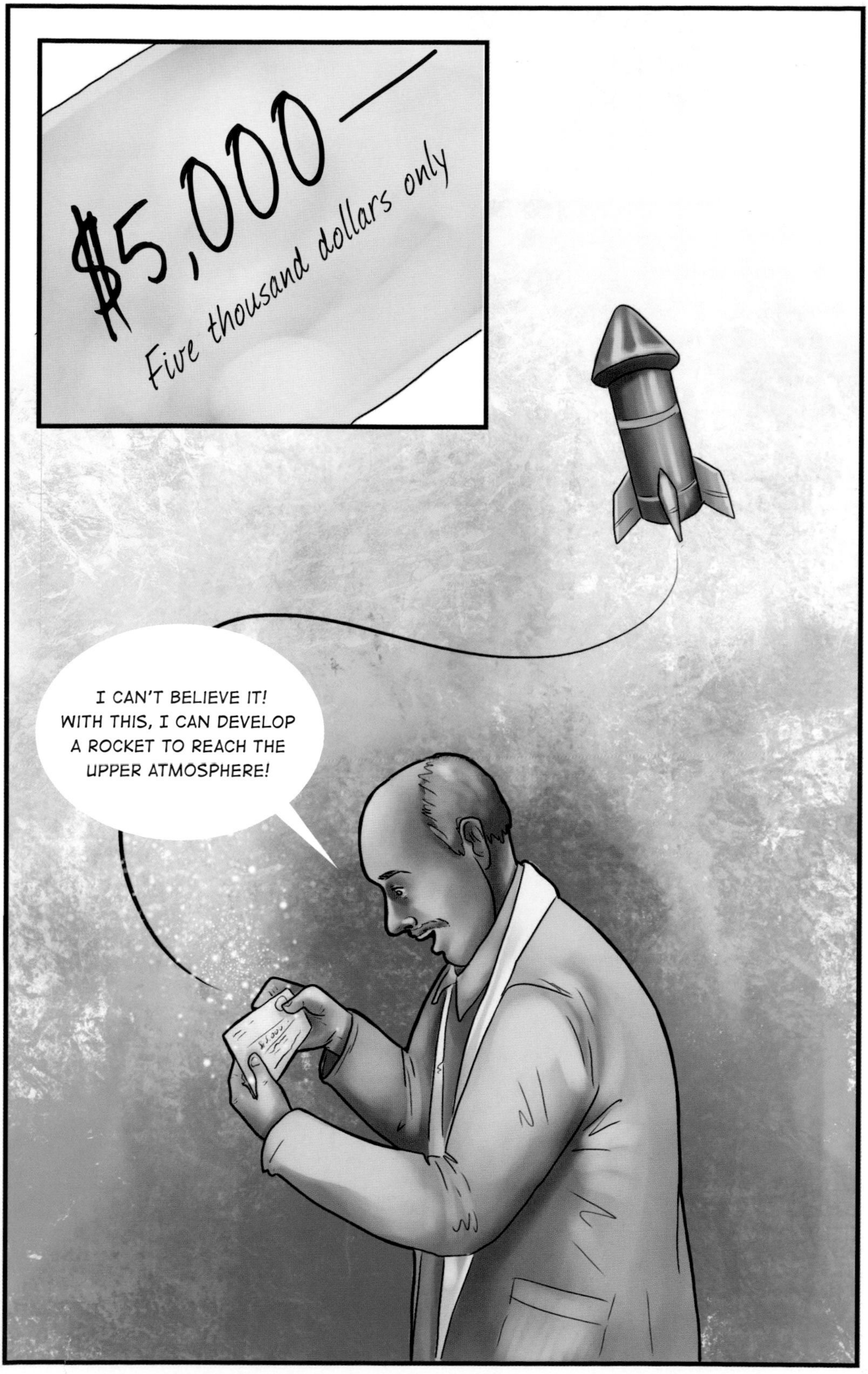
$5,000—
Five thousand dollars only
I CAN'T BELIEVE IT! WITH THIS, I CAN DEVELOP A ROCKET TO REACH THE UPPER ATMOSPHERE!

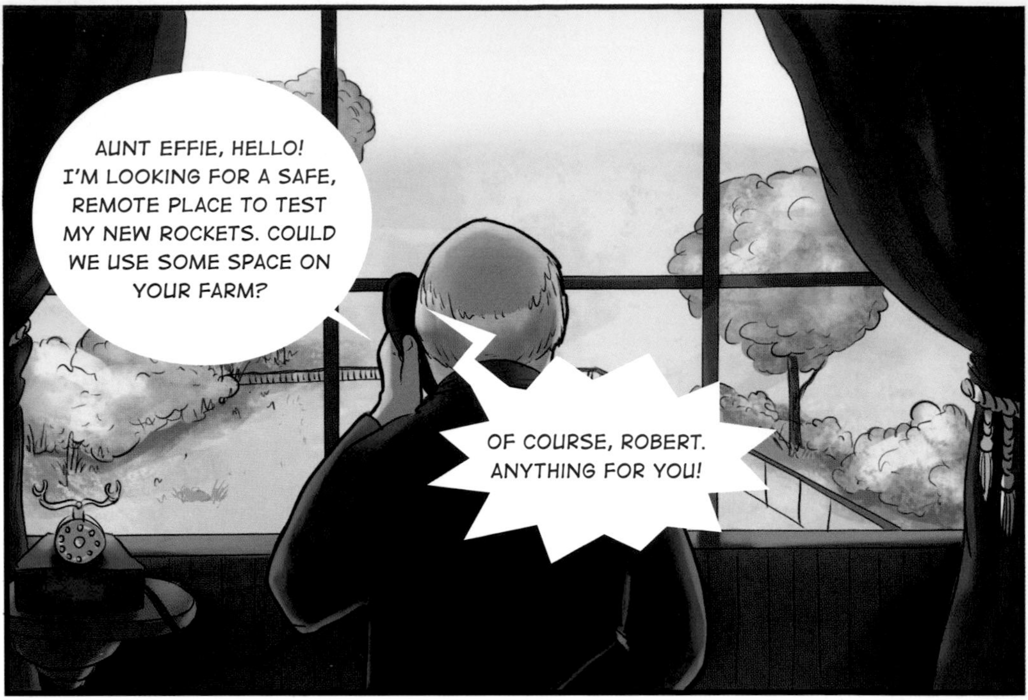
AUNT EFFIE, HELLO! I'M LOOKING FOR A SAFE, REMOTE PLACE TO TEST MY NEW ROCKETS. COULD WE USE SOME SPACE ON YOUR FARM?
OF COURSE, ROBERT. ANYTHING FOR YOU!

ROBERT'S NEW ROCKETS WERE POWERED BY A COMBINATION OF GASOLINE AND LIQUID OXYGEN. ON MARCH 16, 1926, HE SUCCESSFULLY LAUNCHED THE WORLD'S FIRST LIQUID-FUELED ROCKET AT AUBURN, MASSACHUSETTS, AS HIS ASSISTANTS—HENRY SACHS AND PERCY ROOPE—AND HIS WIFE, ESTHER, WATCHED ON.

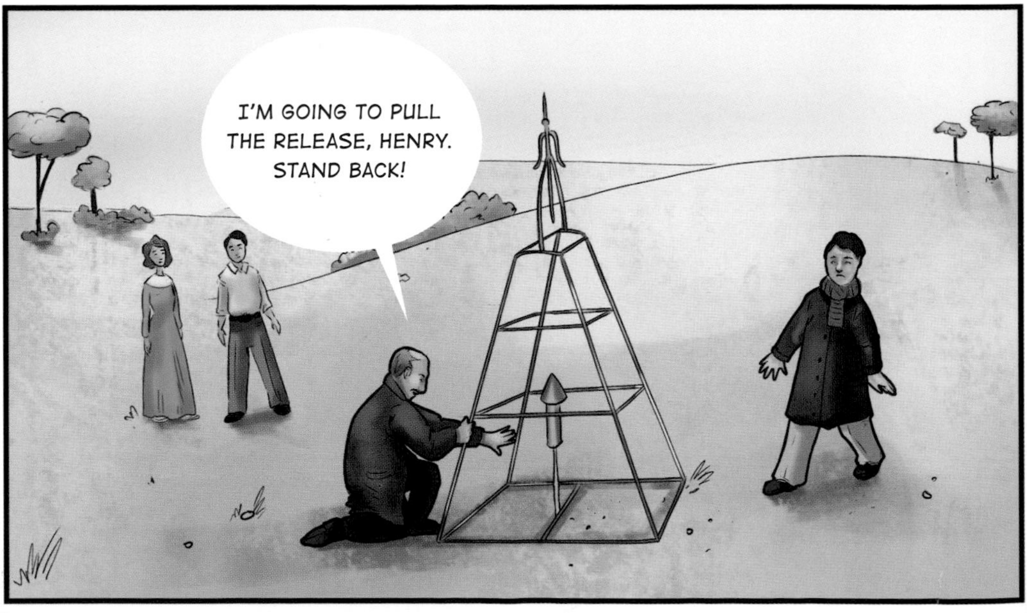
I'M GOING TO PULL THE RELEASE, HENRY. STAND BACK!

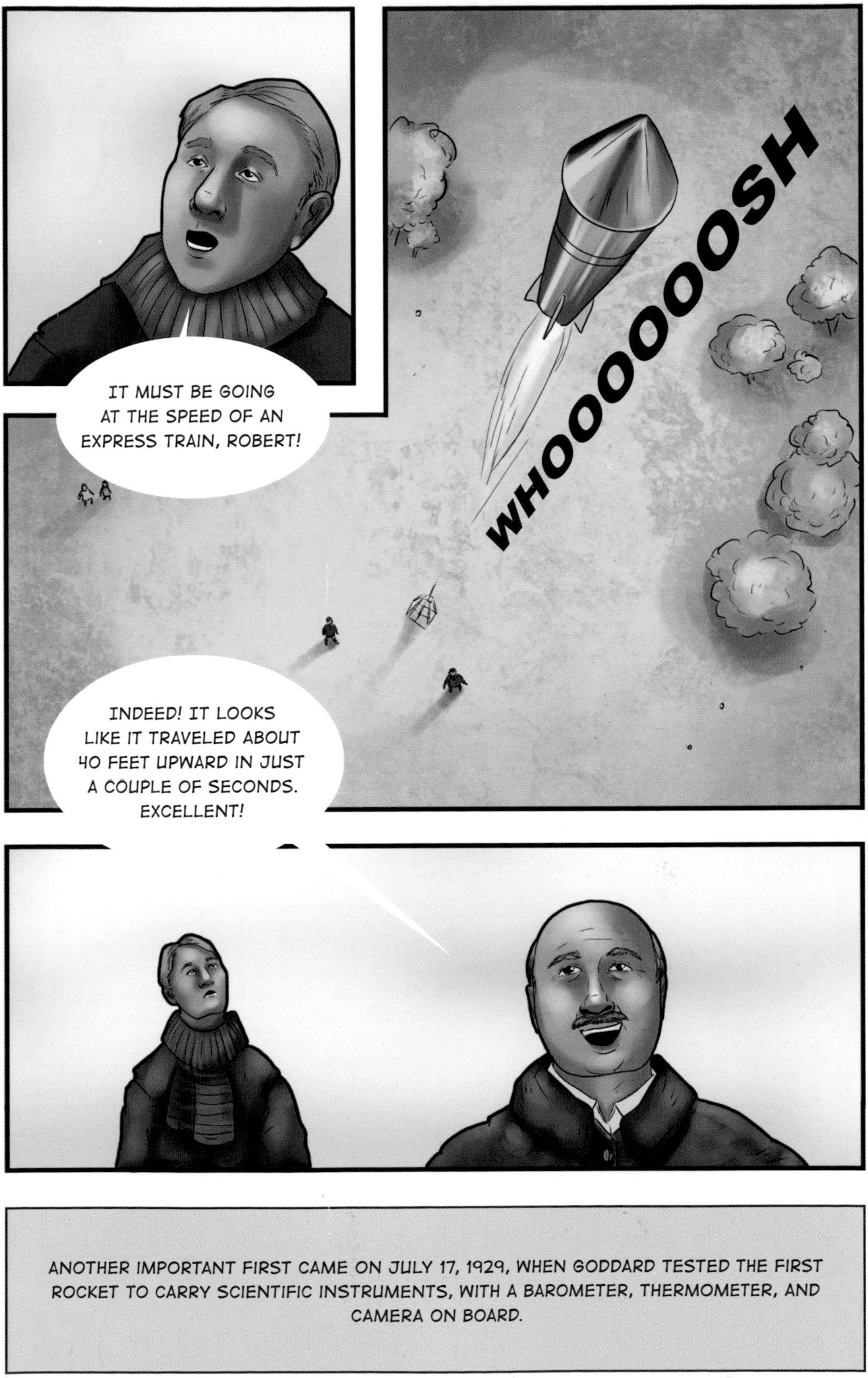
IT MUST BE GOING AT THE SPEED OF AN EXPRESS TRAIN, ROBERT!
WHOOOOOOSH
INDEED! IT LOOKS LIKE IT TRAVELED ABOUT 40 FEET UPWARD IN JUST A COUPLE OF SECONDS. EXCELLENT!
ANOTHER IMPORTANT FIRST CAME ON JULY 17, 1929, WHEN GODDARD TESTED THE FIRST ROCKET TO CARRY SCIENTIFIC INSTRUMENTS, WITH A BAROMETER, THERMOMETER, AND CAMERA ON BOARD.

GODDARD SOON MOVED HIS ROCKET TESTING TO A SITE IN ROSWELL, NEW MEXICO. DURING HIS EXPERIMENTS THERE, HE BECAME THE FIRST TO SHOOT A LIQUID-FUELED ROCKET FASTER THAN THE SPEED OF SOUND. IN 1937, ROBERT'S L-13 ROCKET SMASHED THE SOUND BARRIER—AROUND 767 MPH—AND FLEW 1.7 MILES HIGH.

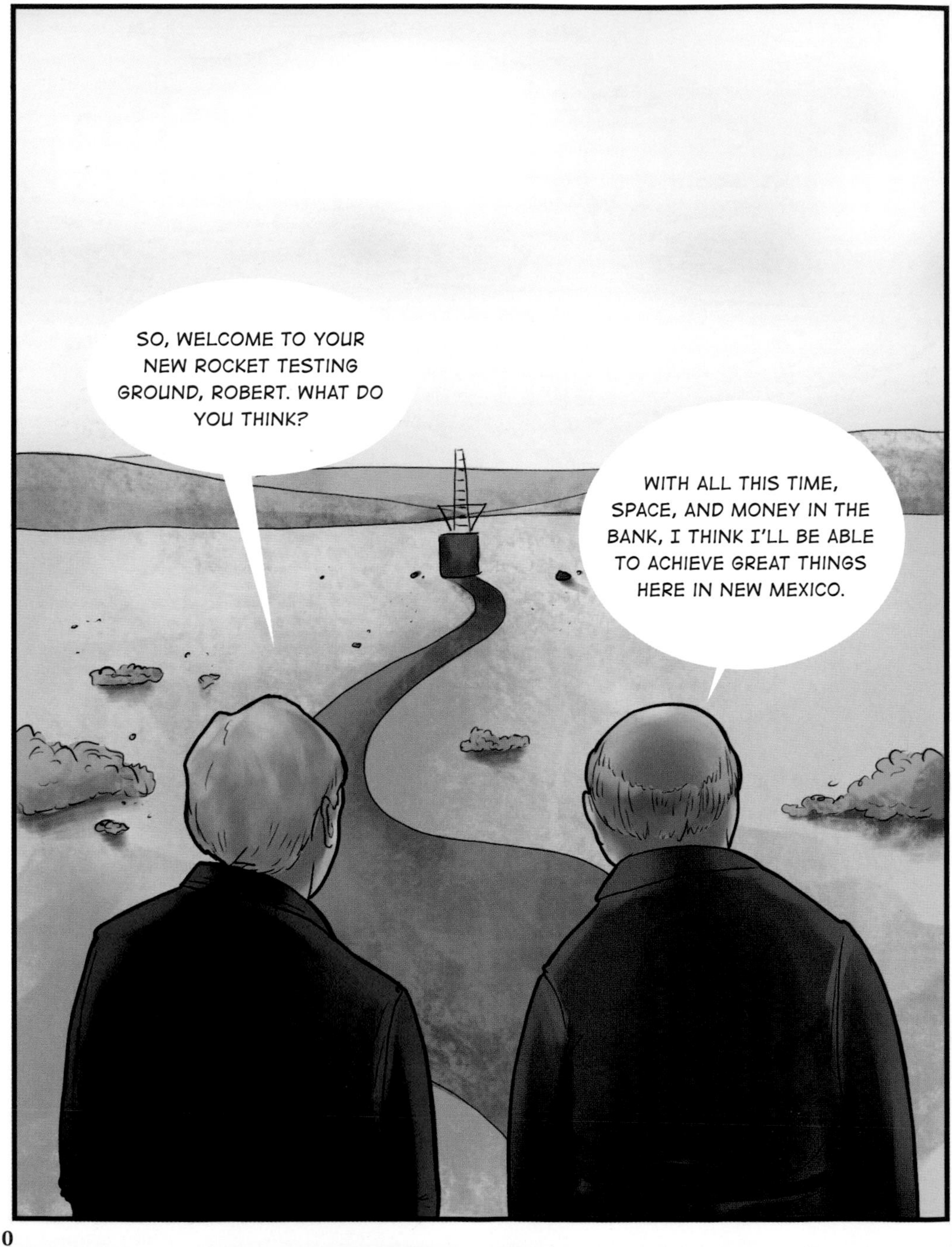
SO, WELCOME TO YOUR NEW ROCKET TESTING GROUND, ROBERT. WHAT DO YOU THINK?
WITH ALL THIS TIME, SPACE, AND MONEY IN THE BANK, I THINK I'LL BE ABLE TO ACHIEVE GREAT THINGS HERE IN NEW MEXICO.

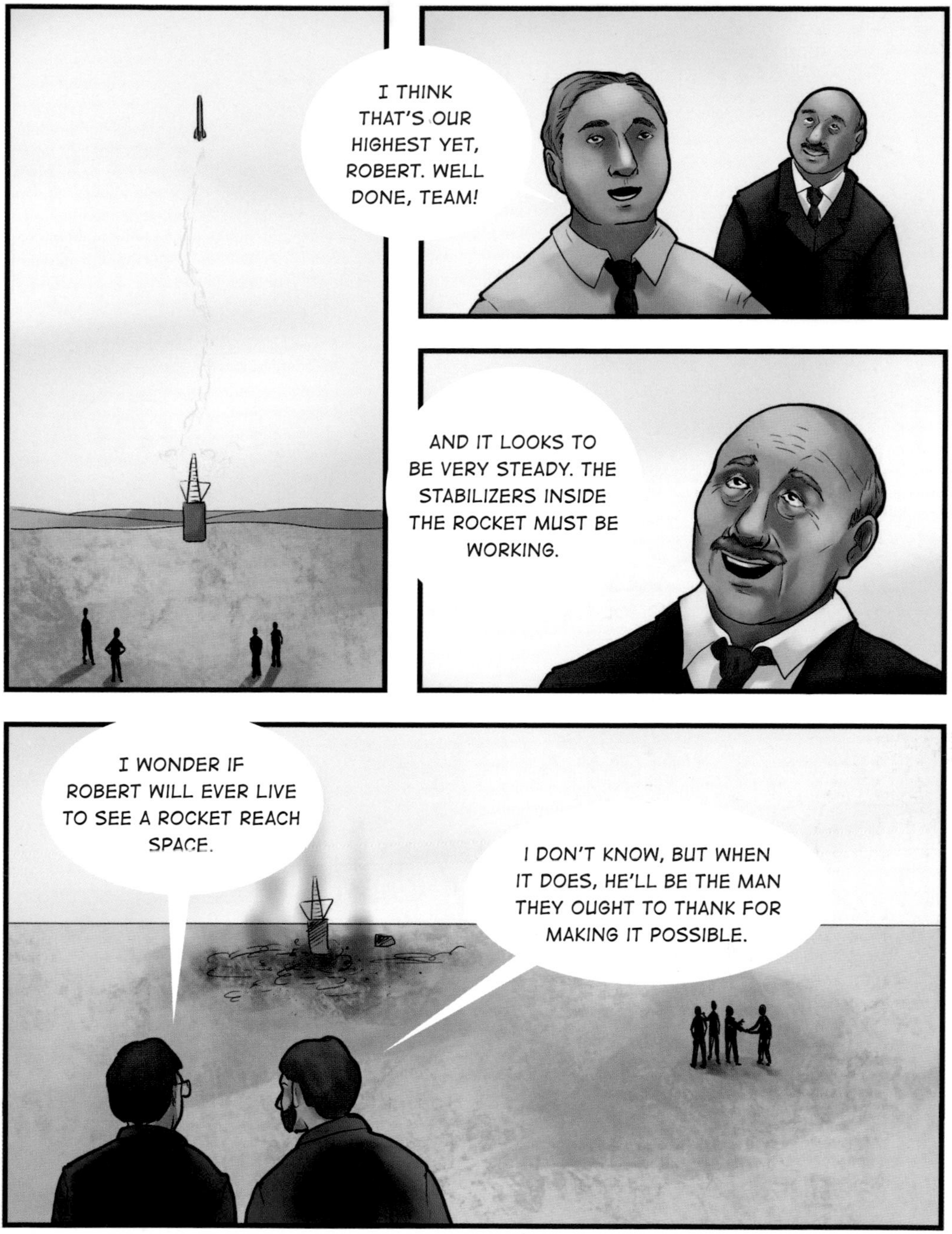
I THINK THAT'S OUR HIGHEST YET, ROBERT. WELL DONE, TEAM!
AND IT LOOKS TO BE VERY STEADY. THE STABILIZERS INSIDE THE ROCKET MUST BE WORKING.
I WONDER IF ROBERT WILL EVER LIVE TO SEE A ROCKET REACH SPACE.
I DON'T KNOW, BUT WHEN IT DOES, HE'LL BE THE MAN THEY OUGHT TO THANK FOR MAKING IT POSSIBLE.

AS THE FIRST SCIENTIST TO SHOOT FOR THE STARS, ROBERT'S WORK PAVED THE WAY FOR SPACEFLIGHT. HE LIVED TO SEE THE GERMAN *V-2* ROCKET REACH SPACE IN 1942—A FEW YEARS BEFORE HIS DEATH. IT TRAVELED FOR 118 MILES BUT ONLY REACHED AN ALTITUDE OF 52.5 MILES DURING ITS FIRST SUCCESSFUL TEST FLIGHT.

SERGEI KOROLEV
(1907–1966)
ARCHITECT OF SPACE EXPLORATION

FROM A YOUNG AGE, SERGEI WAS PASSIONATE ABOUT EXPLORING THE SKIES. WHILE STUDYING AT THE KIEV POLYTECHNIC INSTITUTE IN UKRAINE AS A TEENAGER, HE JOINED A GLIDER CLUB AND BUILT HIS FIRST GLIDER. AT AGE 20, HE MET FELLOW ENTHUSIAST MIKHAIL TIKHONRAVOV AT A GLIDER SHOW. THEY WOULD BECOME FRIENDS AND COLLEAGUES FOR DECADES TO COME.

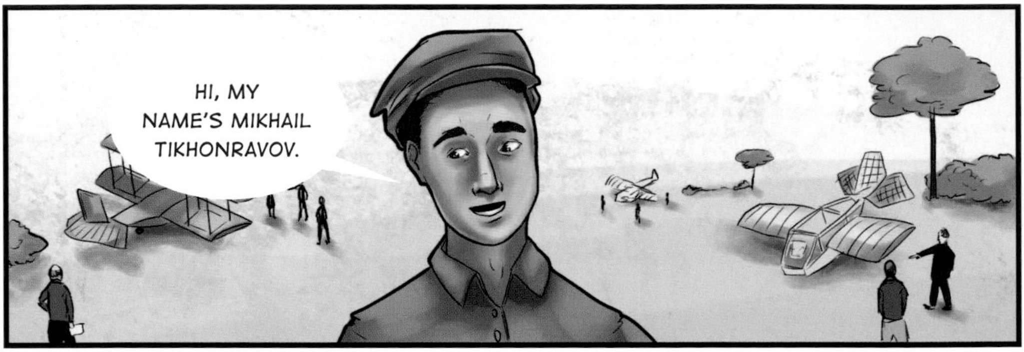
HI, MY NAME'S MIKHAIL TIKHONRAVOV.

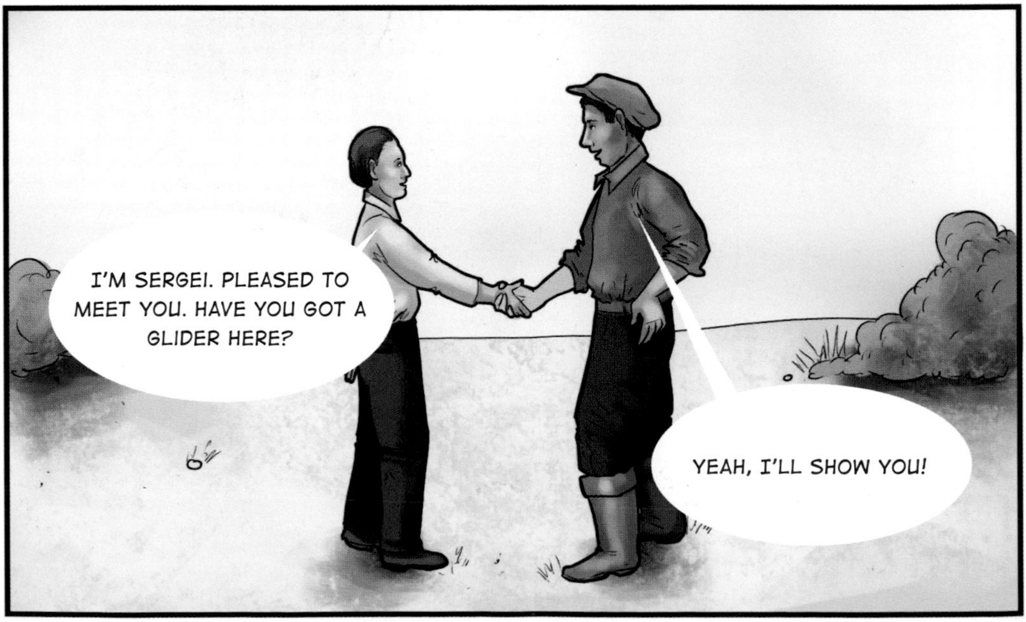
I'M SERGEI. PLEASED TO MEET YOU. HAVE YOU GOT A GLIDER HERE?
YEAH, I'LL SHOW YOU!

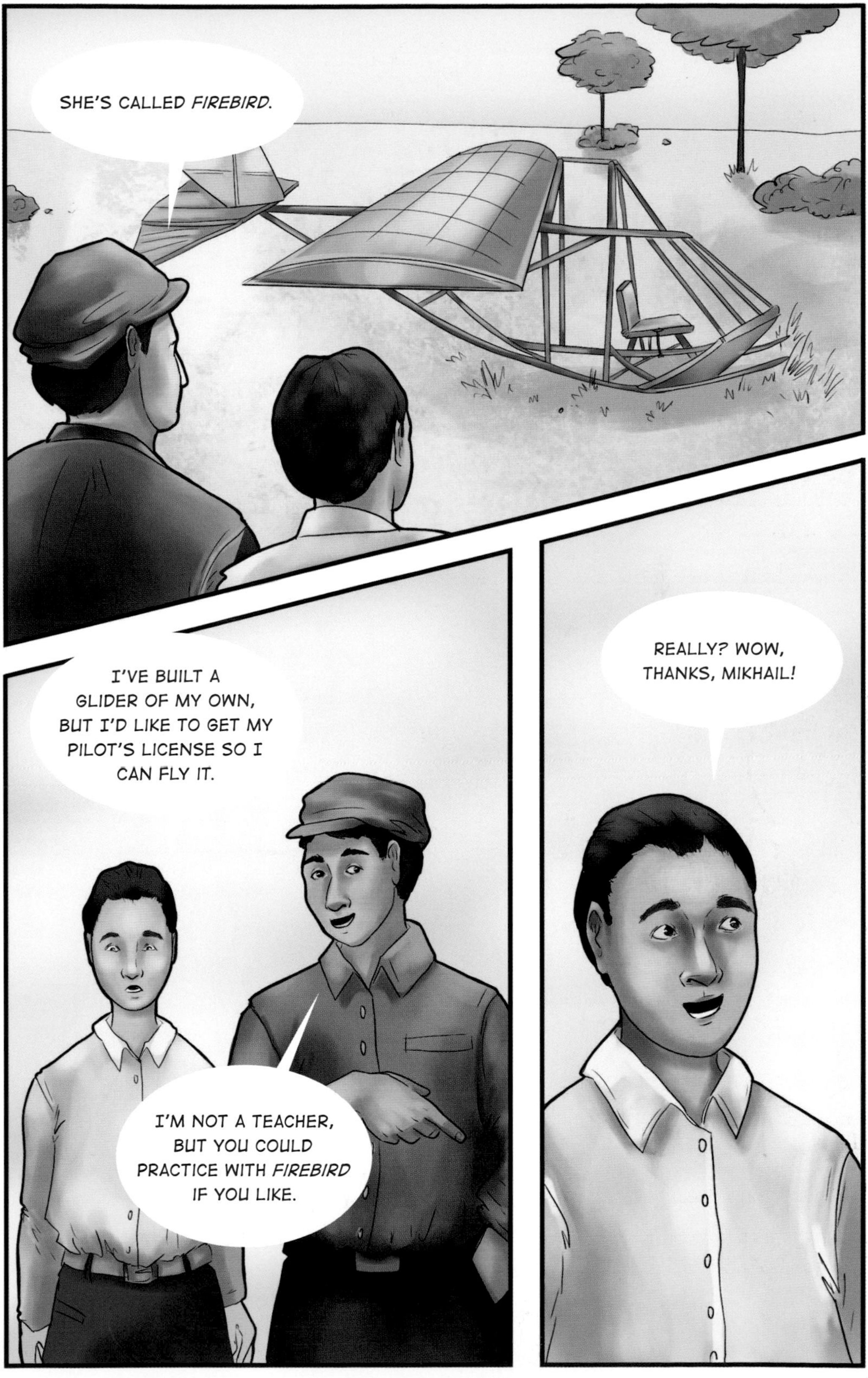
SHE'S CALLED *FIREBIRD*.
I'VE BUILT A GLIDER OF MY OWN, BUT I'D LIKE TO GET MY PILOT'S LICENSE SO I CAN FLY IT.
I'M NOT A TEACHER, BUT YOU COULD PRACTICE WITH *FIREBIRD* IF YOU LIKE.
REALLY? WOW, THANKS, MIKHAIL!

SERGEI GRADUATED FROM ENGINEERING COLLEGE IN 1929, SEVERAL YEARS AFTER RUSSIA BECAME THE SOVIET UNION. WITHIN A COUPLE OF YEARS, HE WAS DESIGNING AIRPLANES AT A FEDERAL RUSSIAN AGENCY. HERE, HE BECAME INTERESTED IN THE IDEA OF SPACEFLIGHT. WITH MIKHAIL TIKHONRAVOV AND RUSSIAN SCIENTIST FRIEDRICH ZANDER, SERGEI STARTED THE GROUP FOR THE STUDY OF REACTIVE MOTION (GIRD) TO FOCUS ON DESIGNING ROCKETS THAT COULD REACH SPACE.

MIKHAIL, I'D LIKE YOU TO MEET FRIEDRICH ZANDER.

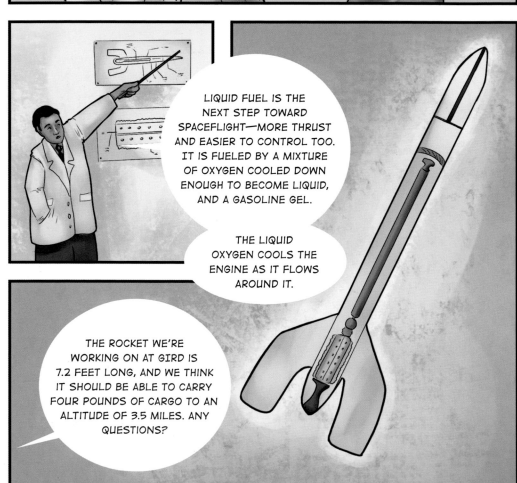

LIQUID FUEL IS THE NEXT STEP TOWARD SPACEFLIGHT—MORE THRUST AND EASIER TO CONTROL TOO. IT IS FUELED BY A MIXTURE OF OXYGEN COOLED DOWN ENOUGH TO BECOME LIQUID, AND A GASOLINE GEL.

THE LIQUID OXYGEN COOLS THE ENGINE AS IT FLOWS AROUND IT.

THE ROCKET WE'RE WORKING ON AT GIRD IS 7.2 FEET LONG, AND WE THINK IT SHOULD BE ABLE TO CARRY FOUR POUNDS OF CARGO TO AN ALTITUDE OF 3.5 MILES. ANY QUESTIONS?

In 1933, the Soviets launched their first rocket—*GIRD-9*. It reached a height of 1,300 feet—a long way short of reaching space!

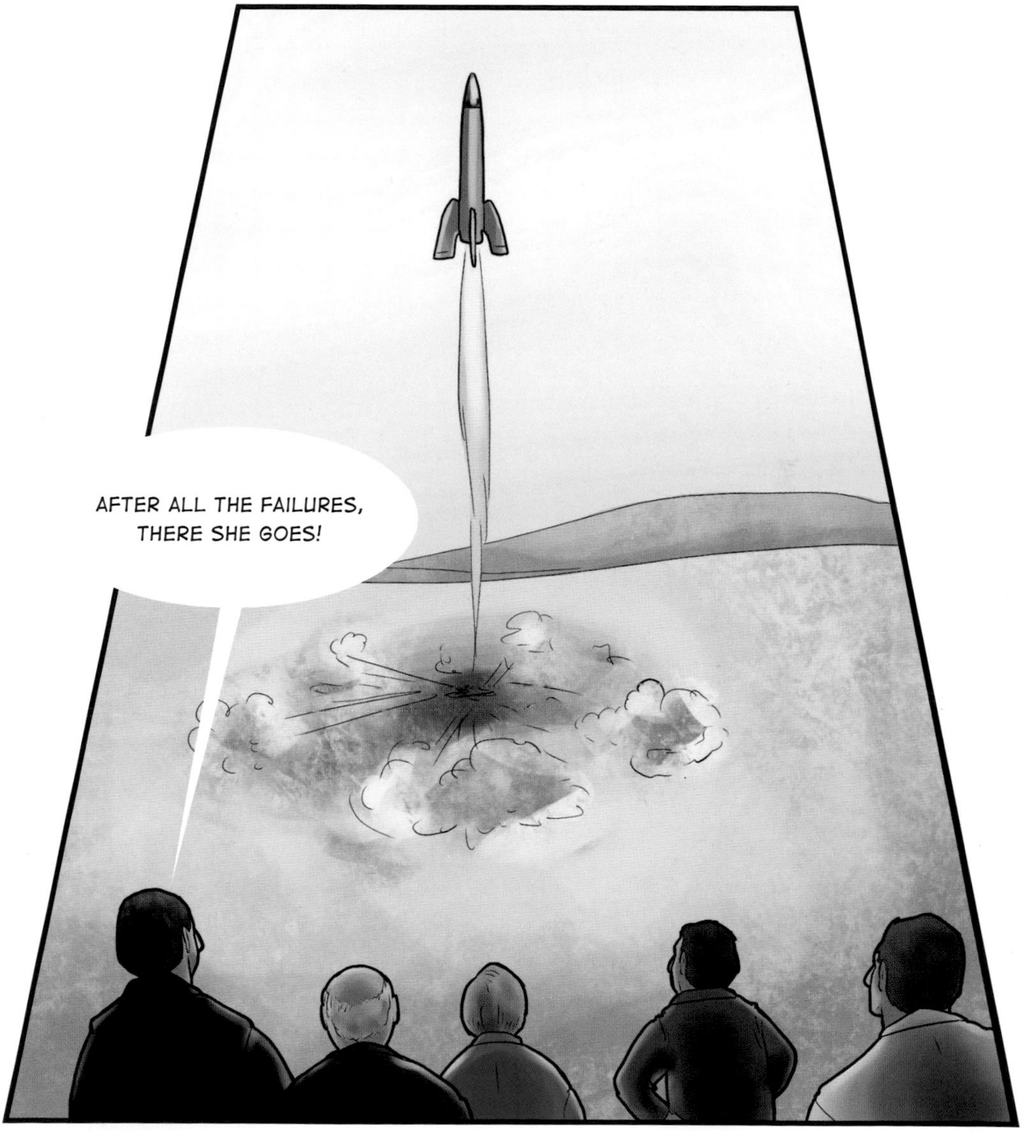
AFTER ALL THE FAILURES, THERE SHE GOES!

Sergei went on to work with other scientists dedicated to achieving space travel. He worked closely with propulsion specialist Valentin Glushko to develop cruise missiles and a rocket-powered glider.

THE 1930s WERE TERRIFYING TIMES IN THE SOVIET UNION. THE COUNTRY'S RULER, JOSEPH STALIN, WAS HUNTING DOWN, TORTURING, AND KILLING PEOPLE THAT OPPOSED HIM UNDER A PROGRAM THAT BECAME KNOWN AS THE GREAT PURGE. IN JUNE 1938, SHORTLY BEFORE THE START OF WORLD WAR II, SERGEI WAS ARRESTED AND THROWN INTO JAIL.

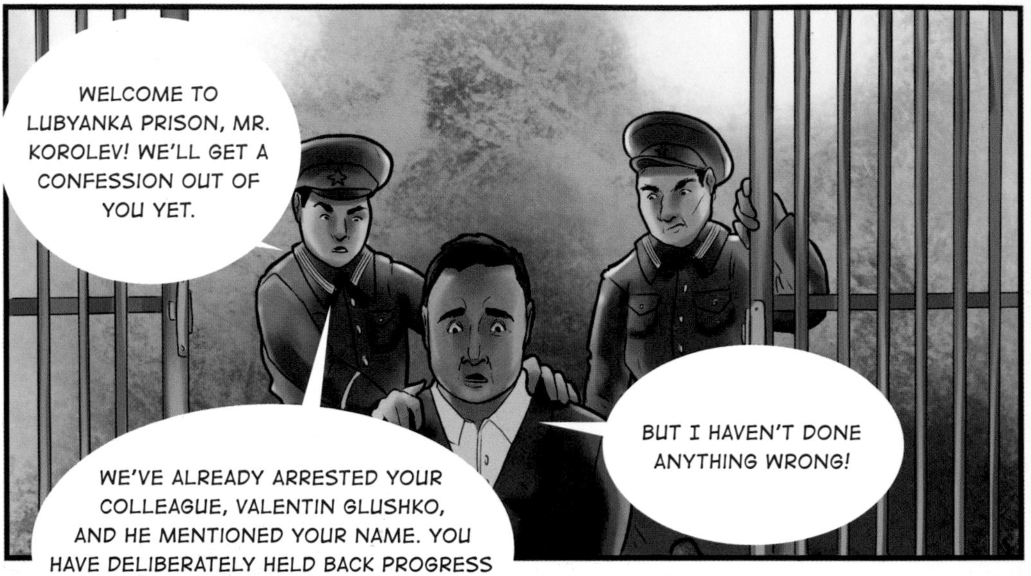
WELCOME TO LUBYANKA PRISON, MR. KOROLEV! WE'LL GET A CONFESSION OUT OF YOU YET.
BUT I HAVEN'T DONE ANYTHING WRONG!
WE'VE ALREADY ARRESTED YOUR COLLEAGUE, VALENTIN GLUSHKO, AND HE MENTIONED YOUR NAME. YOU HAVE DELIBERATELY HELD BACK PROGRESS AT THE RESEARCH INSTITUTE AND WASTED MONEY.

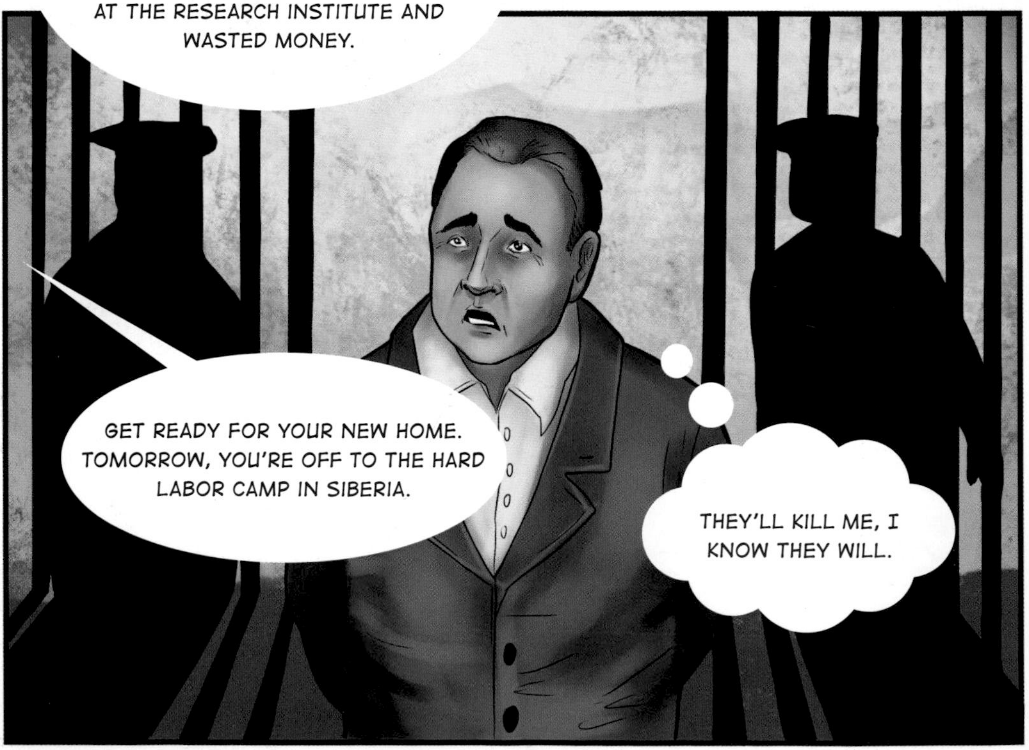
GET READY FOR YOUR NEW HOME. TOMORROW, YOU'RE OFF TO THE HARD LABOR CAMP IN SIBERIA.
THEY'LL KILL ME, I KNOW THEY WILL.

THE FOLLOWING YEAR, SERGEI WAS SENT TO THE KOLYMA LABOR CAMP, WHERE HE WOULD SPEND SEVERAL MONTHS WORKING IN A GOLD MINE UNDER HARSH CONDITIONS. HE SUFFERED MANY INJURIES AND LOST MOST OF HIS TEETH DUE TO MALNUTRITION.

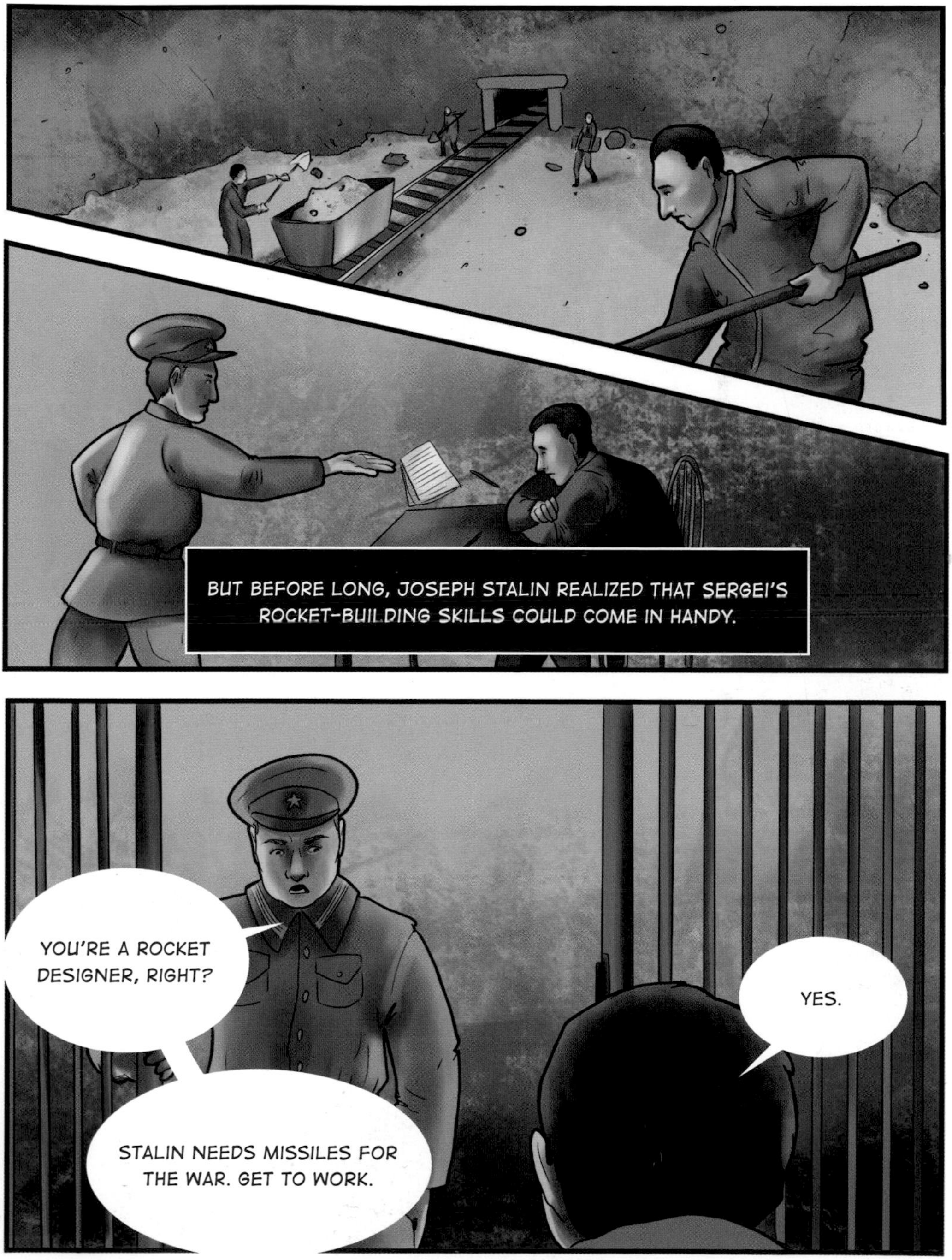
BUT BEFORE LONG, JOSEPH STALIN REALIZED THAT SERGEI'S ROCKET-BUILDING SKILLS COULD COME IN HANDY.
YOU'RE A ROCKET DESIGNER, RIGHT?
YES.
STALIN NEEDS MISSILES FOR THE WAR. GET TO WORK.

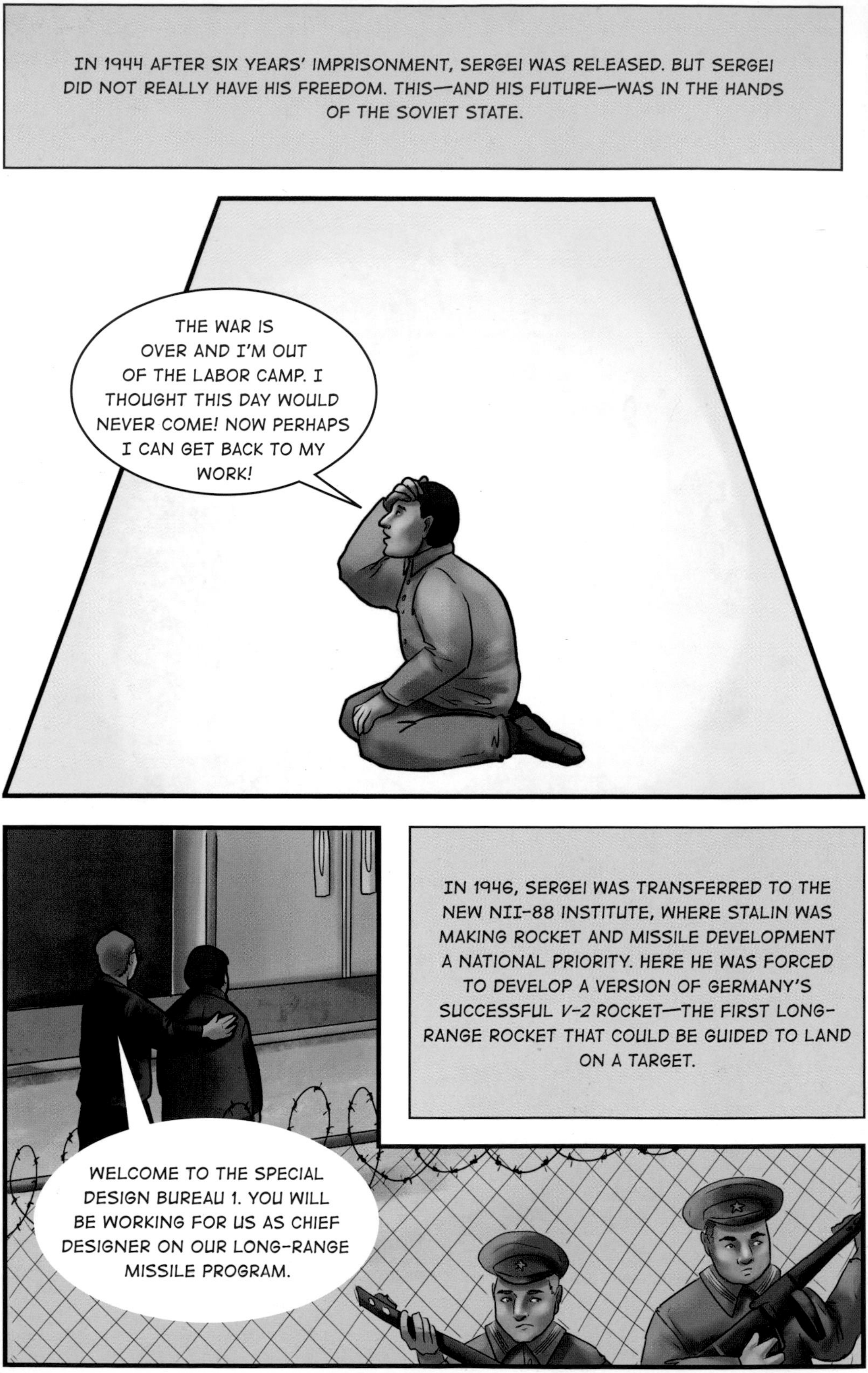
IN 1944 AFTER SIX YEARS' IMPRISONMENT, SERGEI WAS RELEASED. BUT SERGEI DID NOT REALLY HAVE HIS FREEDOM. THIS—AND HIS FUTURE—WAS IN THE HANDS OF THE SOVIET STATE.
THE WAR IS OVER AND I'M OUT OF THE LABOR CAMP. I THOUGHT THIS DAY WOULD NEVER COME! NOW PERHAPS I CAN GET BACK TO MY WORK!
IN 1946, SERGEI WAS TRANSFERRED TO THE NEW NII-88 INSTITUTE, WHERE STALIN WAS MAKING ROCKET AND MISSILE DEVELOPMENT A NATIONAL PRIORITY. HERE HE WAS FORCED TO DEVELOP A VERSION OF GERMANY'S SUCCESSFUL *V-2* ROCKET—THE FIRST LONG-RANGE ROCKET THAT COULD BE GUIDED TO LAND ON A TARGET.
WELCOME TO THE SPECIAL DESIGN BUREAU 1. YOU WILL BE WORKING FOR US AS CHIEF DESIGNER ON OUR LONG-RANGE MISSILE PROGRAM.

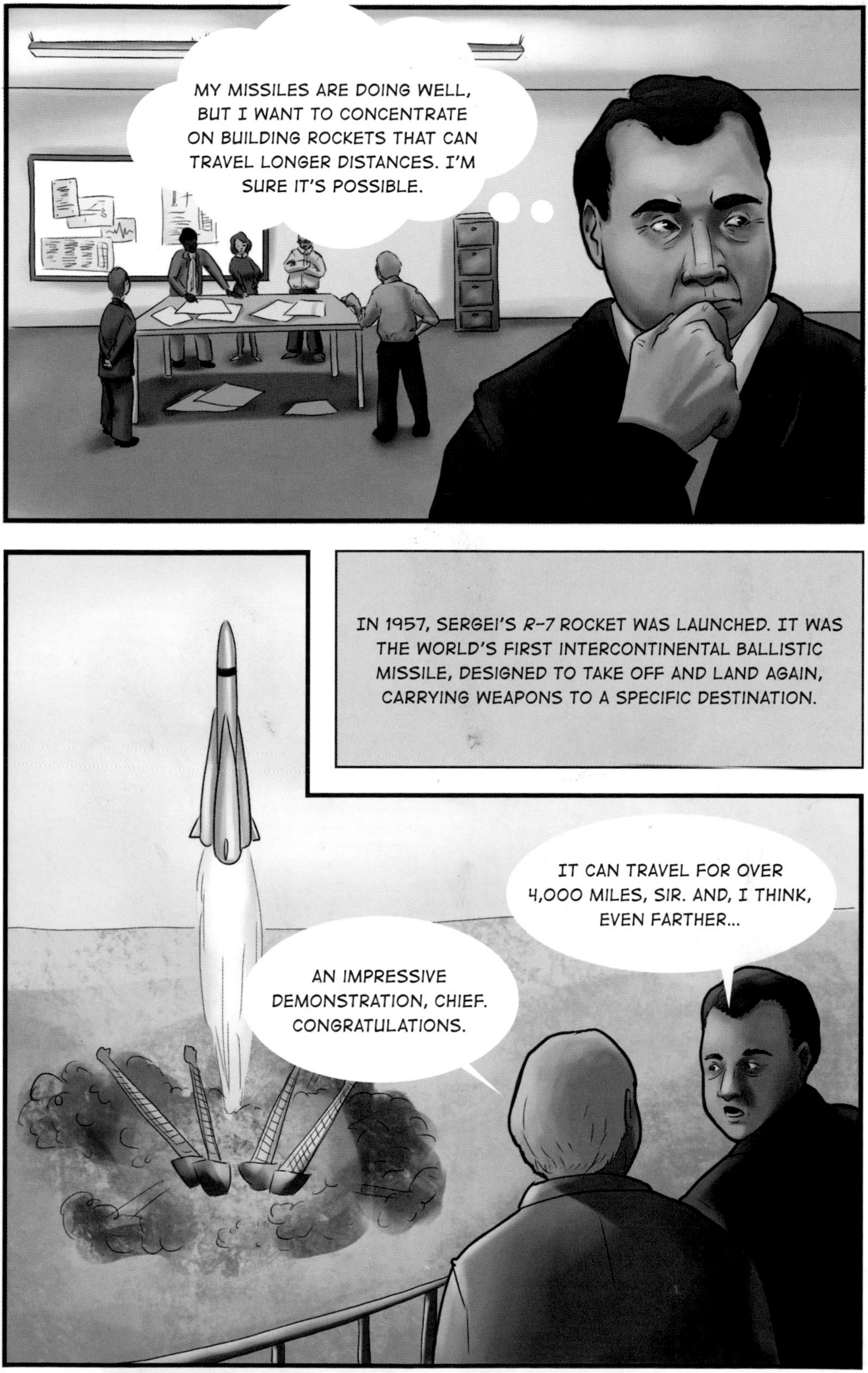
MY MISSILES ARE DOING WELL, BUT I WANT TO CONCENTRATE ON BUILDING ROCKETS THAT CAN TRAVEL LONGER DISTANCES. I'M SURE IT'S POSSIBLE.
IN 1957, SERGEI'S *R-7* ROCKET WAS LAUNCHED. IT WAS THE WORLD'S FIRST INTERCONTINENTAL BALLISTIC MISSILE, DESIGNED TO TAKE OFF AND LAND AGAIN, CARRYING WEAPONS TO A SPECIFIC DESTINATION.
AN IMPRESSIVE DEMONSTRATION, CHIEF. CONGRATULATIONS.
IT CAN TRAVEL FOR OVER 4,000 MILES, SIR. AND, I THINK, EVEN FARTHER...

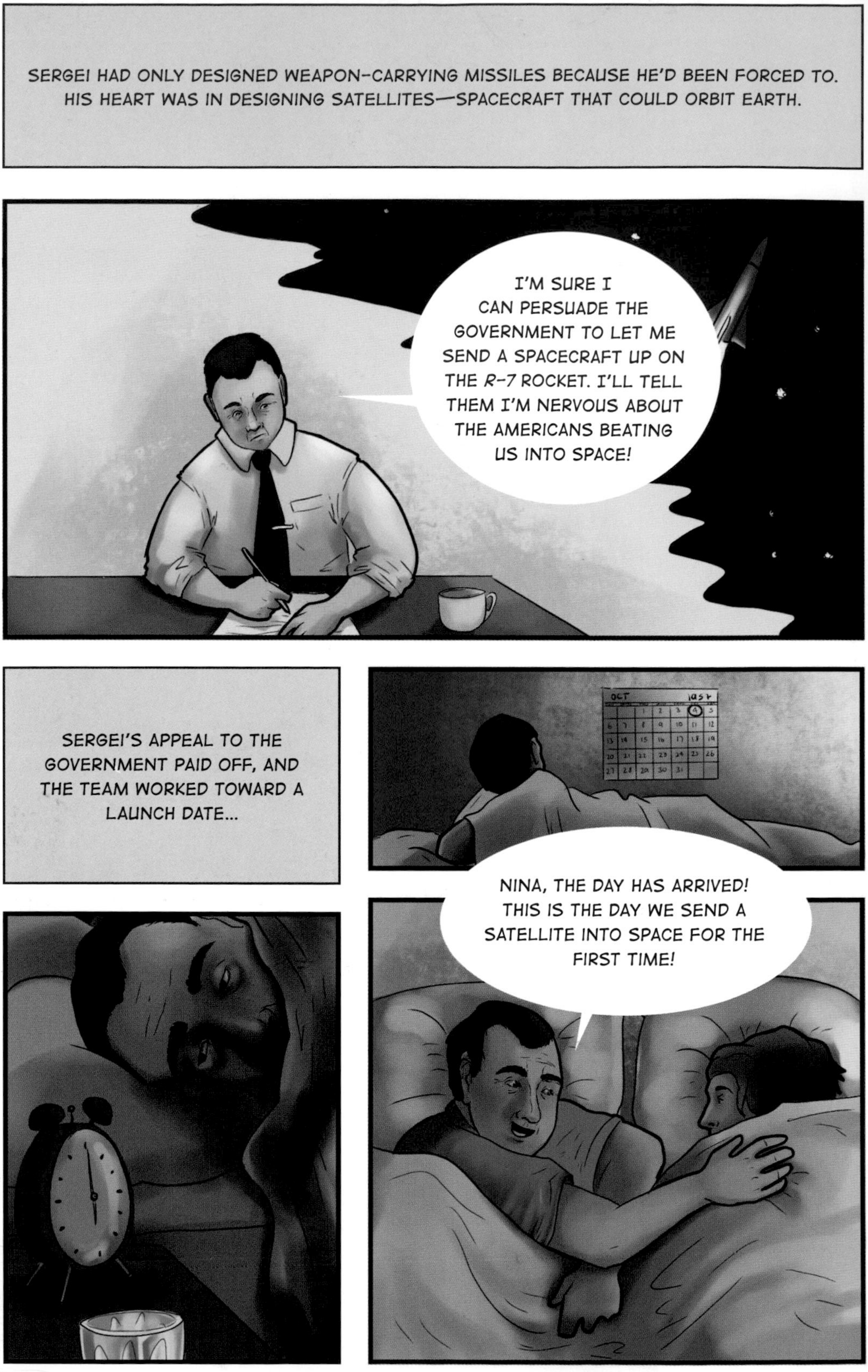
SERGEI HAD ONLY DESIGNED WEAPON-CARRYING MISSILES BECAUSE HE'D BEEN FORCED TO. HIS HEART WAS IN DESIGNING SATELLITES—SPACECRAFT THAT COULD ORBIT EARTH.
I'M SURE I CAN PERSUADE THE GOVERNMENT TO LET ME SEND A SPACECRAFT UP ON THE *R-7* ROCKET. I'LL TELL THEM I'M NERVOUS ABOUT THE AMERICANS BEATING US INTO SPACE!
SERGEI'S APPEAL TO THE GOVERNMENT PAID OFF, AND THE TEAM WORKED TOWARD A LAUNCH DATE...
NINA, THE DAY HAS ARRIVED! THIS IS THE DAY WE SEND A SATELLITE INTO SPACE FOR THE FIRST TIME!

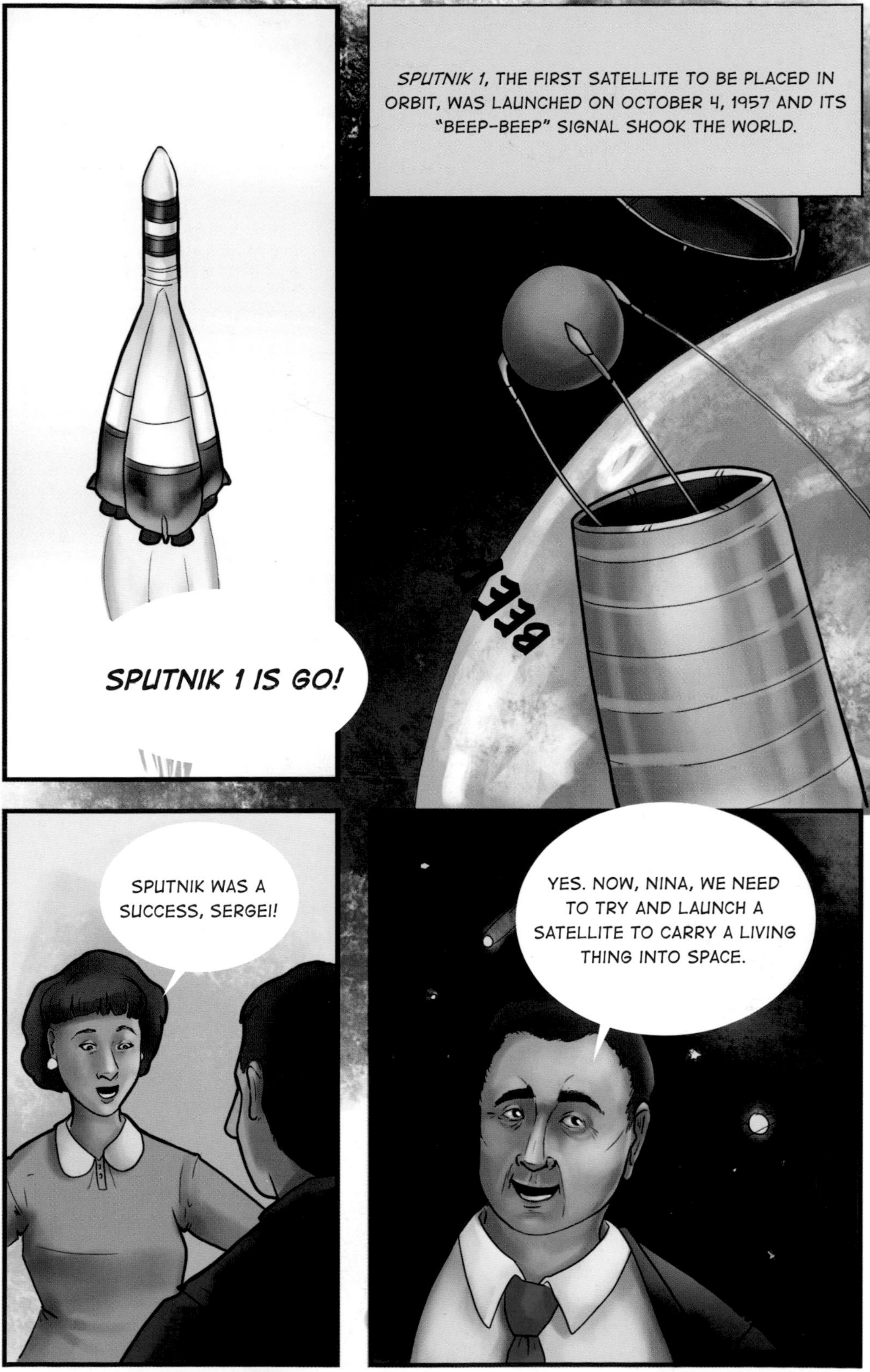
SPUTNIK 1 IS GO!
SPUTNIK 1, THE FIRST SATELLITE TO BE PLACED IN ORBIT, WAS LAUNCHED ON OCTOBER 4, 1957 AND ITS "BEEP-BEEP" SIGNAL SHOOK THE WORLD.
BEEP
SPUTNIK WAS A SUCCESS, SERGEI!
YES. NOW, NINA, WE NEED TO TRY AND LAUNCH A SATELLITE TO CARRY A LIVING THING INTO SPACE.

A MONTH LATER, ON NOVEMBER 3, 1957, KOROLEV'S *SPUTNIK 2* SHOT INTO ORBIT, CARRYING LAIKA THE DOG, THE FIRST ANIMAL TO ORBIT EARTH. THE LAST YEARS OF SERGEI'S LIFE SAW HIM LEAD MANY MORE PIONEERING MISSIONS INTO SPACE, INCLUDING *LUNA 2*, *LUNA 3*, AND *VOSTOK 1*.

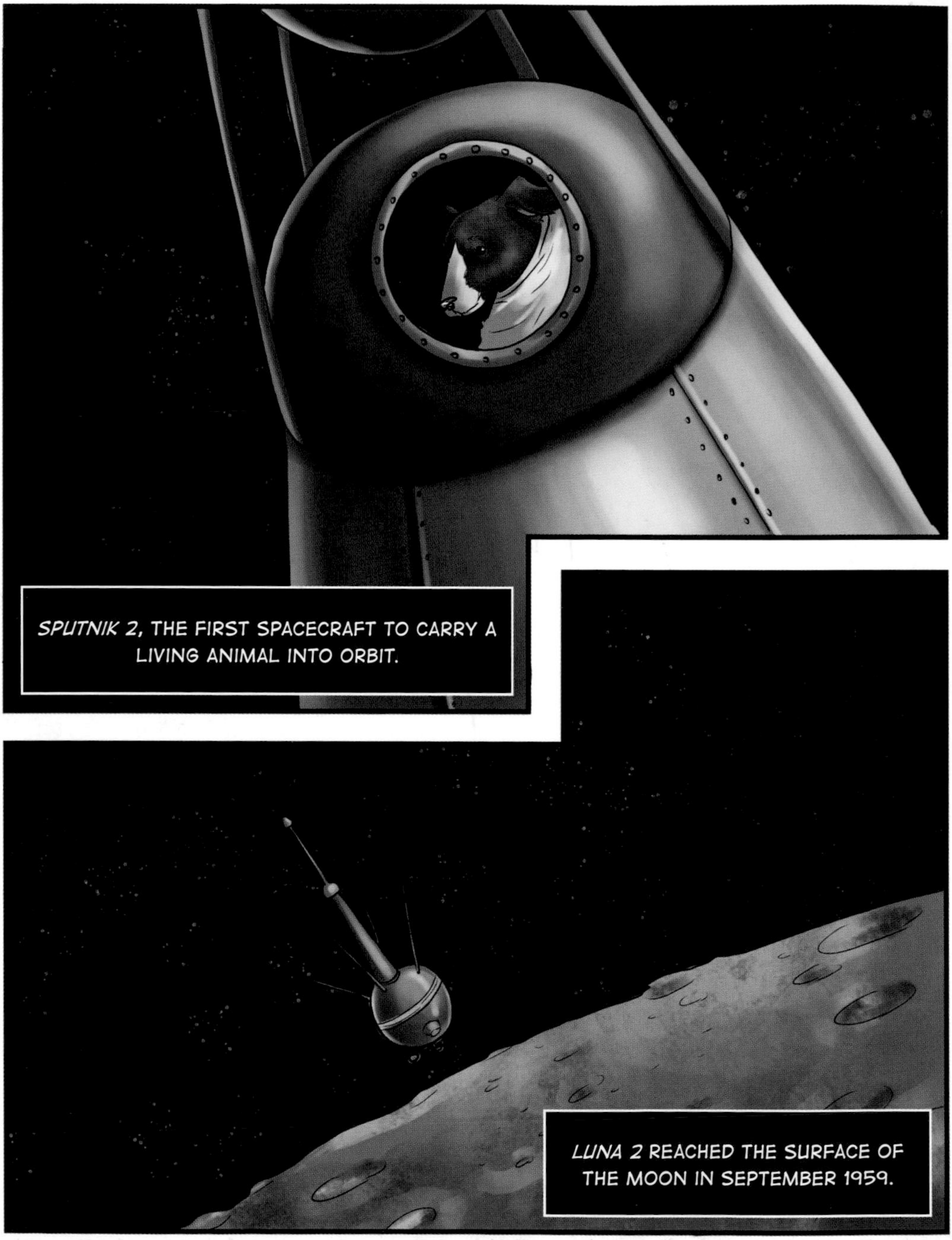
SPUTNIK 2, THE FIRST SPACECRAFT TO CARRY A LIVING ANIMAL INTO ORBIT.
LUNA 2 REACHED THE SURFACE OF THE MOON IN SEPTEMBER 1959.

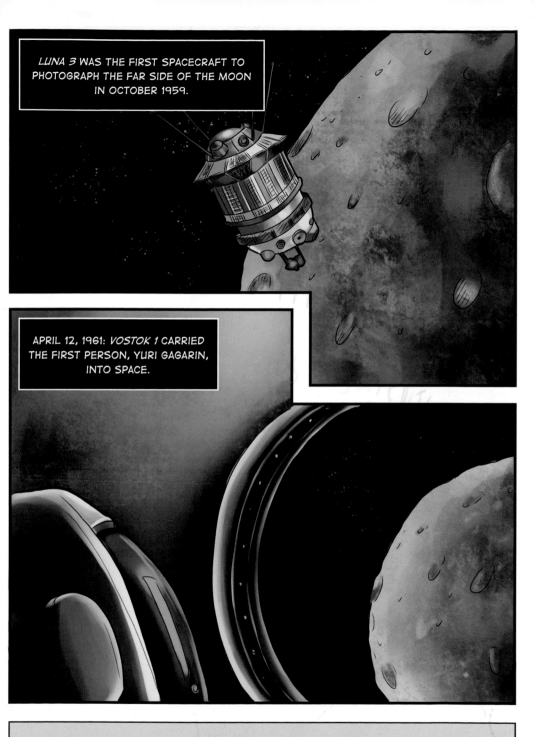

LUNA 3 WAS THE FIRST SPACECRAFT TO PHOTOGRAPH THE FAR SIDE OF THE MOON IN OCTOBER 1959.

APRIL 12, 1961: VOSTOK 1 CARRIED THE FIRST PERSON, YURI GAGARIN, INTO SPACE.

SERGEI'S WORK STARTED AND DROVE FORWARD THE SOVIET SPACE PROGRAM, WHICH ULTIMATELY PUT THE FIRST PERSON INTO SPACE. MANY SAY THAT IF HE'D LIVED LONGER, THE SOVIET UNION, NOT THE U.S., MIGHT HAVE PUT THE FIRST PEOPLE ON THE MOON.

ANIMAL ASTRONAUTS
EARTH'S FIRST SPACE TRAVELERS

SPACE PROGRAMS EAGER TO INTRODUCE A NEW AGE OF EXPLORATION WERE DESPERATE TO PUT A PERSON INTO ORBIT. BUT NO ONE KNEW IF PEOPLE COULD SURVIVE THE TRIP OR EVEN DIGEST FOOD IN SPACE. SO, TESTS BEGAN WITH TINY FRUIT FLIES.

FEBRUARY 20, 1947: FRUIT FLIES BECAME THE FIRST LIVING CREATURES TO TRAVEL INTO OUTER SPACE ON THE *V-2* ROCKET LAUNCHED FROM THE MISSILE RANGE IN WHITE SANDS, NEW MEXICO.

THEY REACHED AN ALTITUDE OF 67 MILES, JUST BEYOND EARTH'S ATMOSPHERE...

...AND WERE RECOVERED ALIVE AFTER PARACHUTING BACK TO EARTH INSIDE A SMALL CAPSULE.

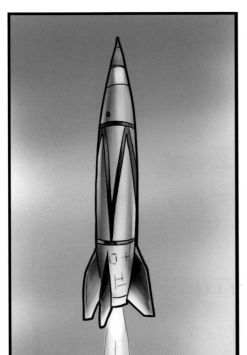

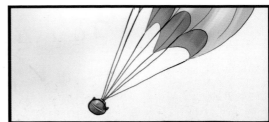

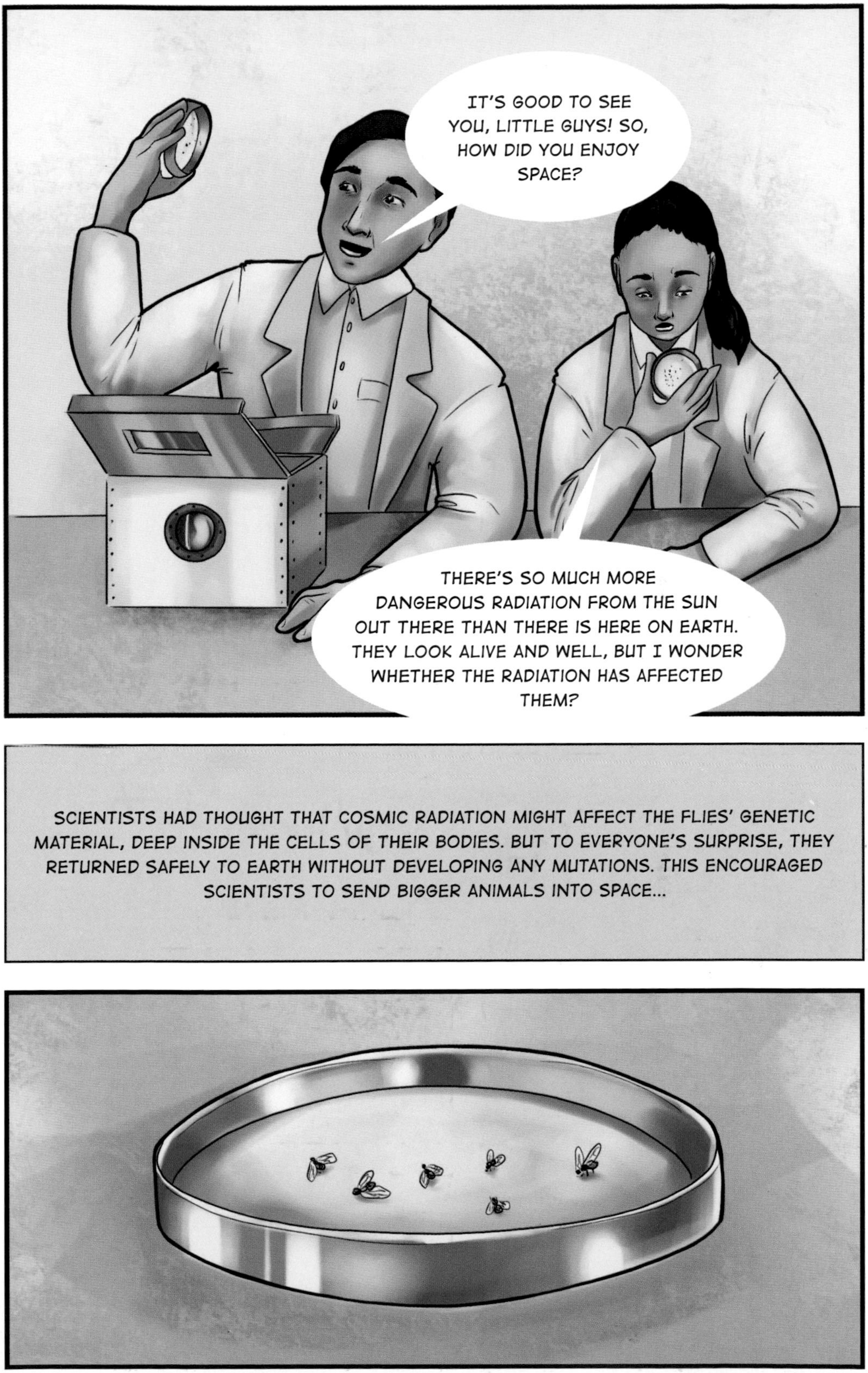
IT'S GOOD TO SEE YOU, LITTLE GUYS! SO, HOW DID YOU ENJOY SPACE?
THERE'S SO MUCH MORE DANGEROUS RADIATION FROM THE SUN OUT THERE THAN THERE IS HERE ON EARTH. THEY LOOK ALIVE AND WELL, BUT I WONDER WHETHER THE RADIATION HAS AFFECTED THEM?
SCIENTISTS HAD THOUGHT THAT COSMIC RADIATION MIGHT AFFECT THE FLIES' GENETIC MATERIAL, DEEP INSIDE THE CELLS OF THEIR BODIES. BUT TO EVERYONE'S SURPRISE, THEY RETURNED SAFELY TO EARTH WITHOUT DEVELOPING ANY MUTATIONS. THIS ENCOURAGED SCIENTISTS TO SEND BIGGER ANIMALS INTO SPACE...

VARIOUS COUNTRIES HAVE SENT ANIMALS INTO SPACE OVER THE YEARS, INCLUDING MANY MONKEYS AND CHIMPANZEES. THE FIRST PRIMATE WAS A RHESUS MONKEY, ALBERT I. THE U.S. SENT HIM INTO FLIGHT ON JUNE 11, 1948, BUT LIKE MANY OTHER ANIMALS, HE DIED ON THE JOURNEY.

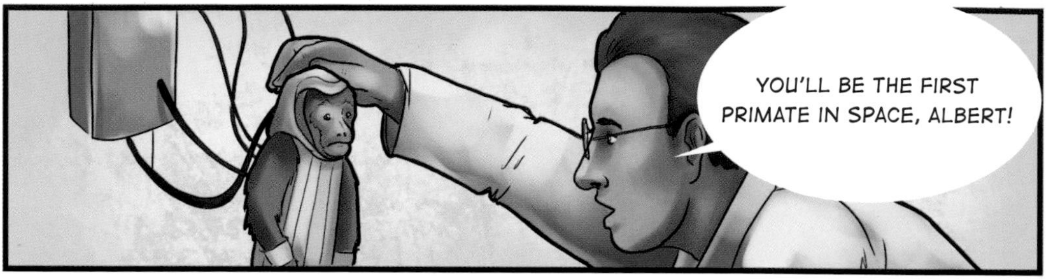
YOU'LL BE THE FIRST PRIMATE IN SPACE, ALBERT!

ELEVEN YEARS LATER, A U.S. MISSION SAW RHESUS MONKEY, ABLE, AND SQUIRREL MONKEY, BAKER, BECOME THE FIRST MAMMALS TO RETURN TO EARTH ALIVE AFTER A TRIP TO SPACE.

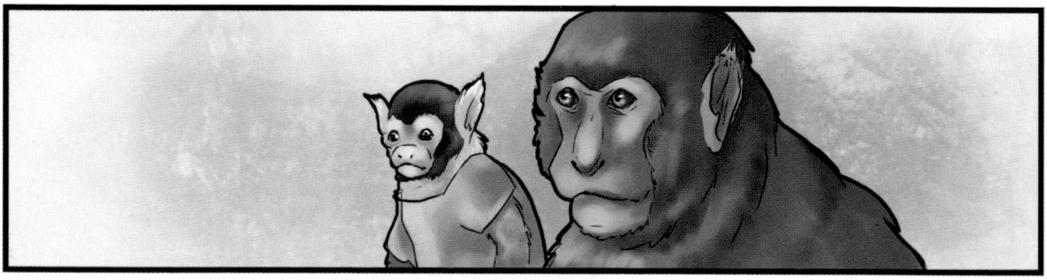

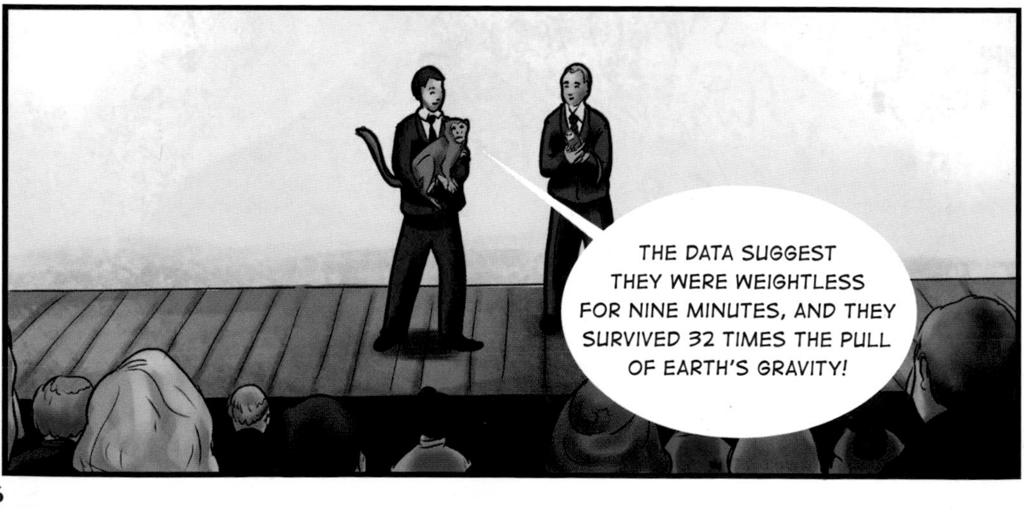
THE DATA SUGGEST THEY WERE WEIGHTLESS FOR NINE MINUTES, AND THEY SURVIVED 32 TIMES THE PULL OF EARTH'S GRAVITY!

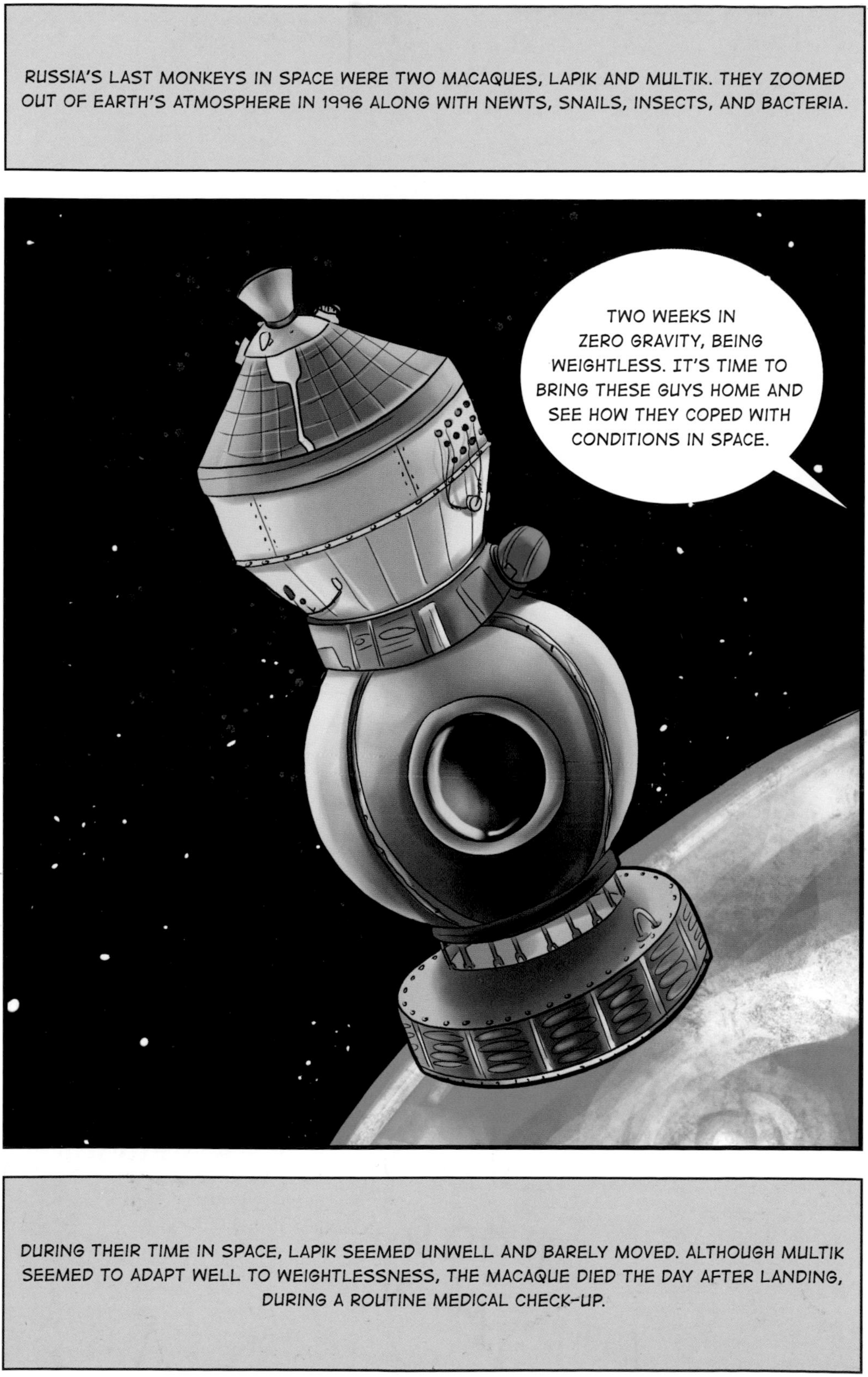
RUSSIA'S LAST MONKEYS IN SPACE WERE TWO MACAQUES, LAPIK AND MULTIK. THEY ZOOMED OUT OF EARTH'S ATMOSPHERE IN 1996 ALONG WITH NEWTS, SNAILS, INSECTS, AND BACTERIA.
TWO WEEKS IN ZERO GRAVITY, BEING WEIGHTLESS. IT'S TIME TO BRING THESE GUYS HOME AND SEE HOW THEY COPED WITH CONDITIONS IN SPACE.
DURING THEIR TIME IN SPACE, LAPIK SEEMED UNWELL AND BARELY MOVED. ALTHOUGH MULTIK SEEMED TO ADAPT WELL TO WEIGHTLESSNESS, THE MACAQUE DIED THE DAY AFTER LANDING, DURING A ROUTINE MEDICAL CHECK-UP.

IN THE 1950s, RUSSIA LAUNCHED A TOTAL OF 12 DOGS ON VARIOUS SUBORBITAL FLIGHTS. LAIKA THE DOG WAS ONE OF THE MOST FAMOUS ANIMALS TO TRAVEL INTO SPACE. SHE WAS THE FIRST ANIMAL TO ORBIT EARTH IN 1957.

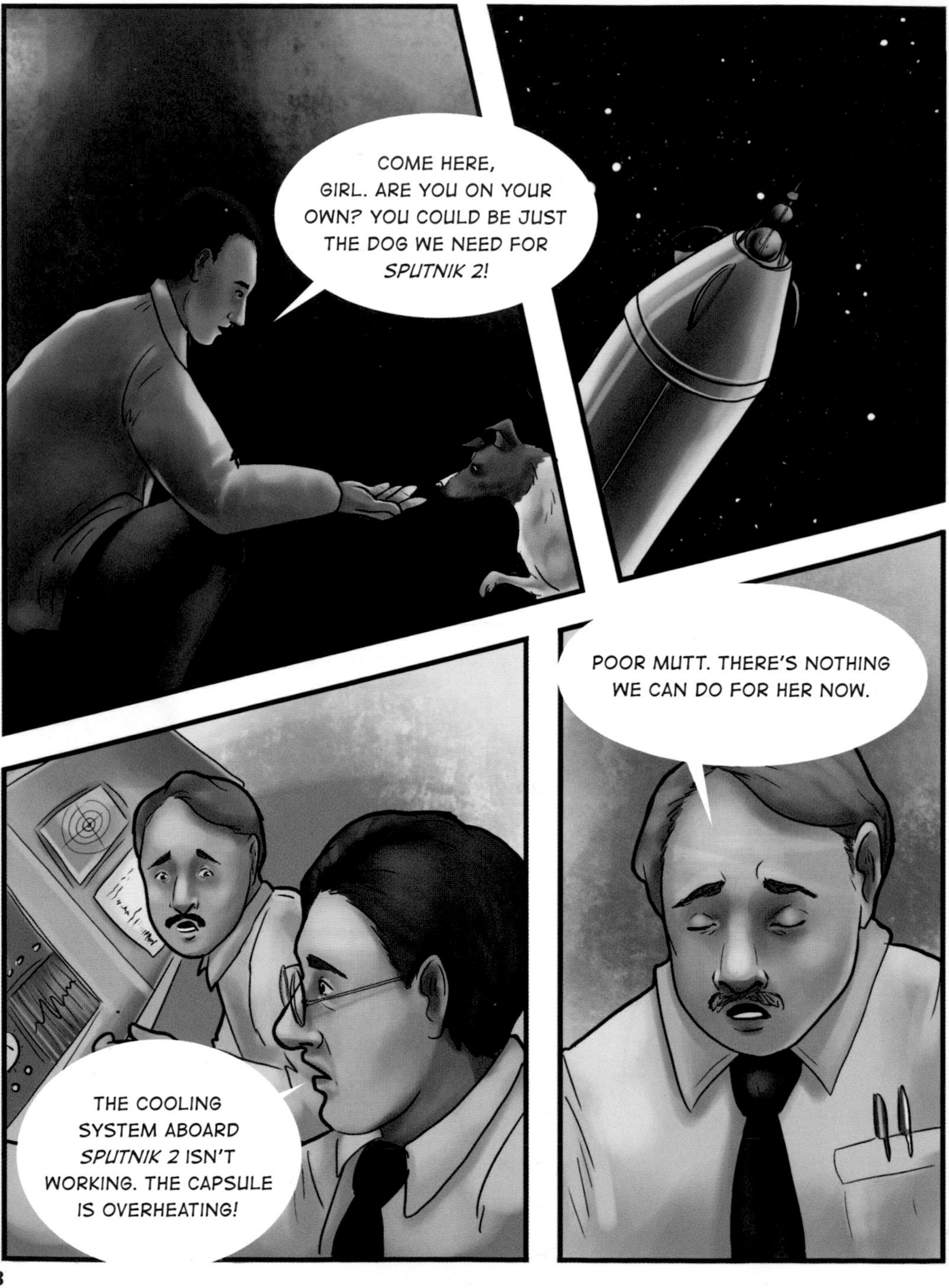
COME HERE, GIRL. ARE YOU ON YOUR OWN? YOU COULD BE JUST THE DOG WE NEED FOR *SPUTNIK 2*!
THE COOLING SYSTEM ABOARD *SPUTNIK 2* ISN'T WORKING. THE CAPSULE IS OVERHEATING!
POOR MUTT. THERE'S NOTHING WE CAN DO FOR HER NOW.

LAIKA DIED SEVERAL HOURS INTO THE FLIGHT FROM STRESS AND HEAT. A TRIBUTE TO HER WAS UNVEILED IN APRIL 2008, NEAR THE MILITARY RESEARCH CENTER IN MOSCOW THAT PREPARED HER FLIGHT INTO SPACE.

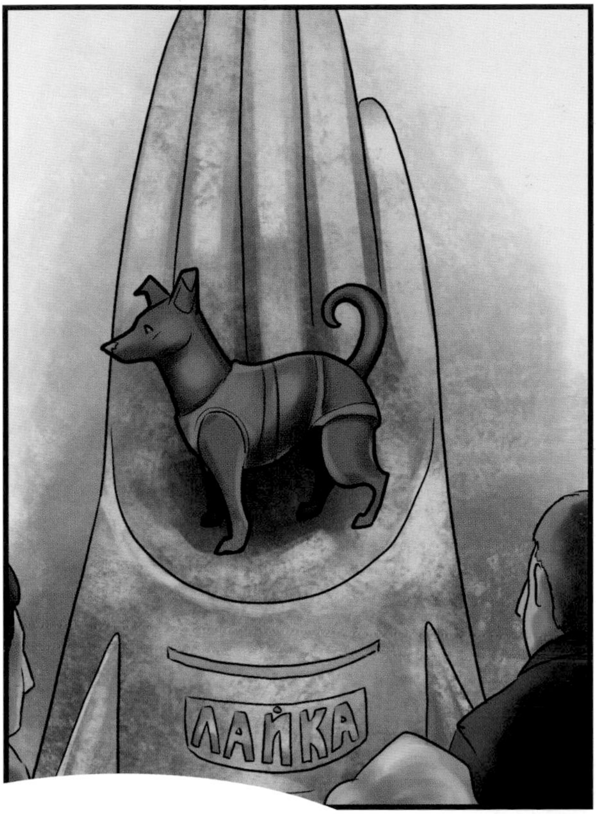
ЛАЙКА

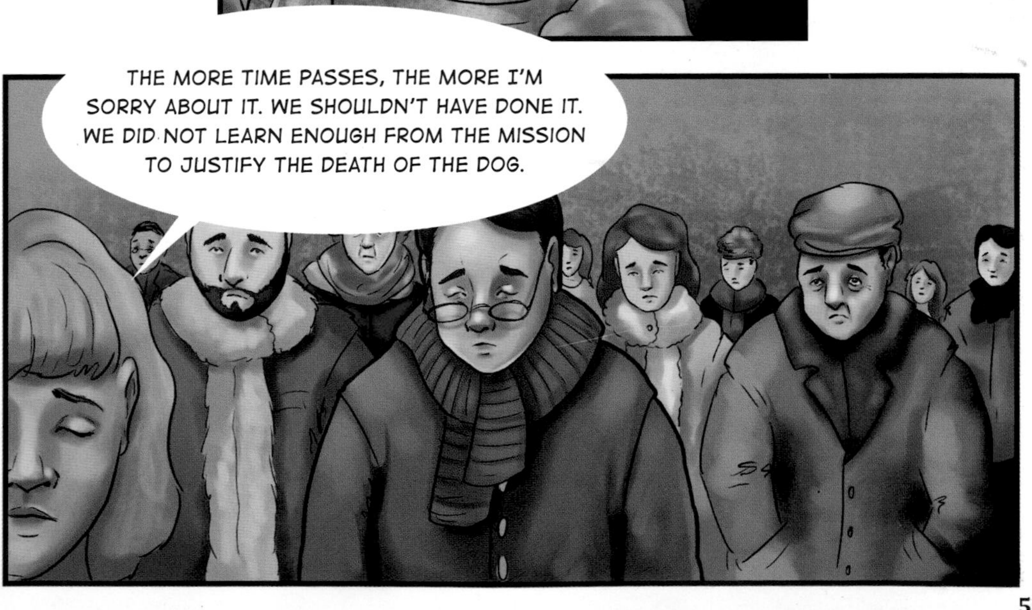
THE MORE TIME PASSES, THE MORE I'M SORRY ABOUT IT. WE SHOULDN'T HAVE DONE IT. WE DID NOT LEARN ENOUGH FROM THE MISSION TO JUSTIFY THE DEATH OF THE DOG.

THE FIRST ANIMALS TO ORBIT EARTH AND SURVIVE WERE THE DOGS BELKA AND STRELKA. THEIR CO-PASSENGERS ON RUSSIA'S *SPUTNIK 5* IN AUGUST 1960 WERE A RABBIT, MICE, RATS, AND PLANTS.

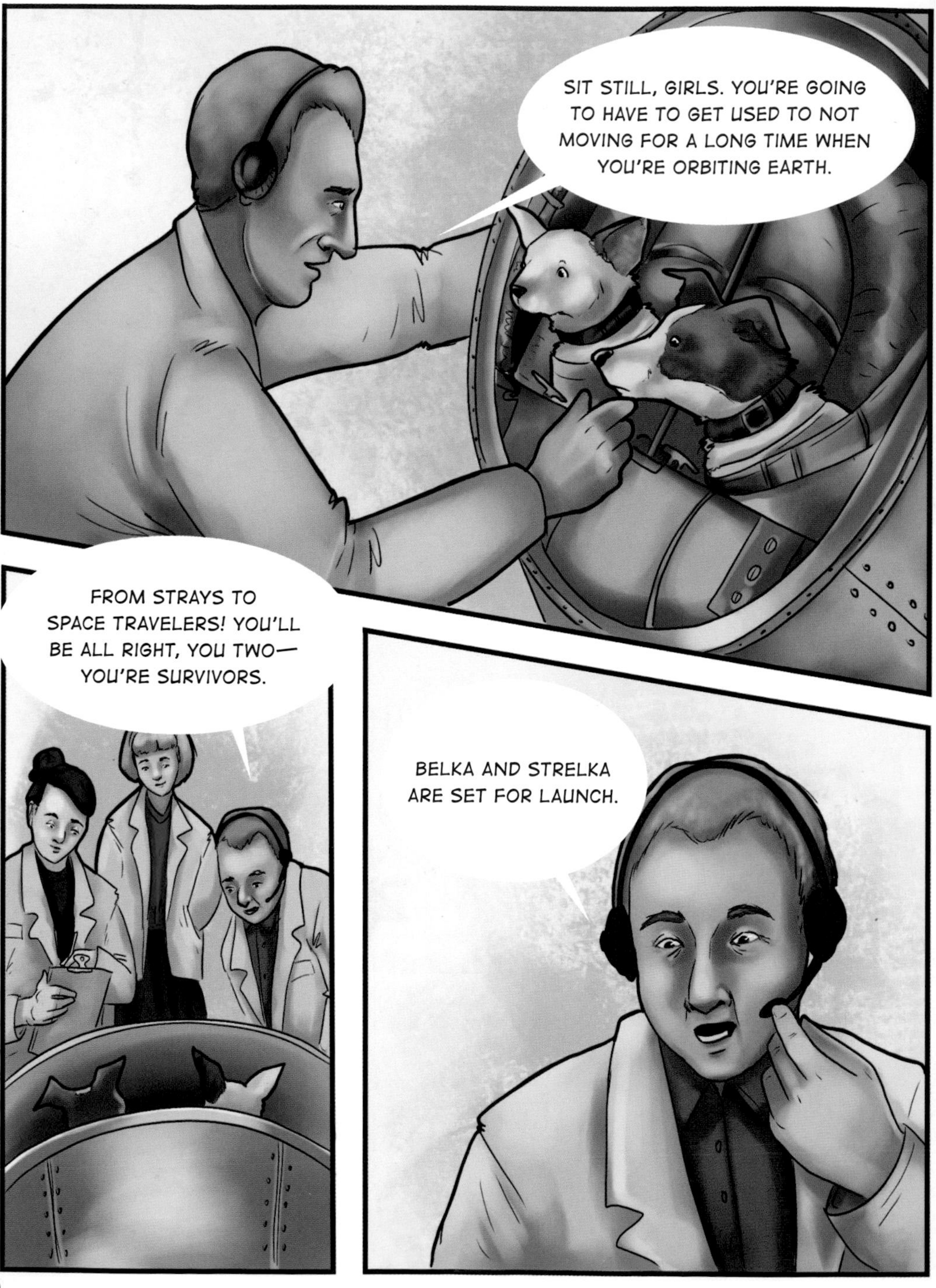
SIT STILL, GIRLS. YOU'RE GOING TO HAVE TO GET USED TO NOT MOVING FOR A LONG TIME WHEN YOU'RE ORBITING EARTH.
FROM STRAYS TO SPACE TRAVELERS! YOU'LL BE ALL RIGHT, YOU TWO—YOU'RE SURVIVORS.
BELKA AND STRELKA ARE SET FOR LAUNCH.

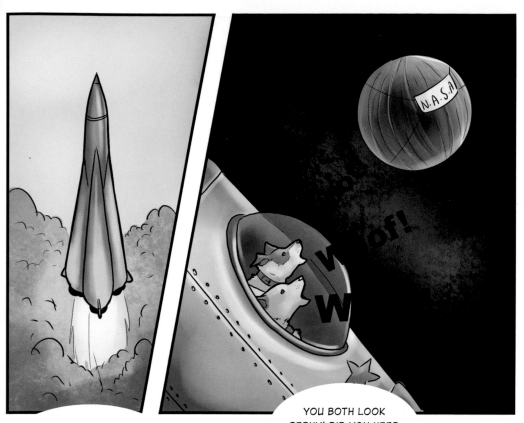

HA! I CAN HEAR THE DOGS BARKING AT NASA'S ECHO COMMUNICATIONS SATELLITE!

YOU BOTH LOOK PERKY! DID YOU KEEP EACH OTHER COMPANY?

STRELKA LATER GAVE BIRTH TO A LITTER OF HEALTHY PUPPIES, AND BOTH OF THE SPACE DOGS LIVED INTO OLD AGE. THEIR BODIES HAVE BEEN PRESERVED AND PUT ON DISPLAY IN RUSSIA'S MUSEUM OF COSMONAUTS.

IN 1961, CHIMPANZEE HAM WAS KIDNAPPED BY POACHERS FROM HIS HOME IN THE JUNGLES OF CAMEROON, A COUNTRY IN AFRICA, AND TRANSFERRED TO A FARM IN FLORIDA. PURCHASED BY THE U.S. AIR FORCE WHEN HE WAS TWO YEARS OLD, HAM BECAME THE FIRST ANIMAL TRAINED TO PERFORM TASKS ON BOARD A SPACECRAFT RATHER THAN SIMPLY RIDE IN IT.

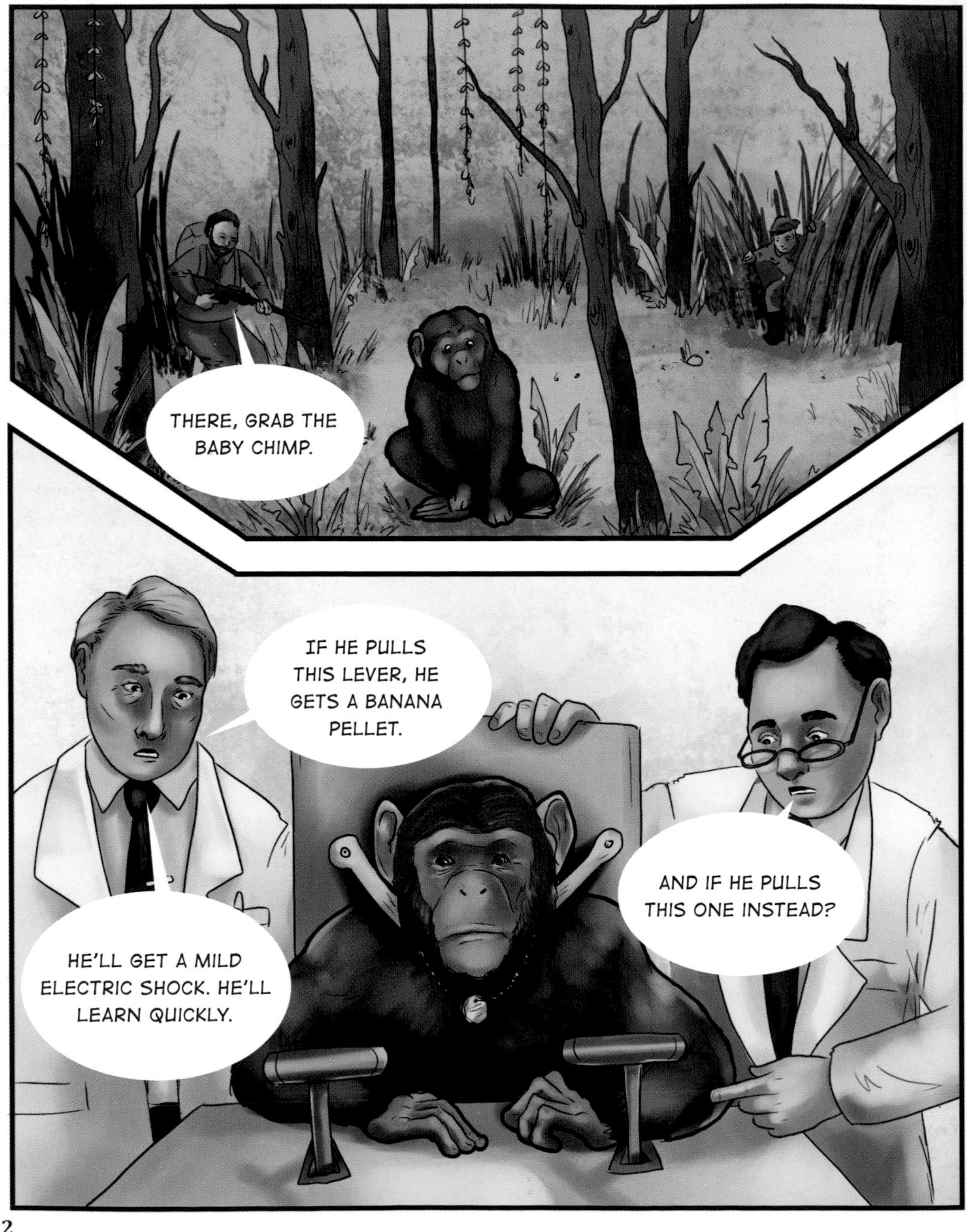
THERE, GRAB THE BABY CHIMP.
IF HE PULLS THIS LEVER, HE GETS A BANANA PELLET.
AND IF HE PULLS THIS ONE INSTEAD?
HE'LL GET A MILD ELECTRIC SHOCK. HE'LL LEARN QUICKLY.

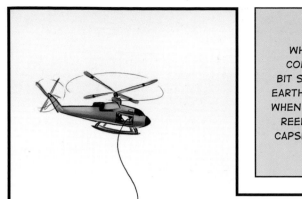

WHILE IN SPACE, HAM SUCCESSFULLY COMPLETED ALL HIS TASKS—IF A TINY BIT SLOWER THAN HE HAD DONE THEM ON EARTH. HIS SPACESUIT KEPT HIM ALIVE EVEN WHEN THE CAPSULE LOST PRESSURE. AFTER REENTERING EARTH'S ATMOSPHERE, THE CAPSULE LANDED IN THE ATLANTIC OCEAN.

QUICK, WE NEED TO GET HAM OUT OF THERE BEFORE HE DROWNS!

ALTHOUGH THE CAPSULE STARTED FLOODING WITH SEAWATER, A RESCUE HELICOPTER MANAGED TO REACH HAM JUST IN TIME. HE RECOVERED ABOARD THE U.S.S. DONNER. HAM WAS TIRED AND HAD LOST A LOT OF WATER FROM HIS BODY, BUT OTHERWISE HEALTHY.

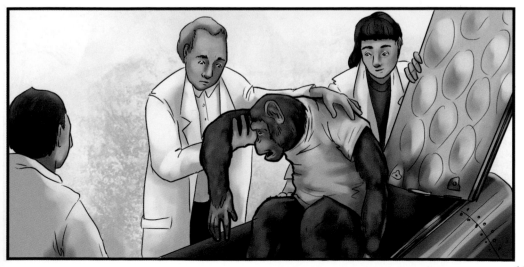

EVEN AFTER PEOPLE STARTED VISITING SPACE, A VARIETY OF ANIMALS, INCLUDING FROGS, SPIDERS, RABBITS, TURTLES, INSECTS, FISH, JELLYFISH, AMOEBAS, AND ALGAE HAVE CONTINUED TO BE SENT INTO ORBIT BY VARIOUS SPACE PROGRAMS AROUND THE WORLD. SCIENTISTS WATCHED CLOSELY TO SEE HOW THEY BEHAVED IN SPACE'S VERY LOW GRAVITY.

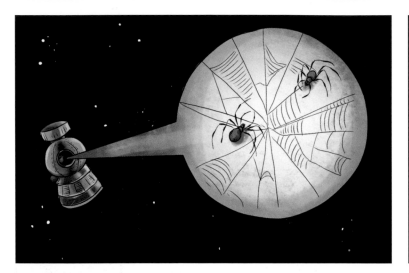

IN 1973, TWO FEMALE EUROPEAN GARDEN SPIDERS NAMED ARABELLA AND ANITA SPUN WEBS IN SPACE. AT FIRST THEIR WEBS WERE LOPSIDED. BUT THEY GOT THE HANG OF IT AFTER A FEW DAYS.

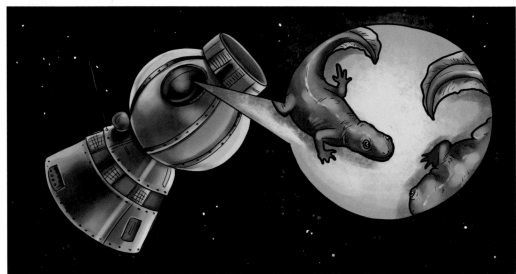

IN 1985, TEN NEWTS HAD THEIR FRONT LEGS CUT OFF BEFORE THEIR JOURNEY INTO SPACE ABOARD THE BION SATELLITE. SCIENTISTS WANTED TO SEE IF THEIR LEGS WOULD GROW BACK LIKE THEY USUALLY DO. IN SPACE, THEIR LEGS REGENERATED FASTER THAN NORMAL.

IN 1988, FROG EGGS WERE SENT INTO SPACE. THEY HATCHED INTO TADPOLES AS NORMAL.

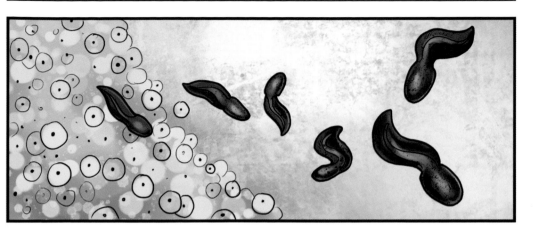

IN 2007, MICROSCOPIC CREATURES KNOWN AS WATER BEARS, OR TARDIGRADES, SPENT TEN DAYS IN OPEN SPACE, ON THE OUTSIDE OF THE SATELLITE. THEY WERE EXPOSED TO POWERFUL COSMIC RAYS FROM THE SUN AND FREEZING TEMPERATURES. YET, MOST OF THEM SURVIVED!

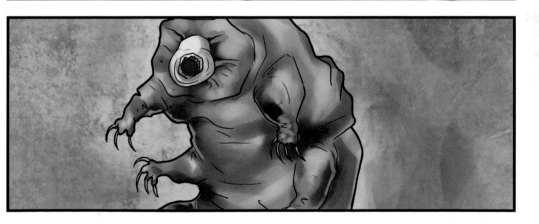

SUCCESSFULLY RETRIEVING ANIMALS FROM SPACE GAVE SPACE PROGRAMS THE CONFIDENCE TO SEND PEOPLE, BUT MANY OF THESE MISSIONS ARE NOW CONSIDERED TO HAVE BEEN CRUEL. EXPERIMENTS ABOARD THE INTERNATIONAL SPACE STATION CONTINUE TO INVESTIGATE HOW SIMPLE ANIMALS AND PLANTS REACT TO CONDITIONS IN SPACE.

YURI GAGARIN
(1934–1968)
FIRST PERSON IN SPACE

BORN IN RUSSIA IN 1934, YURI GAGARIN'S EARLY YEARS WERE DIFFICULT. IN 1941, WHEN HE WAS SEVEN YEARS OLD, THE GERMANS TOOK CONTROL OF HIS FAMILY HOME DURING WORLD WAR II.

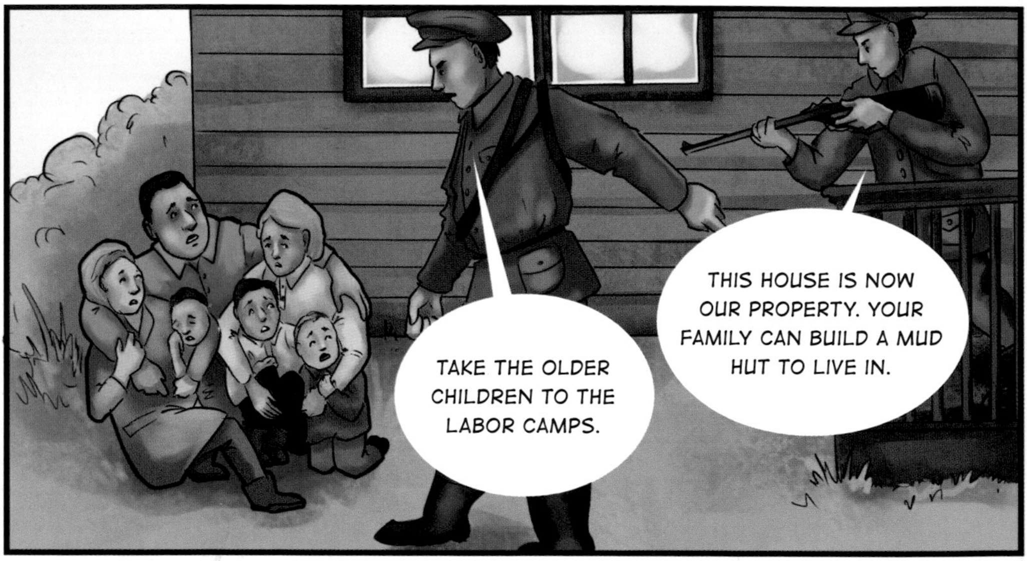
TAKE THE OLDER CHILDREN TO THE LABOR CAMPS.
THIS HOUSE IS NOW OUR PROPERTY. YOUR FAMILY CAN BUILD A MUD HUT TO LIVE IN.

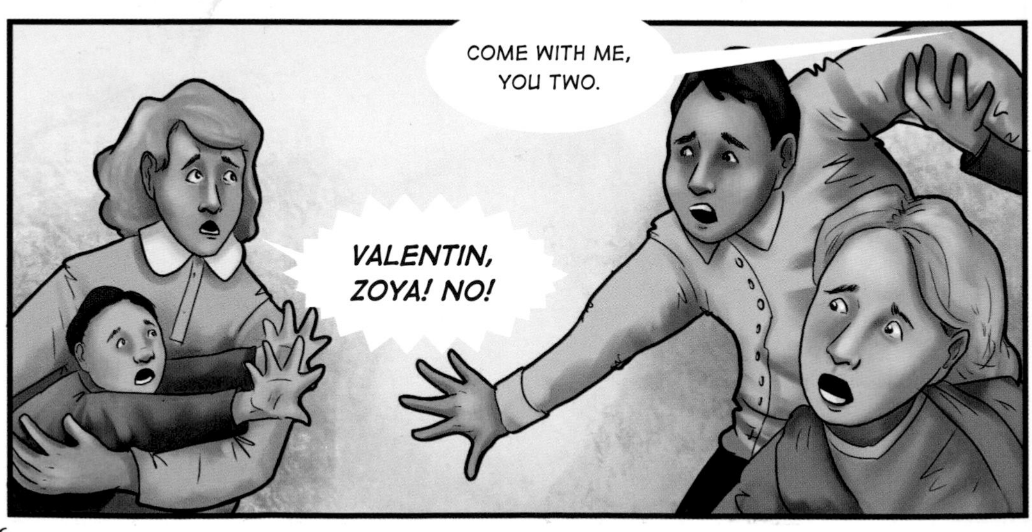
COME WITH ME, YOU TWO.
VALENTIN, ZOYA! NO!

WITH HIS OLDER SIBLINGS TAKEN AWAY, YOUNG YURI HELPED HIS MOTHER AND FATHER TO DIG A MUD SHELTER, WHERE THEY WERE TO LIVE, INTO A HILL BEHIND THEIR OLD HOME.

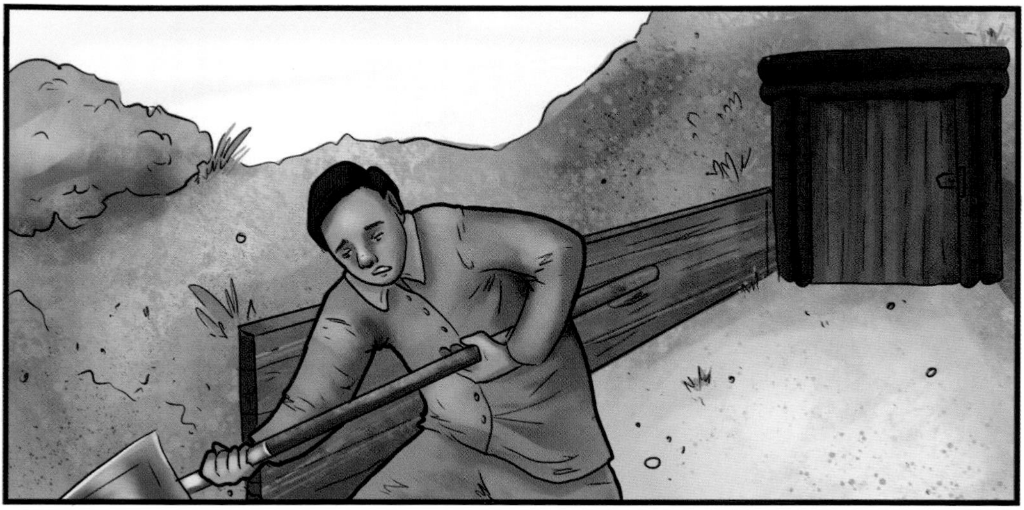

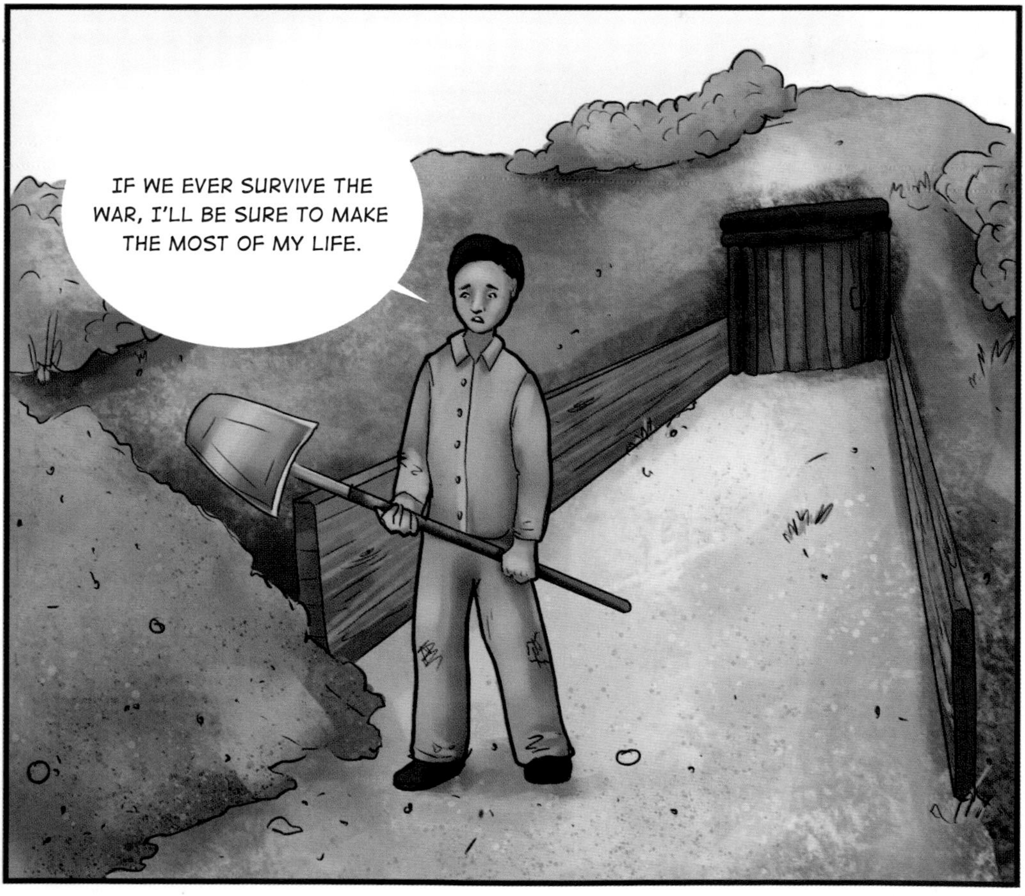
IF WE EVER SURVIVE THE WAR, I'LL BE SURE TO MAKE THE MOST OF MY LIFE.

AFTER THE WAR ENDED IN 1945, YURI'S BROTHER AND SISTER RETURNED HOME, AND THE FAMILY MOVED TO A NEW TOWN IN 1946. YURI ENROLLED AT THE SARATOV TECHNICAL COLLEGE. WHILE HE WAS THERE, HE LEARNED TO FLY.

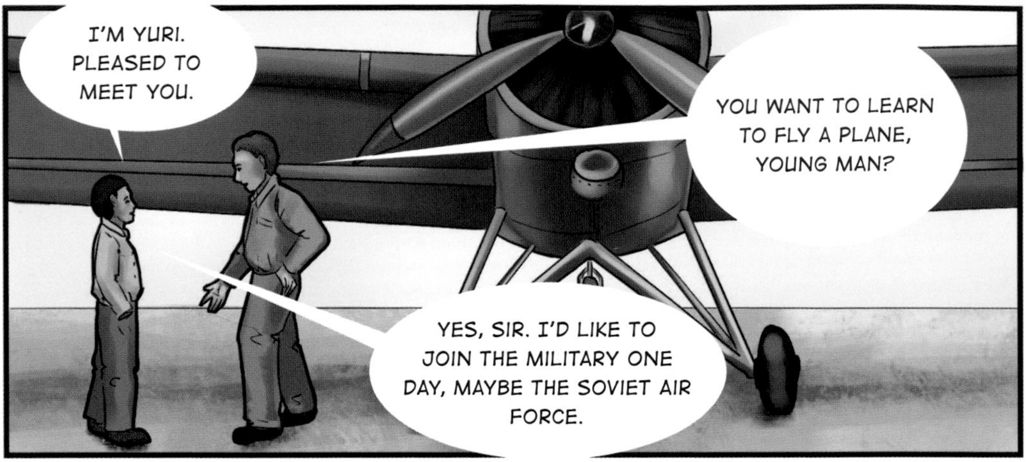

I'M YURI. PLEASED TO MEET YOU.
YOU WANT TO LEARN TO FLY A PLANE, YOUNG MAN?
YES, SIR. I'D LIKE TO JOIN THE MILITARY ONE DAY, MAYBE THE SOVIET AIR FORCE.

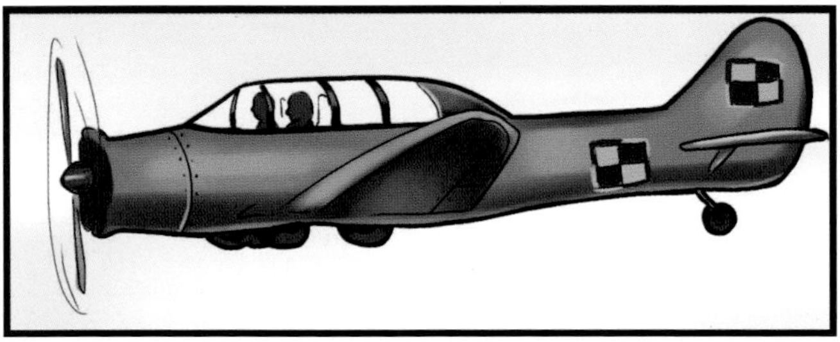

IN 1955, YURI SOLOED IN A YAK-18 TRAINER AIRCRAFT OVER THE VOLGA RIVER BEFORE HE JOINED THE AIR FORCE.

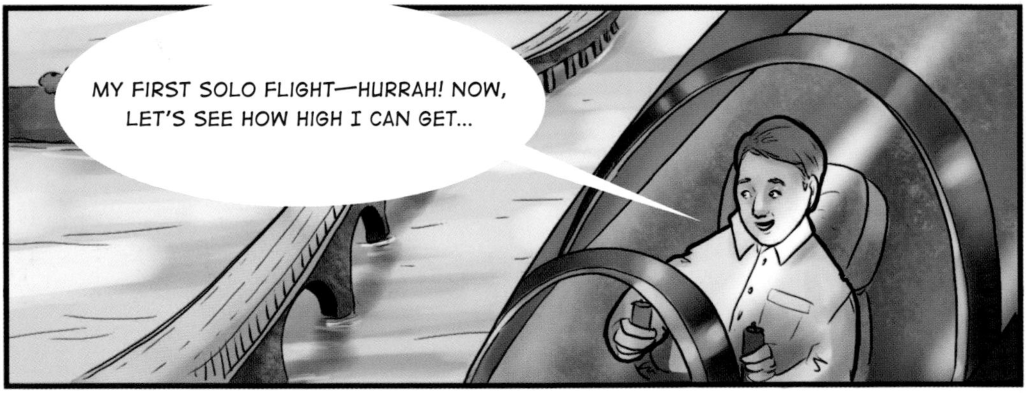

MY FIRST SOLO FLIGHT—HURRAH! NOW, LET'S SEE HOW HIGH I CAN GET...

AFTER GRADUATING, YURI DECIDED TO JOIN THE SOVIET AIR FORCE.

In November 1957, Yuri gained his flying wings with top honors from Orenburg Aviation School. It was also on this same day that he married his wife, Valentina.

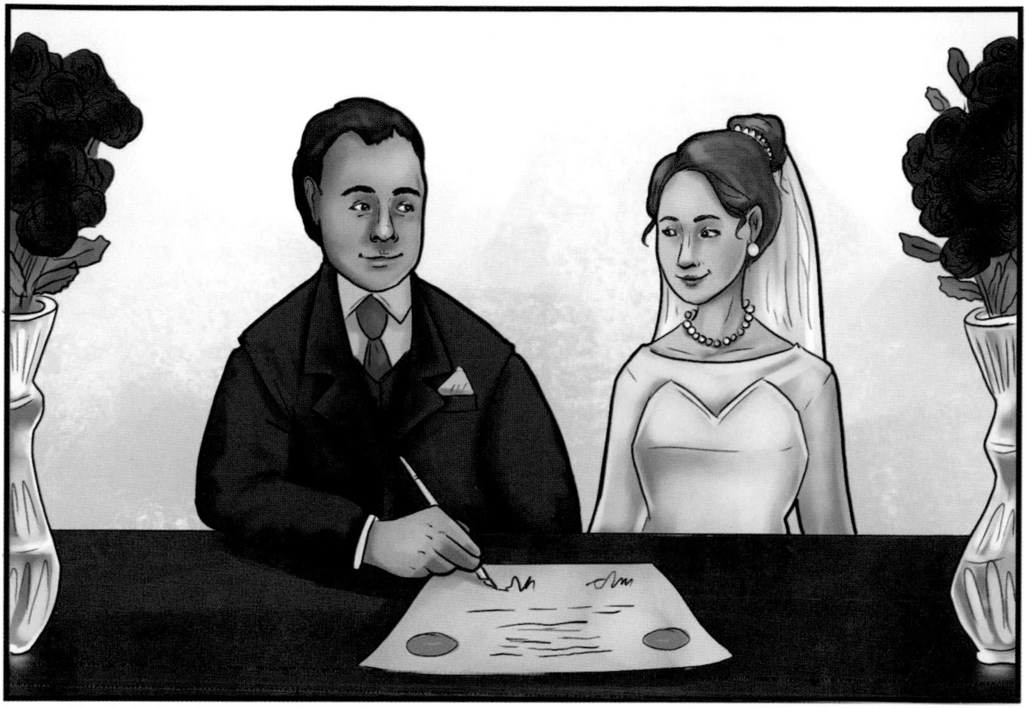

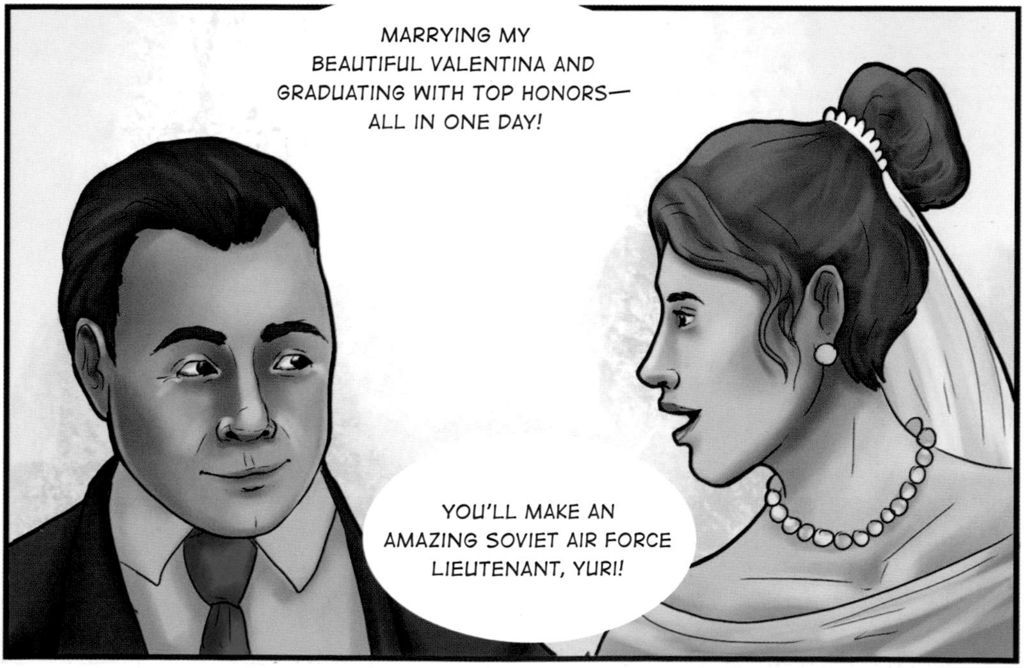
MARRYING MY BEAUTIFUL VALENTINA AND GRADUATING WITH TOP HONORS—ALL IN ONE DAY!
YOU'LL MAKE AN AMAZING SOVIET AIR FORCE LIEUTENANT, YURI!

IN 1960, KONSTANTIN VERSHININ SELECTED YURI AND 19 OTHER PILOTS TO JOIN THE SOVIET SPACE PROGRAM. THEN YURI JOINED A MORE ELITE GROUP, THE SOCHI SIX. ONE OF THEM WOULD BECOME THE FIRST COSMONAUT—THE RUSSIAN NAME FOR AN ASTRONAUT.

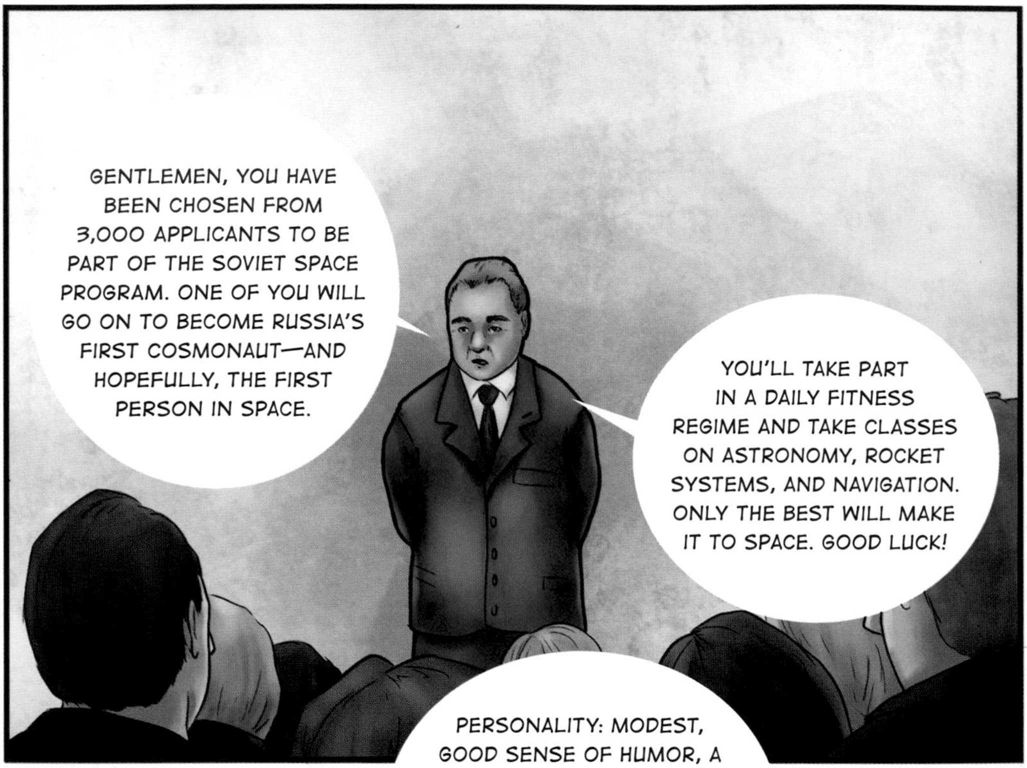
GENTLEMEN, YOU HAVE BEEN CHOSEN FROM 3,000 APPLICANTS TO BE PART OF THE SOVIET SPACE PROGRAM. ONE OF YOU WILL GO ON TO BECOME RUSSIA'S FIRST COSMONAUT—AND HOPEFULLY, THE FIRST PERSON IN SPACE.
YOU'LL TAKE PART IN A DAILY FITNESS REGIME AND TAKE CLASSES ON ASTRONOMY, ROCKET SYSTEMS, AND NAVIGATION. ONLY THE BEST WILL MAKE IT TO SPACE. GOOD LUCK!

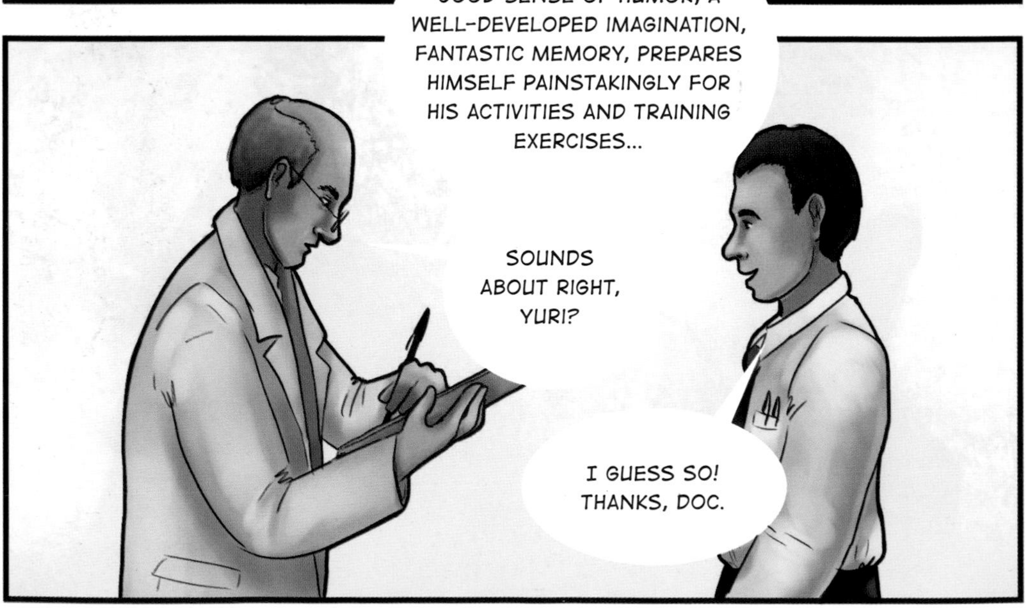
PERSONALITY: MODEST, GOOD SENSE OF HUMOR, A WELL-DEVELOPED IMAGINATION, FANTASTIC MEMORY, PREPARES HIMSELF PAINSTAKINGLY FOR HIS ACTIVITIES AND TRAINING EXERCISES...
SOUNDS ABOUT RIGHT, YURI?
I GUESS SO! THANKS, DOC.

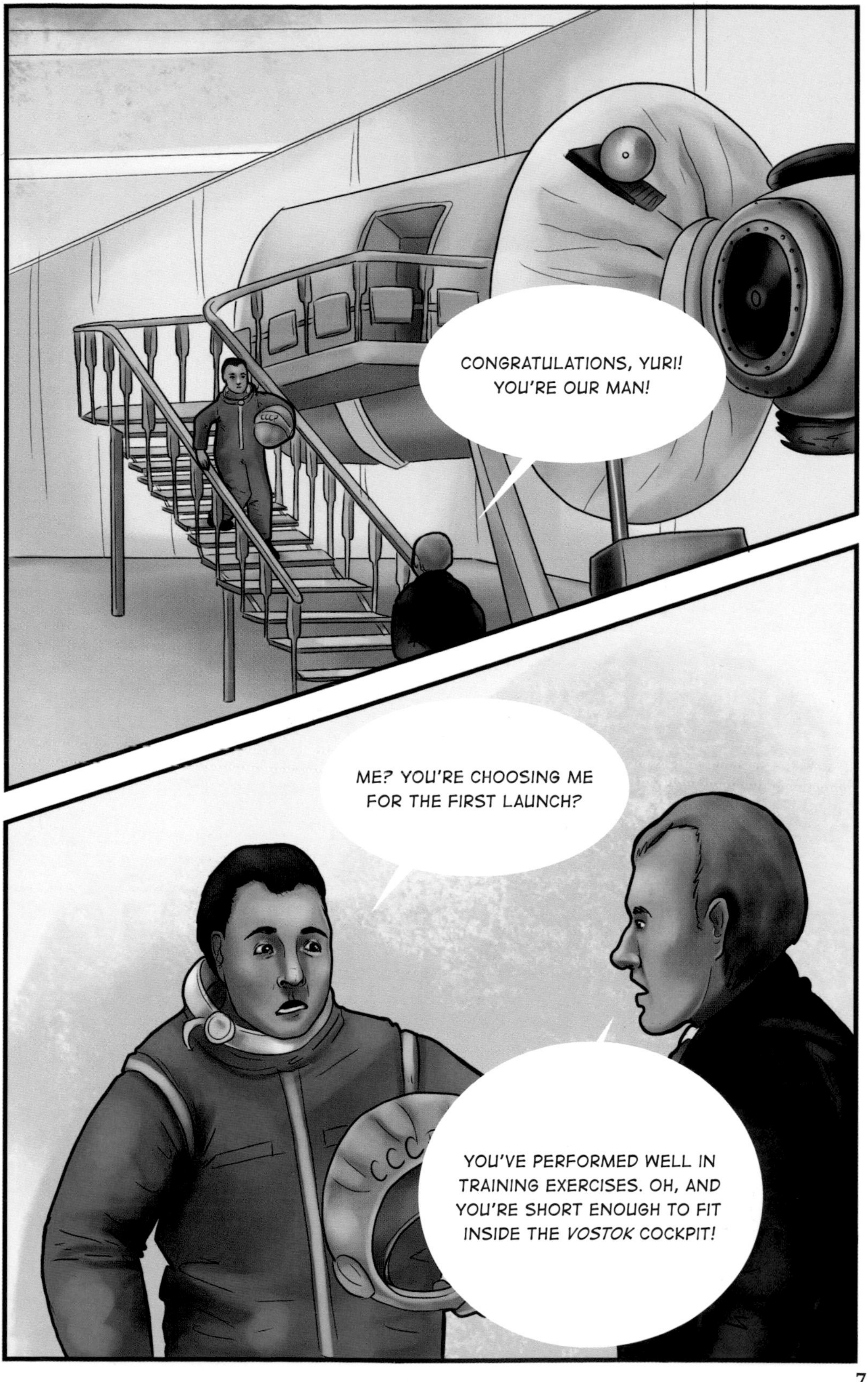
CONGRATULATIONS, YURI! YOU'RE OUR MAN!
ME? YOU'RE CHOOSING ME FOR THE FIRST LAUNCH?
YOU'VE PERFORMED WELL IN TRAINING EXERCISES. OH, AND YOU'RE SHORT ENOUGH TO FIT INSIDE THE *VOSTOK* COCKPIT!

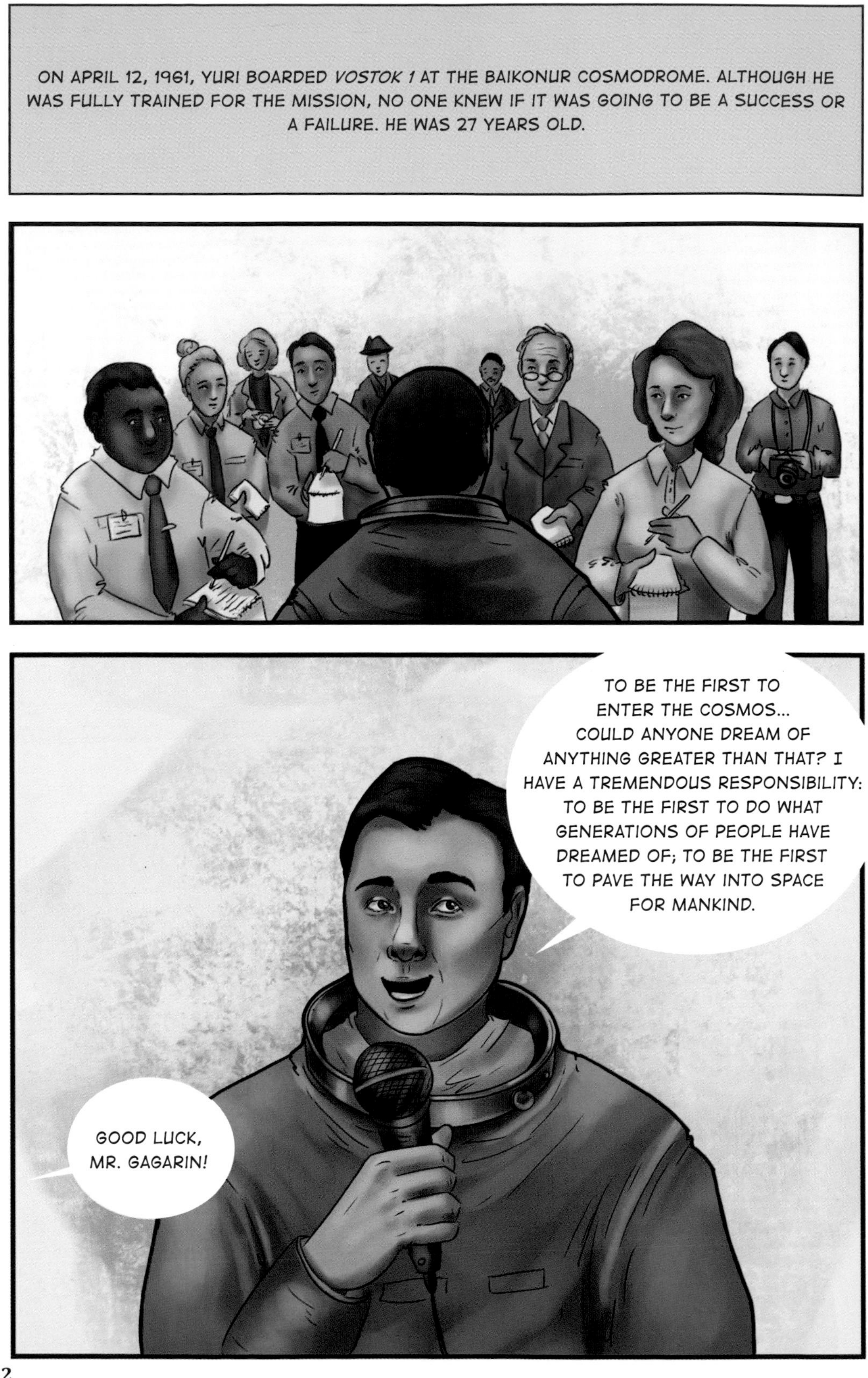
ON APRIL 12, 1961, YURI BOARDED *VOSTOK 1* AT THE BAIKONUR COSMODROME. ALTHOUGH HE WAS FULLY TRAINED FOR THE MISSION, NO ONE KNEW IF IT WAS GOING TO BE A SUCCESS OR A FAILURE. HE WAS 27 YEARS OLD.
TO BE THE FIRST TO ENTER THE COSMOS... COULD ANYONE DREAM OF ANYTHING GREATER THAN THAT? I HAVE A TREMENDOUS RESPONSIBILITY: TO BE THE FIRST TO DO WHAT GENERATIONS OF PEOPLE HAVE DREAMED OF; TO BE THE FIRST TO PAVE THE WAY INTO SPACE FOR MANKIND.
GOOD LUCK, MR. GAGARIN!

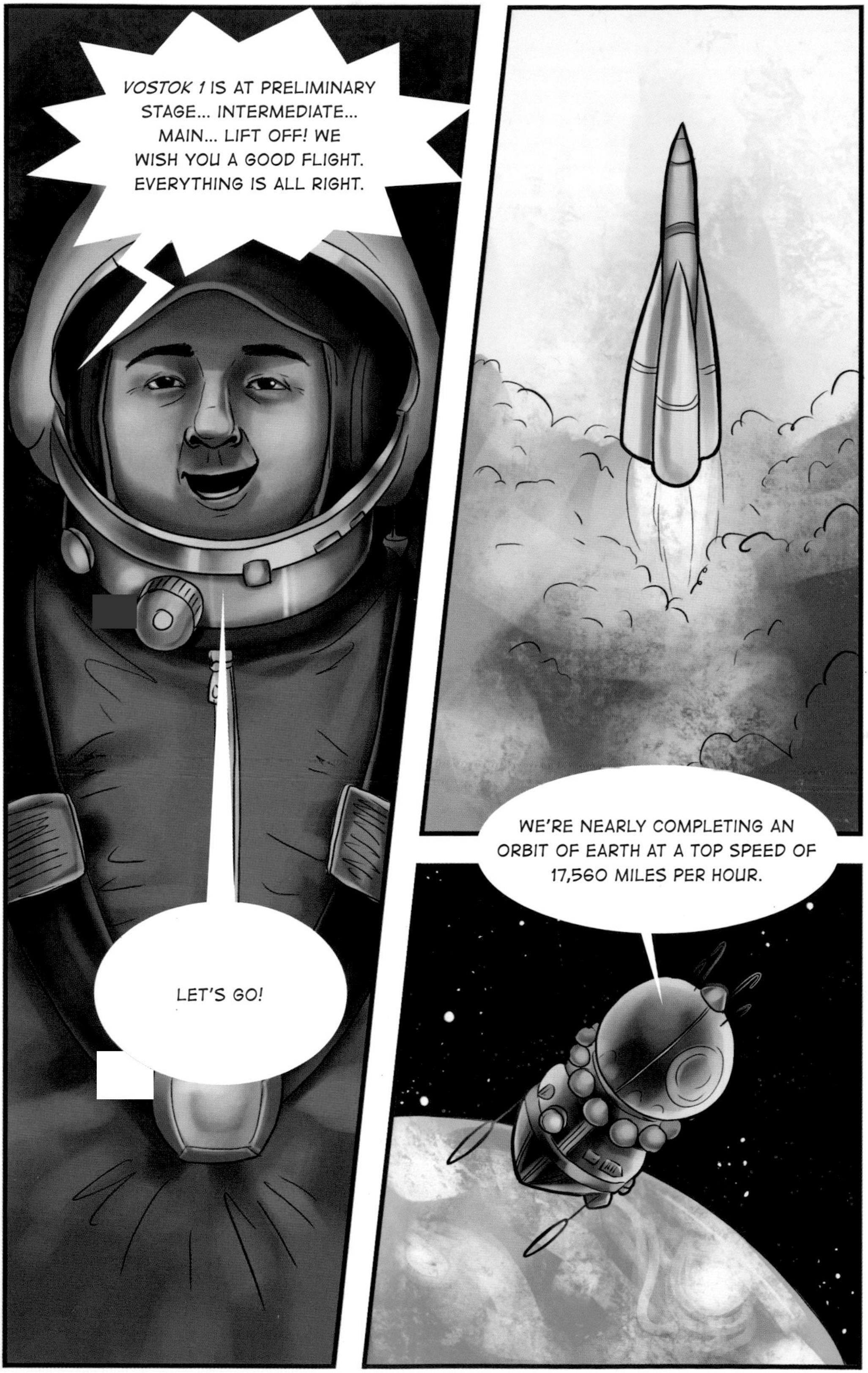
VOSTOK 1 IS AT PRELIMINARY STAGE... INTERMEDIATE... MAIN... LIFT OFF! WE WISH YOU A GOOD FLIGHT. EVERYTHING IS ALL RIGHT.
LET'S GO!
WE'RE NEARLY COMPLETING AN ORBIT OF EARTH AT A TOP SPEED OF 17,560 MILES PER HOUR.

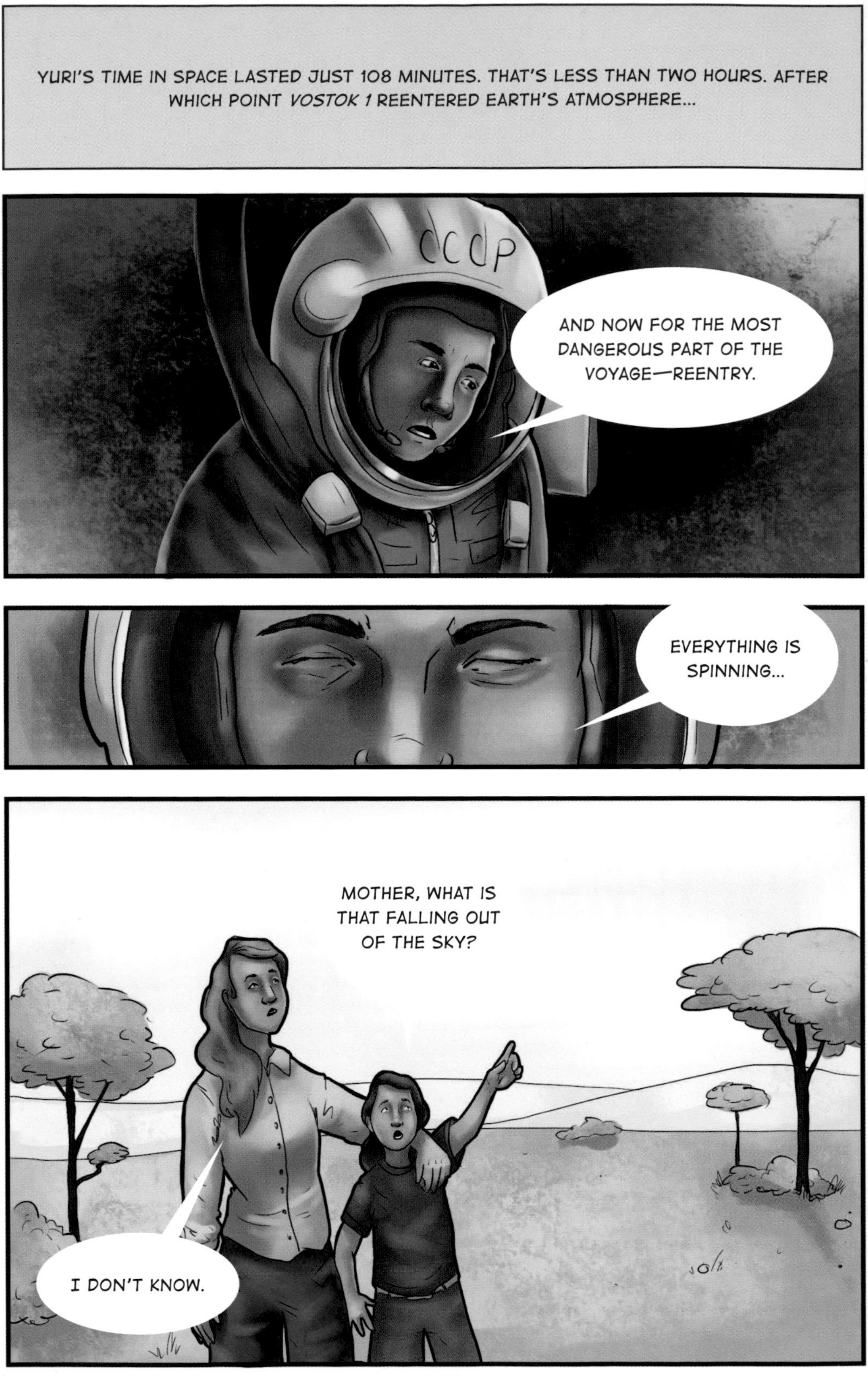
YURI'S TIME IN SPACE LASTED JUST 108 MINUTES. THAT'S LESS THAN TWO HOURS. AFTER WHICH POINT *VOSTOK 1* REENTERED EARTH'S ATMOSPHERE...
AND NOW FOR THE MOST DANGEROUS PART OF THE VOYAGE—REENTRY.
EVERYTHING IS SPINNING...
MOTHER, WHAT IS THAT FALLING OUT OF THE SKY?
I DON'T KNOW.

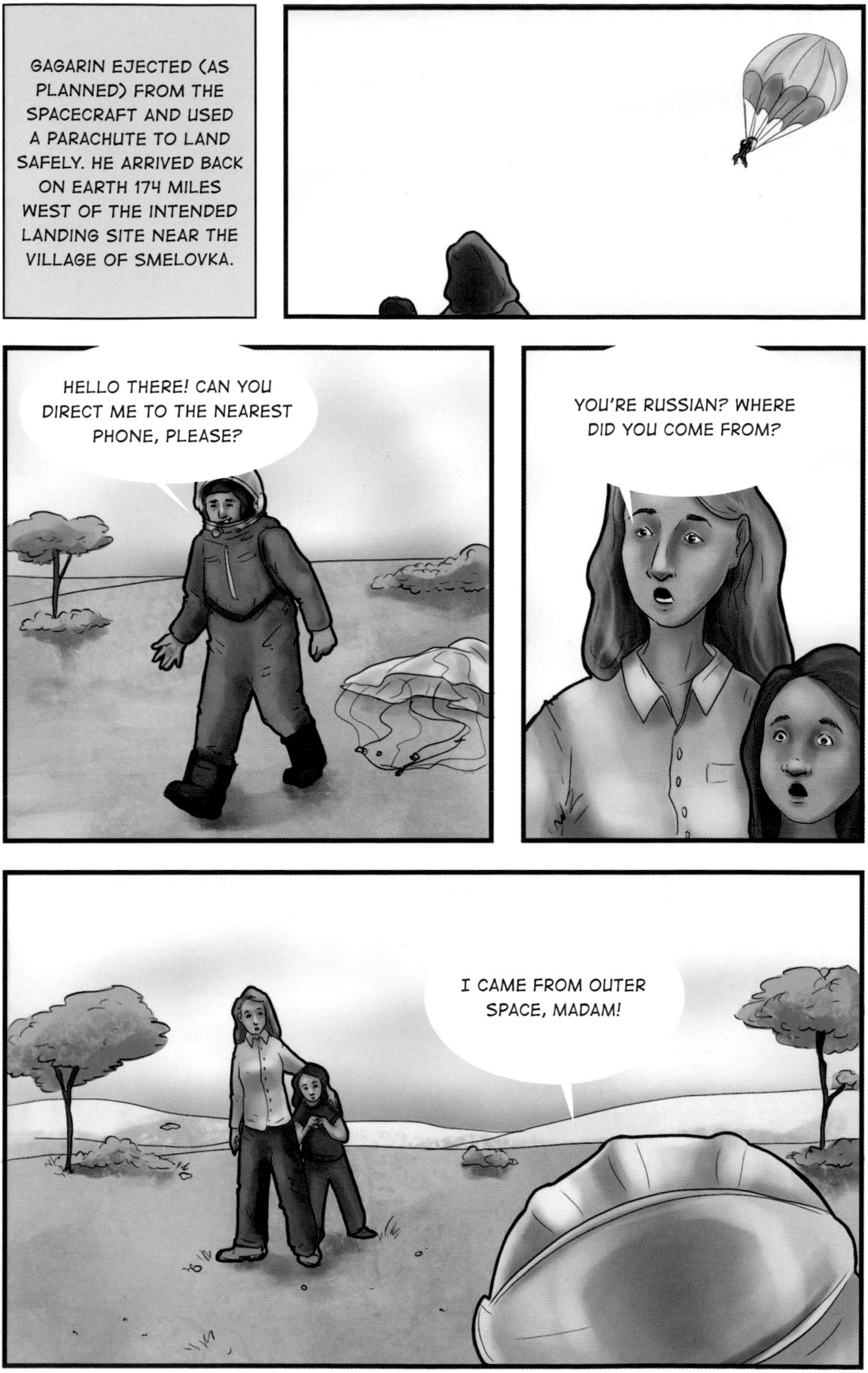
GAGARIN EJECTED (AS PLANNED) FROM THE SPACECRAFT AND USED A PARACHUTE TO LAND SAFELY. HE ARRIVED BACK ON EARTH 174 MILES WEST OF THE INTENDED LANDING SITE NEAR THE VILLAGE OF SMELOVKA.
HELLO THERE! CAN YOU DIRECT ME TO THE NEAREST PHONE, PLEASE?
YOU'RE RUSSIAN? WHERE DID YOU COME FROM?
I CAME FROM OUTER SPACE, MADAM!

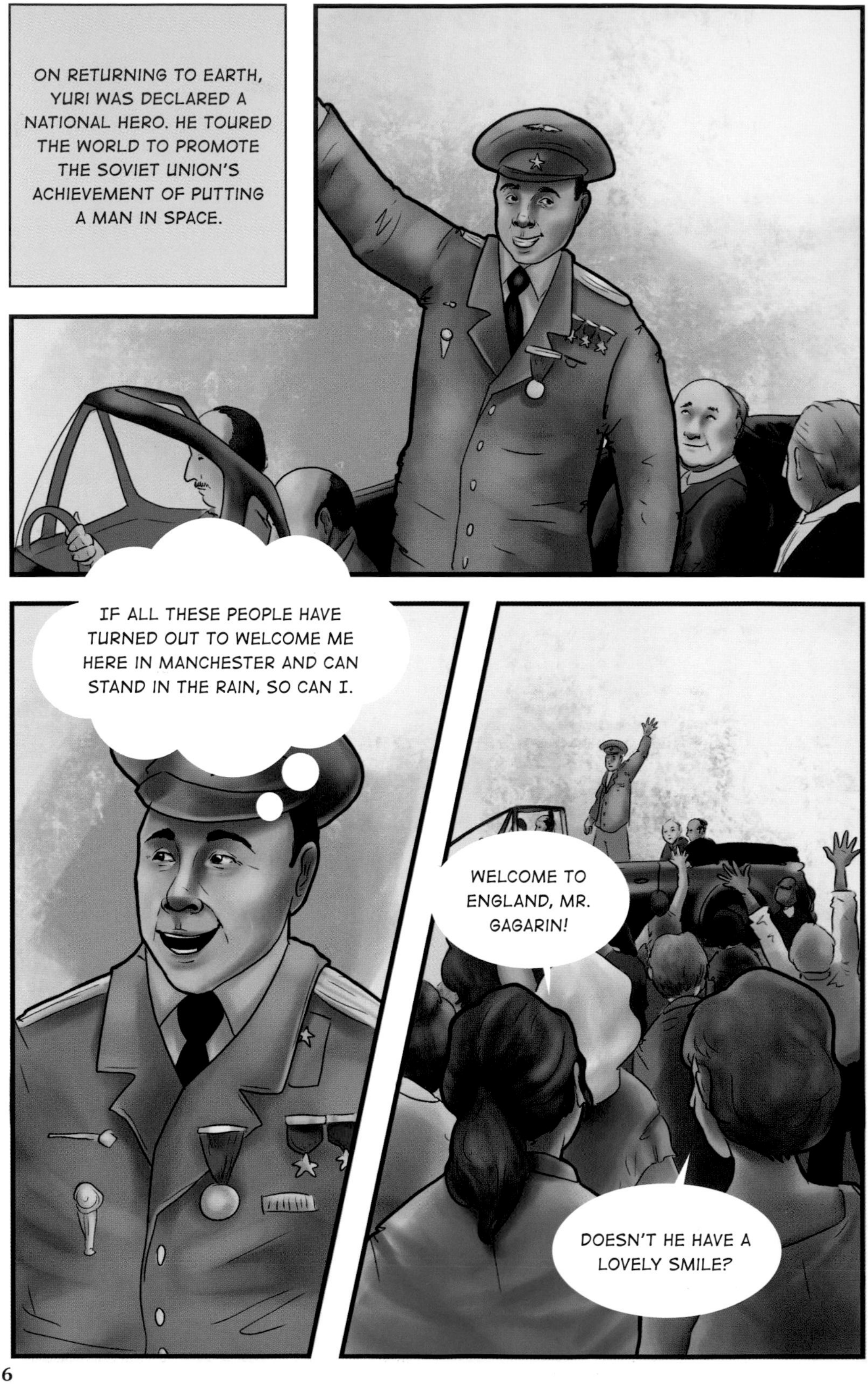
ON RETURNING TO EARTH, YURI WAS DECLARED A NATIONAL HERO. HE TOURED THE WORLD TO PROMOTE THE SOVIET UNION'S ACHIEVEMENT OF PUTTING A MAN IN SPACE.
IF ALL THESE PEOPLE HAVE TURNED OUT TO WELCOME ME HERE IN MANCHESTER AND CAN STAND IN THE RAIN, SO CAN I.
WELCOME TO ENGLAND, MR. GAGARIN!
DOESN'T HE HAVE A LOVELY SMILE?

AS THE DEPUTY TRAINING DIRECTOR AT THE STAR CITY TRAINING BASE IN MOSCOW, YURI WORKED WITH THE CHIEF DESIGNER OF THE SOVIET SPACE PROGRAM, SERGEI KOROLEV, TO PREPARE COSMONAUTS FOR FUTURE MISSIONS.

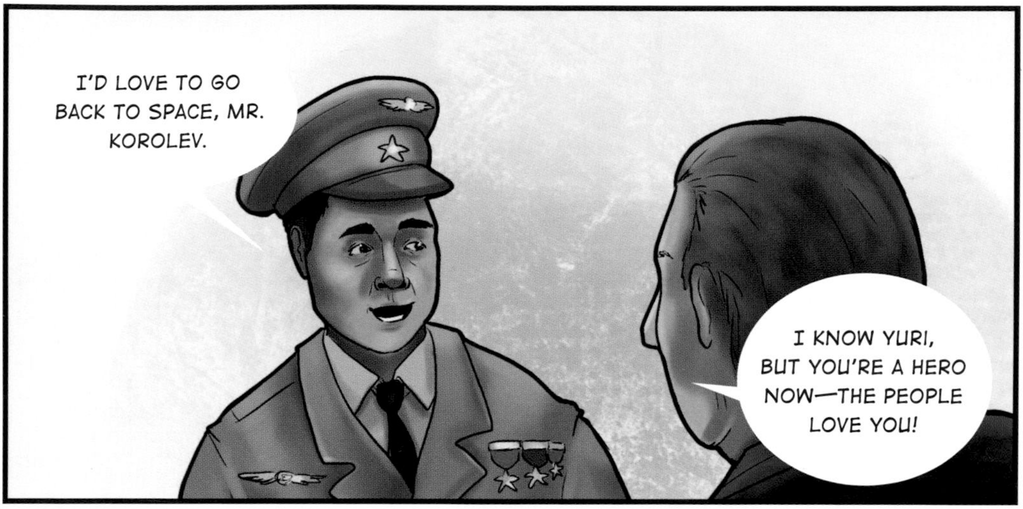
I'D LOVE TO GO BACK TO SPACE, MR. KOROLEV.
I KNOW YURI, BUT YOU'RE A HERO NOW—THE PEOPLE LOVE YOU!

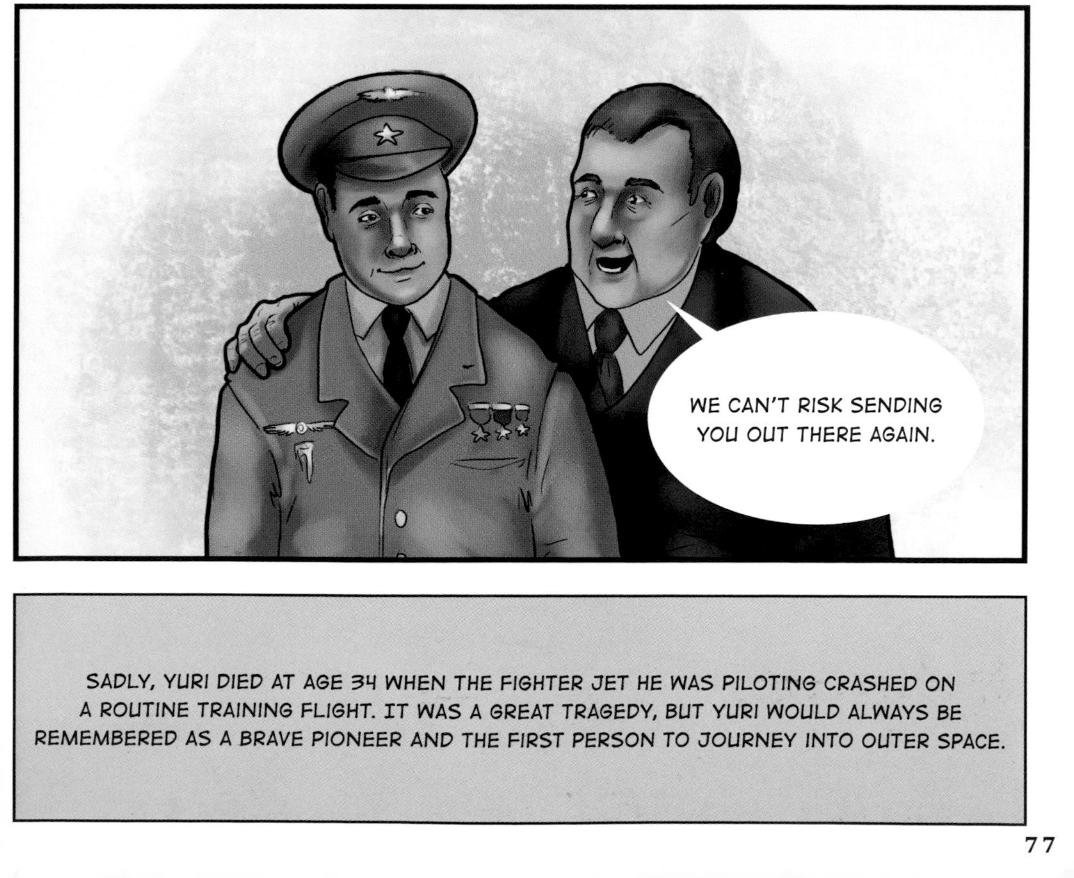
WE CAN'T RISK SENDING YOU OUT THERE AGAIN.

SADLY, YURI DIED AT AGE 34 WHEN THE FIGHTER JET HE WAS PILOTING CRASHED ON A ROUTINE TRAINING FLIGHT. IT WAS A GREAT TRAGEDY, BUT YURI WOULD ALWAYS BE REMEMBERED AS A BRAVE PIONEER AND THE FIRST PERSON TO JOURNEY INTO OUTER SPACE.

VALENTINA TERESHKOVA
(1937–present)
FIRST WOMAN IN SPACE

VALENTINA TERESHKOVA WAS BORN INTO A POOR FAMILY IN CENTRAL RUSSIA. HER FATHER WAS KILLED FIGHTING IN WORLD WAR II, SO VALENTINA, HER YOUNGER BROTHER, AND HER OLDER SISTER WERE RAISED BY HER MOTHER ALONE.

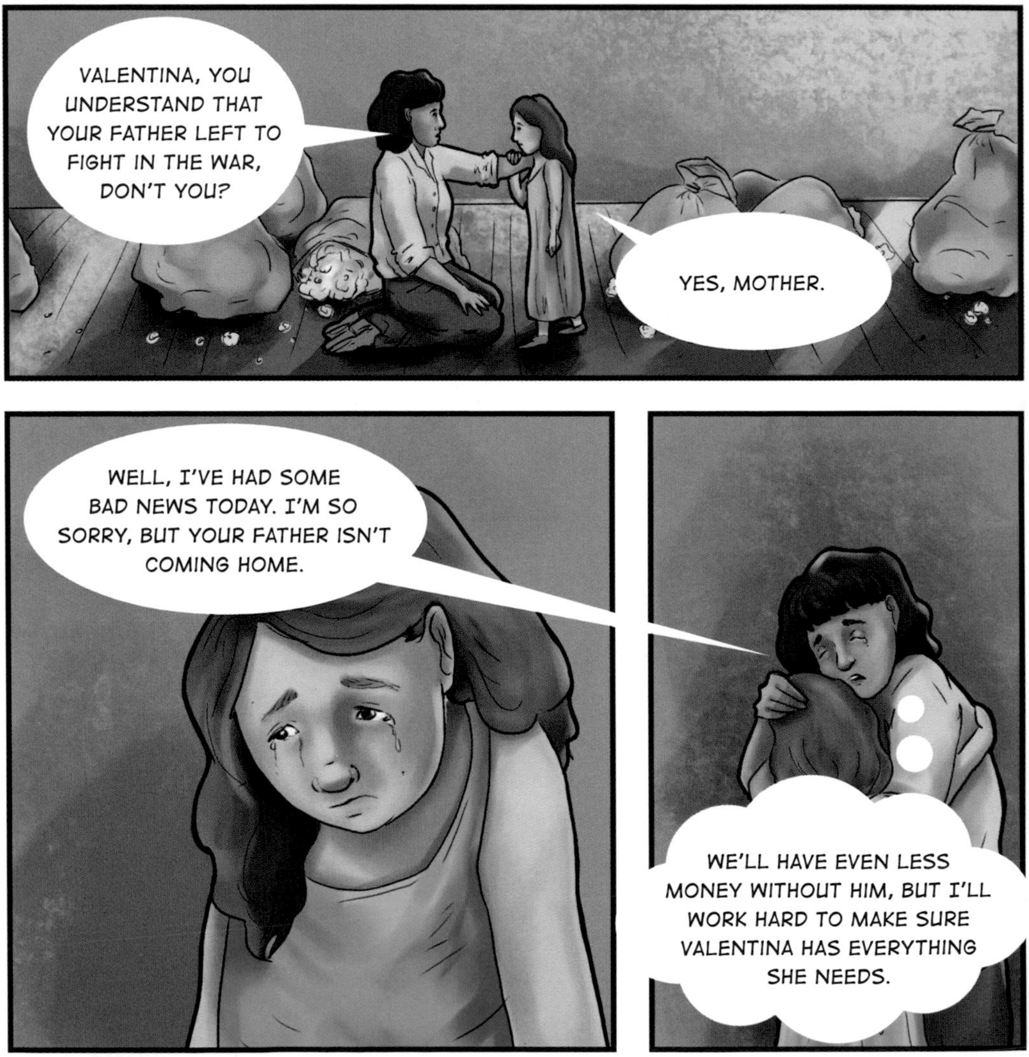
VALENTINA, YOU UNDERSTAND THAT YOUR FATHER LEFT TO FIGHT IN THE WAR, DON'T YOU?
YES, MOTHER.
WELL, I'VE HAD SOME BAD NEWS TODAY. I'M SO SORRY, BUT YOUR FATHER ISN'T COMING HOME.
WE'LL HAVE EVEN LESS MONEY WITHOUT HIM, BUT I'LL WORK HARD TO MAKE SURE VALENTINA HAS EVERYTHING SHE NEEDS.

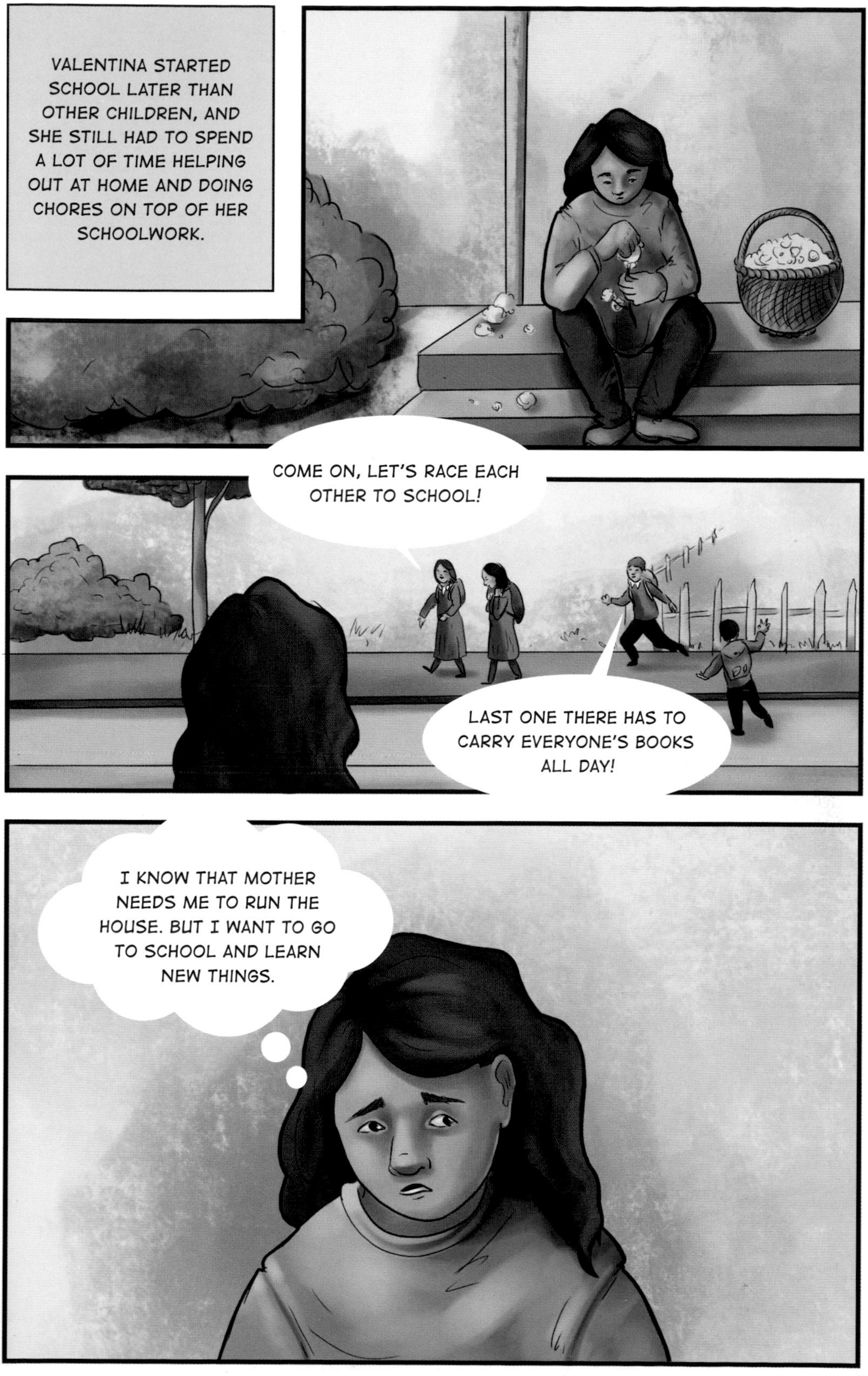
VALENTINA STARTED SCHOOL LATER THAN OTHER CHILDREN, AND SHE STILL HAD TO SPEND A LOT OF TIME HELPING OUT AT HOME AND DOING CHORES ON TOP OF HER SCHOOLWORK.
COME ON, LET'S RACE EACH OTHER TO SCHOOL!
LAST ONE THERE HAS TO CARRY EVERYONE'S BOOKS ALL DAY!
I KNOW THAT MOTHER NEEDS ME TO RUN THE HOUSE. BUT I WANT TO GO TO SCHOOL AND LEARN NEW THINGS.

VALENTINA LEFT SCHOOL AT AGE 16 AND STARTED WORKING AT THE COTTON MILL WITH HER MOTHER. BUT SHE KEPT STUDYING IN HER FREE TIME BY TAKING COURSES TAUGHT THROUGH THE MAIL AND LATER SHE GRADUATED FROM TECHNICAL SCHOOL.

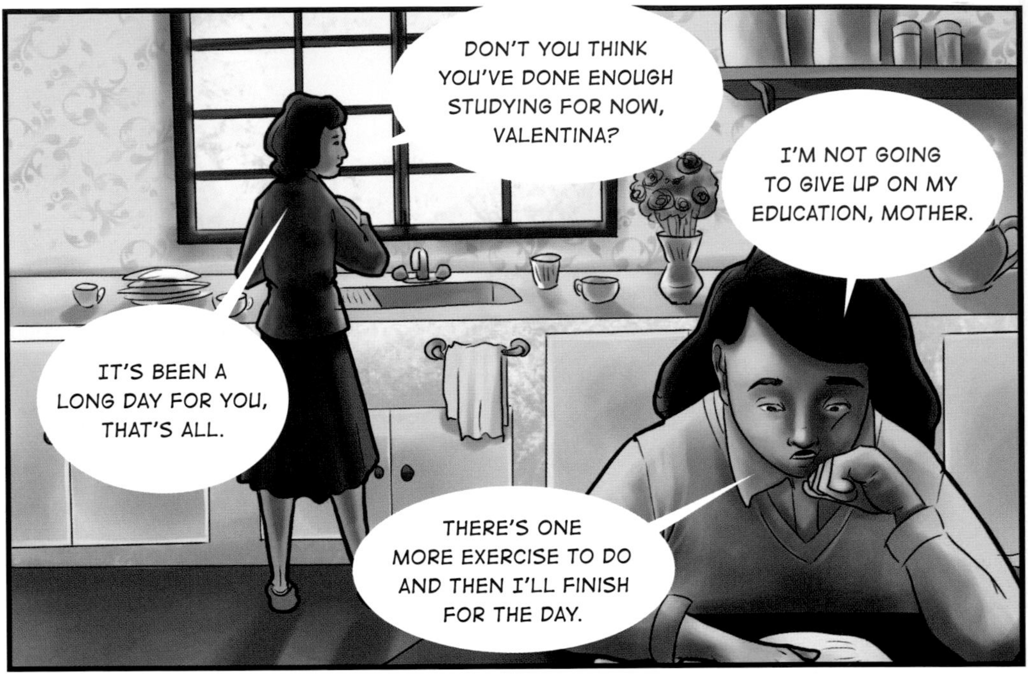
DON'T YOU THINK YOU'VE DONE ENOUGH STUDYING FOR NOW, VALENTINA?
I'M NOT GOING TO GIVE UP ON MY EDUCATION, MOTHER.
IT'S BEEN A LONG DAY FOR YOU, THAT'S ALL.
THERE'S ONE MORE EXERCISE TO DO AND THEN I'LL FINISH FOR THE DAY.

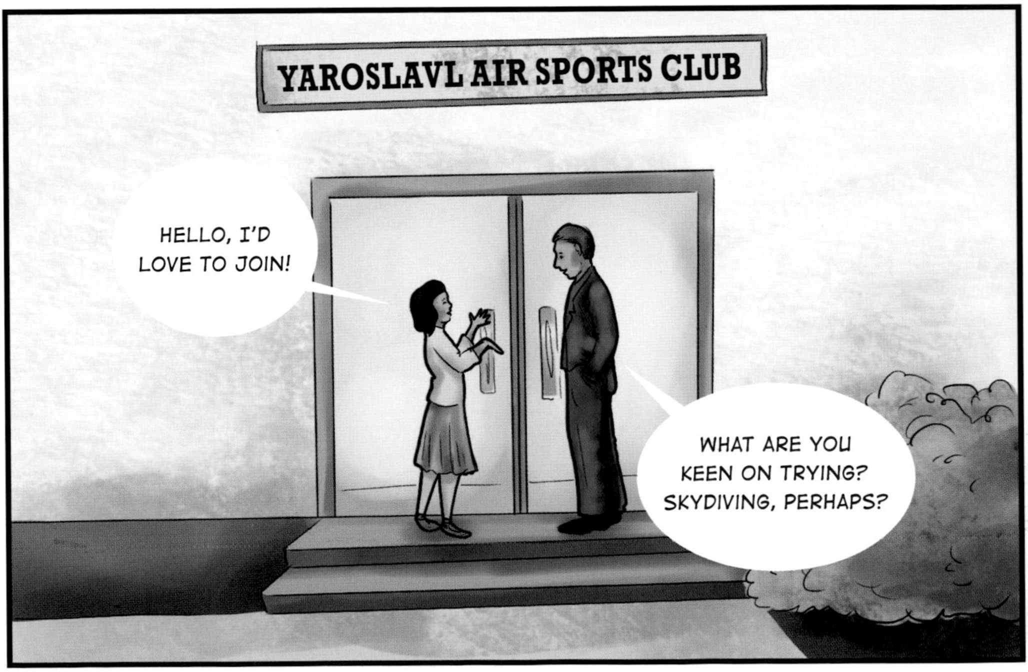
YAROSLAVL AIR SPORTS CLUB
HELLO, I'D LOVE TO JOIN!
WHAT ARE YOU KEEN ON TRYING? SKYDIVING, PERHAPS?

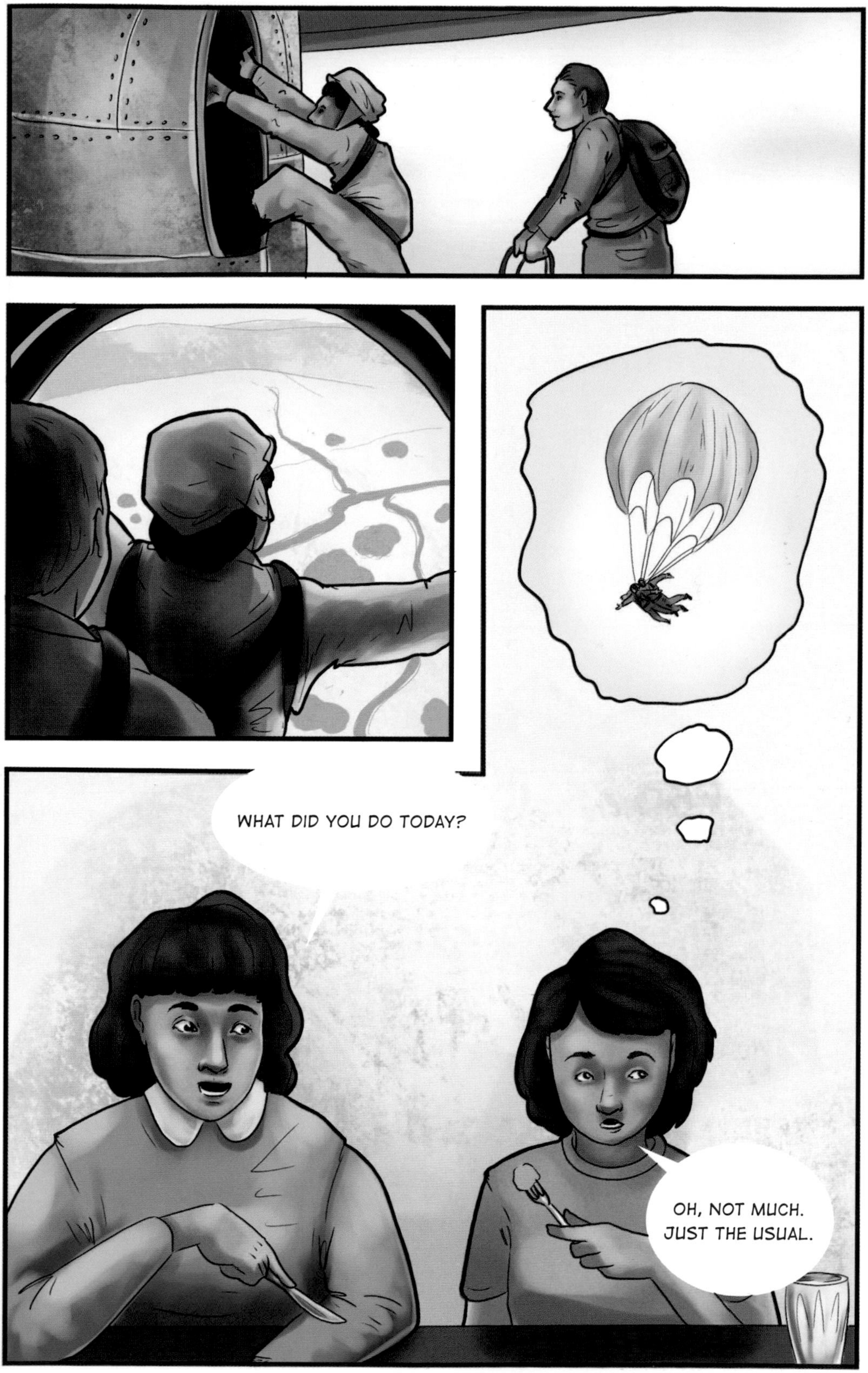
WHAT DID YOU DO TODAY?
OH, NOT MUCH. JUST THE USUAL.

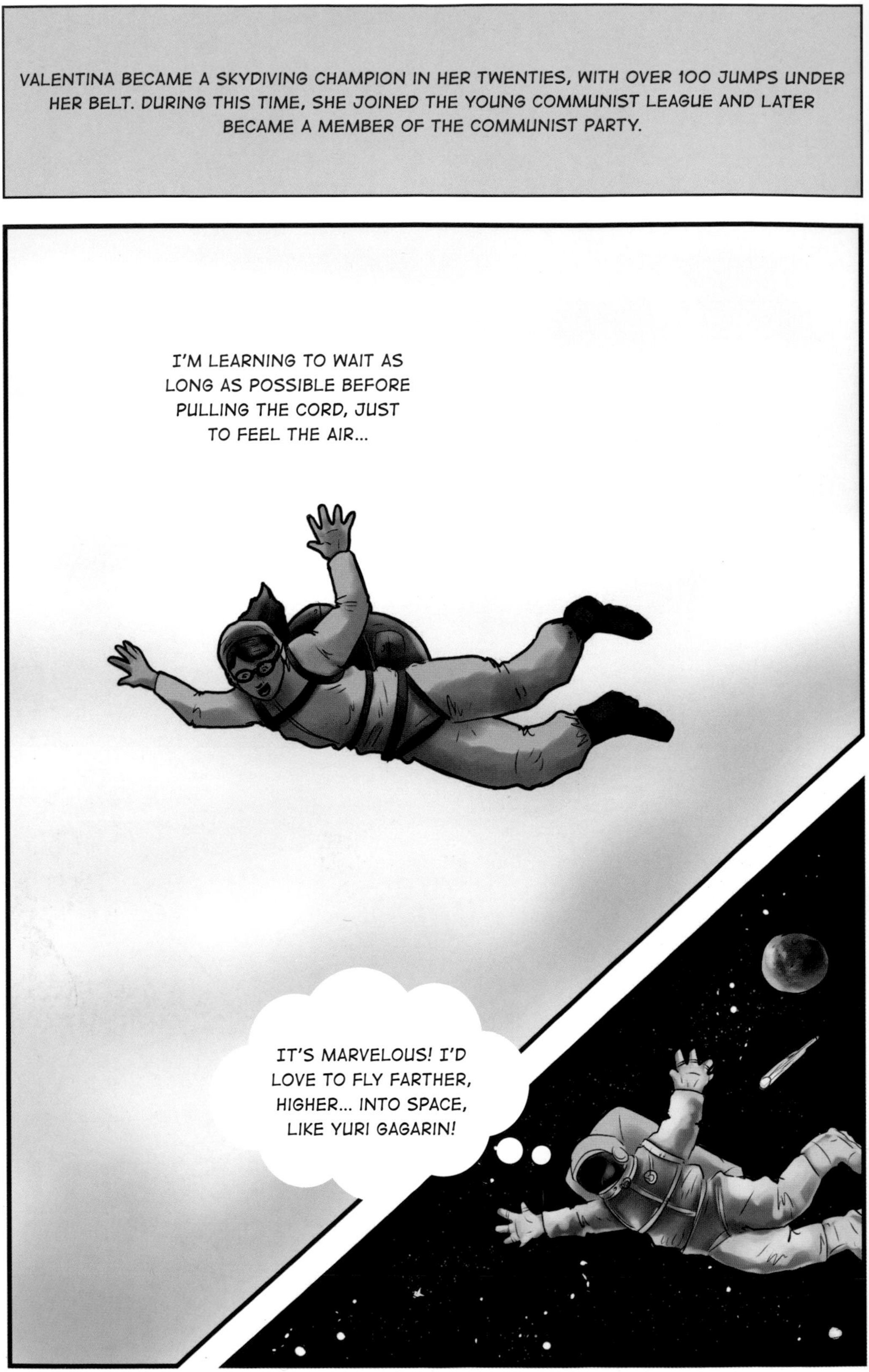
VALENTINA BECAME A SKYDIVING CHAMPION IN HER TWENTIES, WITH OVER 100 JUMPS UNDER HER BELT. DURING THIS TIME, SHE JOINED THE YOUNG COMMUNIST LEAGUE AND LATER BECAME A MEMBER OF THE COMMUNIST PARTY.
I'M LEARNING TO WAIT AS LONG AS POSSIBLE BEFORE PULLING THE CORD, JUST TO FEEL THE AIR...
IT'S MARVELOUS! I'D LOVE TO FLY FARTHER, HIGHER... INTO SPACE, LIKE YURI GAGARIN!

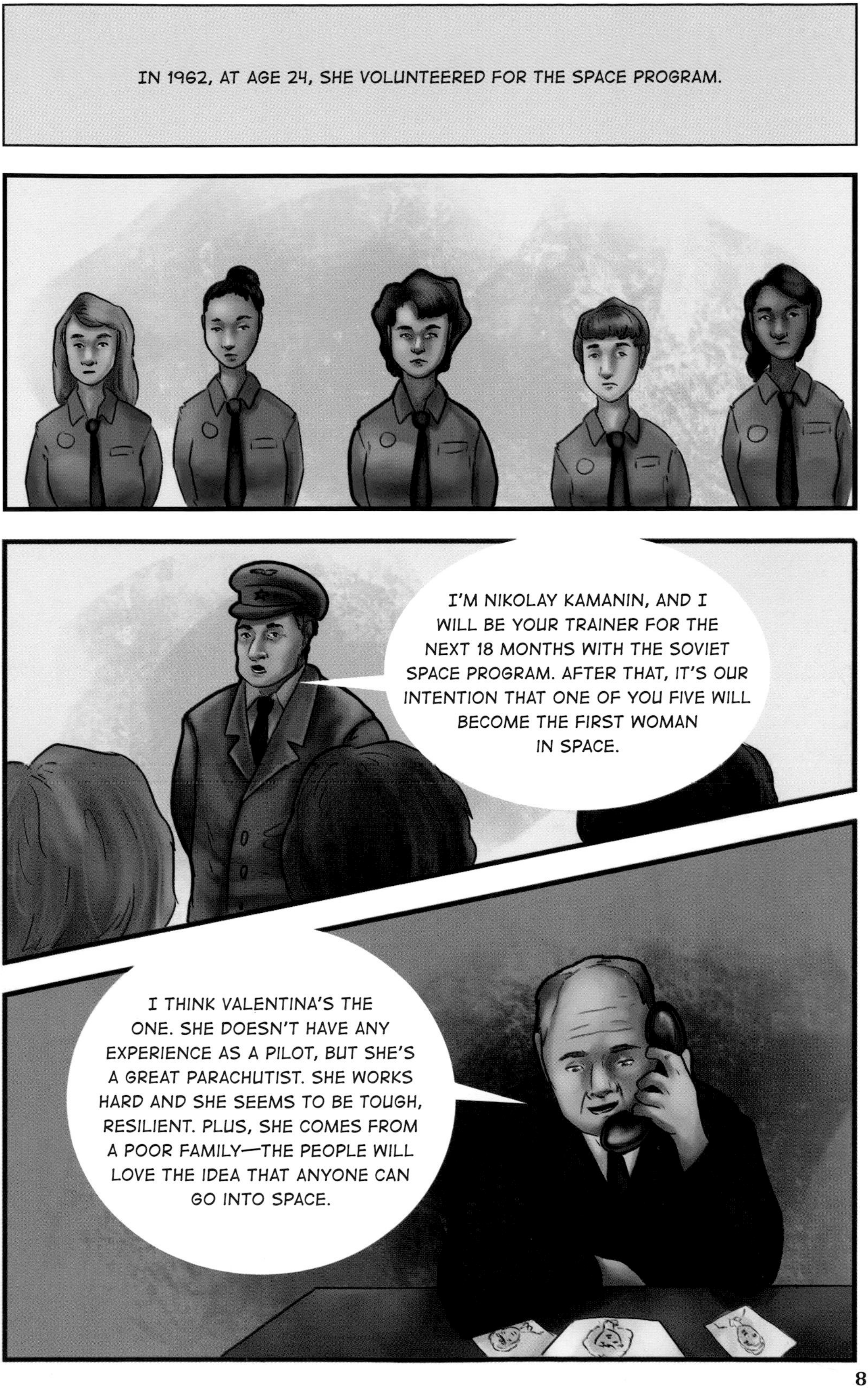
IN 1962, AT AGE 24, SHE VOLUNTEERED FOR THE SPACE PROGRAM.
I'M NIKOLAY KAMANIN, AND I WILL BE YOUR TRAINER FOR THE NEXT 18 MONTHS WITH THE SOVIET SPACE PROGRAM. AFTER THAT, IT'S OUR INTENTION THAT ONE OF YOU FIVE WILL BECOME THE FIRST WOMAN IN SPACE.
I THINK VALENTINA'S THE ONE. SHE DOESN'T HAVE ANY EXPERIENCE AS A PILOT, BUT SHE'S A GREAT PARACHUTIST. SHE WORKS HARD AND SHE SEEMS TO BE TOUGH, RESILIENT. PLUS, SHE COMES FROM A POOR FAMILY—THE PEOPLE WILL LOVE THE IDEA THAT ANYONE CAN GO INTO SPACE.

ON JUNE 16, 1963, AT THE AGE OF 26, VALENTINA BECAME THE FIRST WOMAN TO TRAVEL IN SPACE, ABOARD THE RUSSIAN SPACECRAFT *VOSTOK 6*. WHEN SHE LEFT HOME THAT MORNING, SHE LIED TO HER MOTHER, SAYING SHE WAS GOING SKYDIVING.

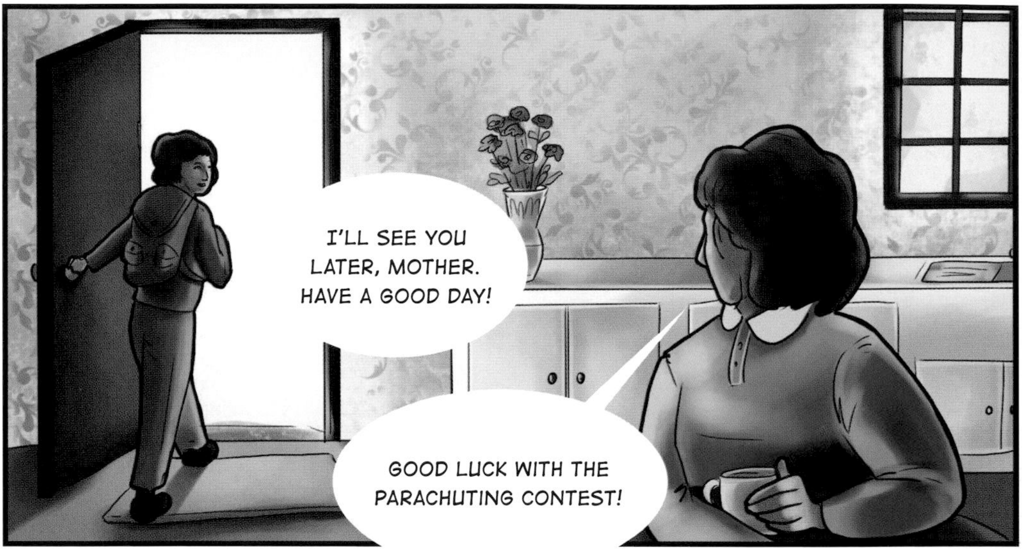
I'LL SEE YOU LATER, MOTHER. HAVE A GOOD DAY!
GOOD LUCK WITH THE PARACHUTING CONTEST!

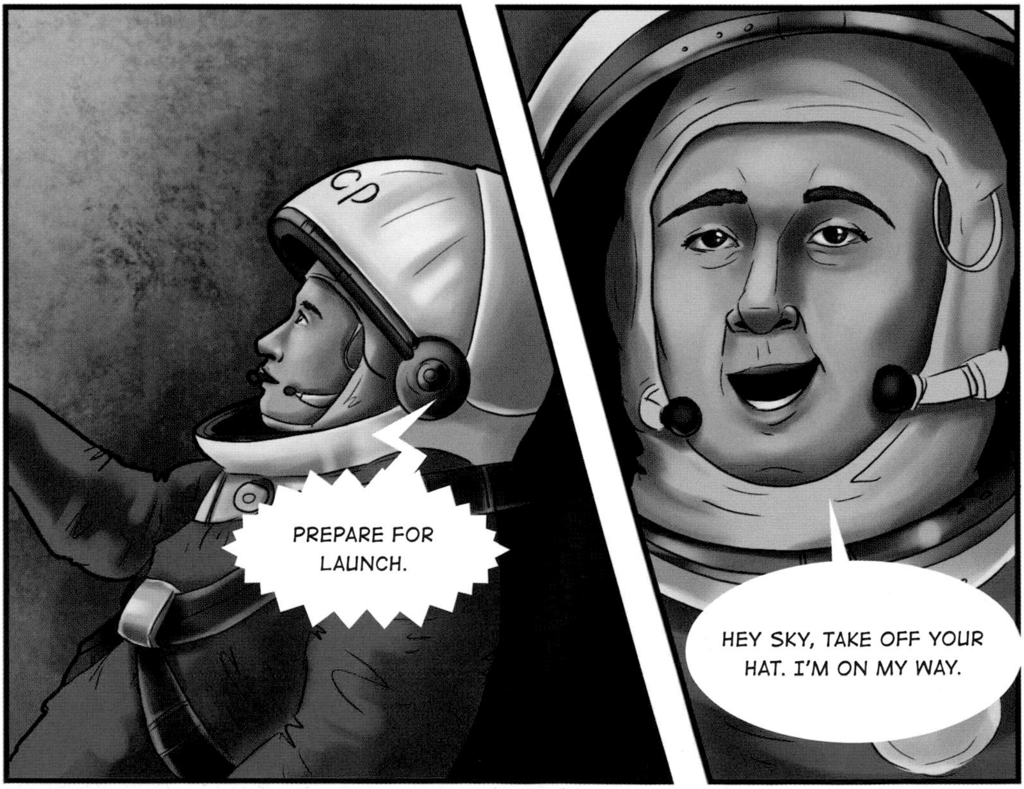
CP
PREPARE FOR LAUNCH.
HEY SKY, TAKE OFF YOUR HAT. I'M ON MY WAY.

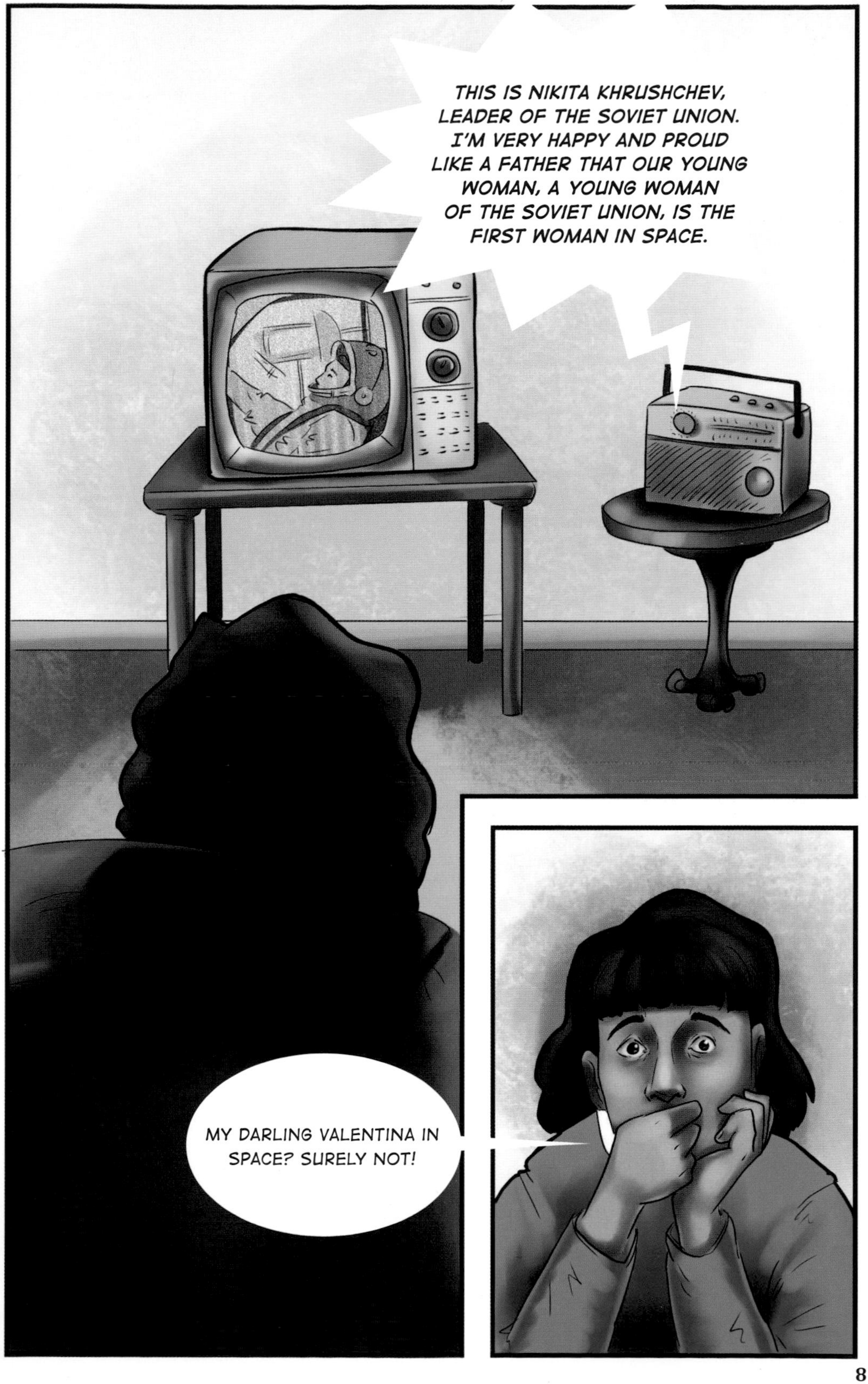
THIS IS NIKITA KHRUSHCHEV, LEADER OF THE SOVIET UNION. I'M VERY HAPPY AND PROUD LIKE A FATHER THAT OUR YOUNG WOMAN, A YOUNG WOMAN OF THE SOVIET UNION, IS THE FIRST WOMAN IN SPACE.
MY DARLING VALENTINA IN SPACE? SURELY NOT!

ALL ON HER OWN INSIDE *VOSTOK 6*, VALENTINA ORBITED EARTH 48 TIMES IN JUST UNDER THREE DAYS—FAR LONGER THAN ANYONE ELSE HAD EVER SPENT IN SPACE. CONDITIONS INSIDE THE SPACECRAFT WERE UNCOMFORTABLE.

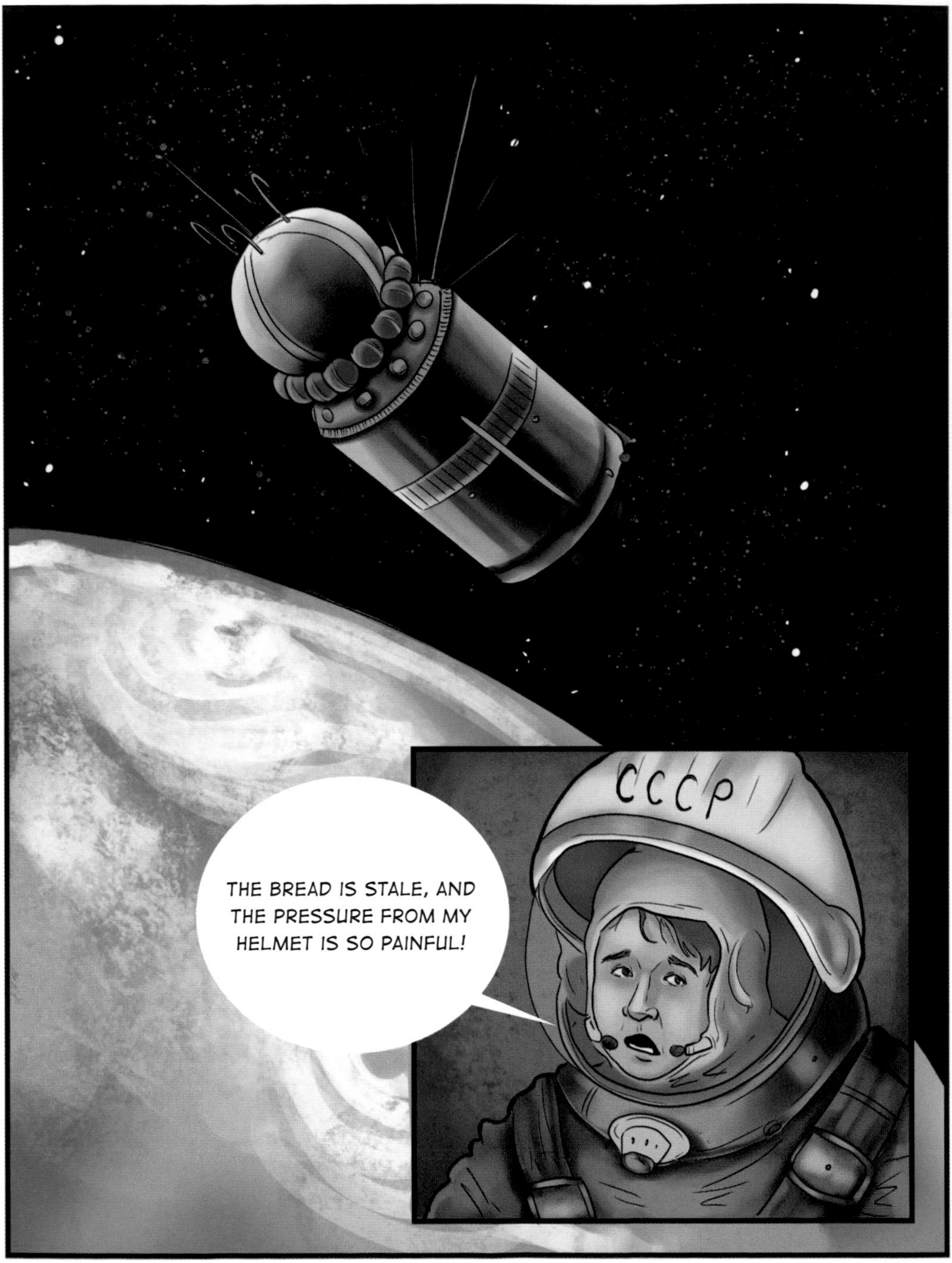
CCCP
THE BREAD IS STALE, AND THE PRESSURE FROM MY HELMET IS SO PAINFUL!

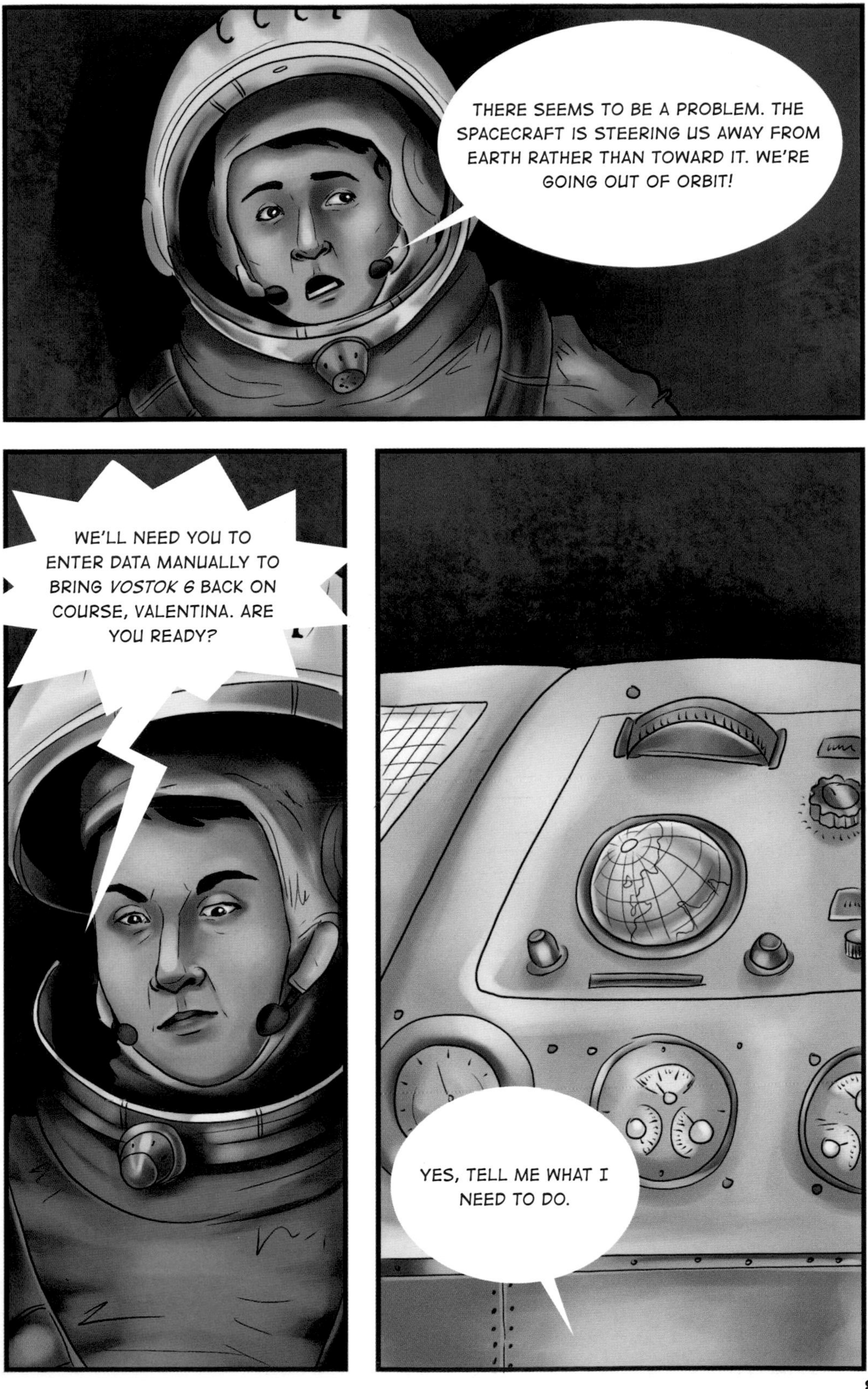
THERE SEEMS TO BE A PROBLEM. THE SPACECRAFT IS STEERING US AWAY FROM EARTH RATHER THAN TOWARD IT. WE'RE GOING OUT OF ORBIT!
WE'LL NEED YOU TO ENTER DATA MANUALLY TO BRING *VOSTOK 6* BACK ON COURSE, VALENTINA. ARE YOU READY?
YES, TELL ME WHAT I NEED TO DO.

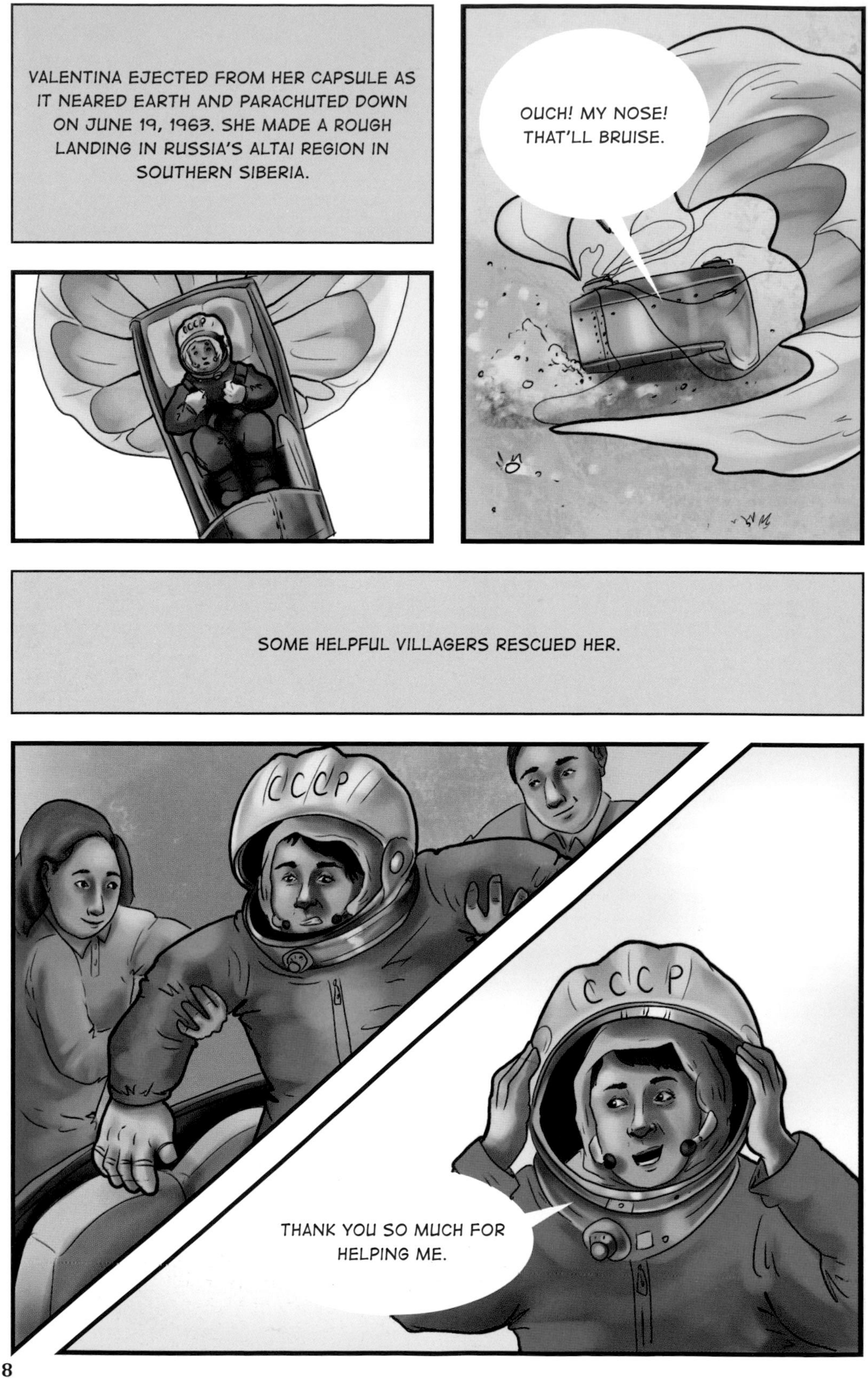
VALENTINA EJECTED FROM HER CAPSULE AS IT NEARED EARTH AND PARACHUTED DOWN ON JUNE 19, 1963. SHE MADE A ROUGH LANDING IN RUSSIA'S ALTAI REGION IN SOUTHERN SIBERIA.
OUCH! MY NOSE! THAT'LL BRUISE.
SOME HELPFUL VILLAGERS RESCUED HER.
THANK YOU SO MUCH FOR HELPING ME.

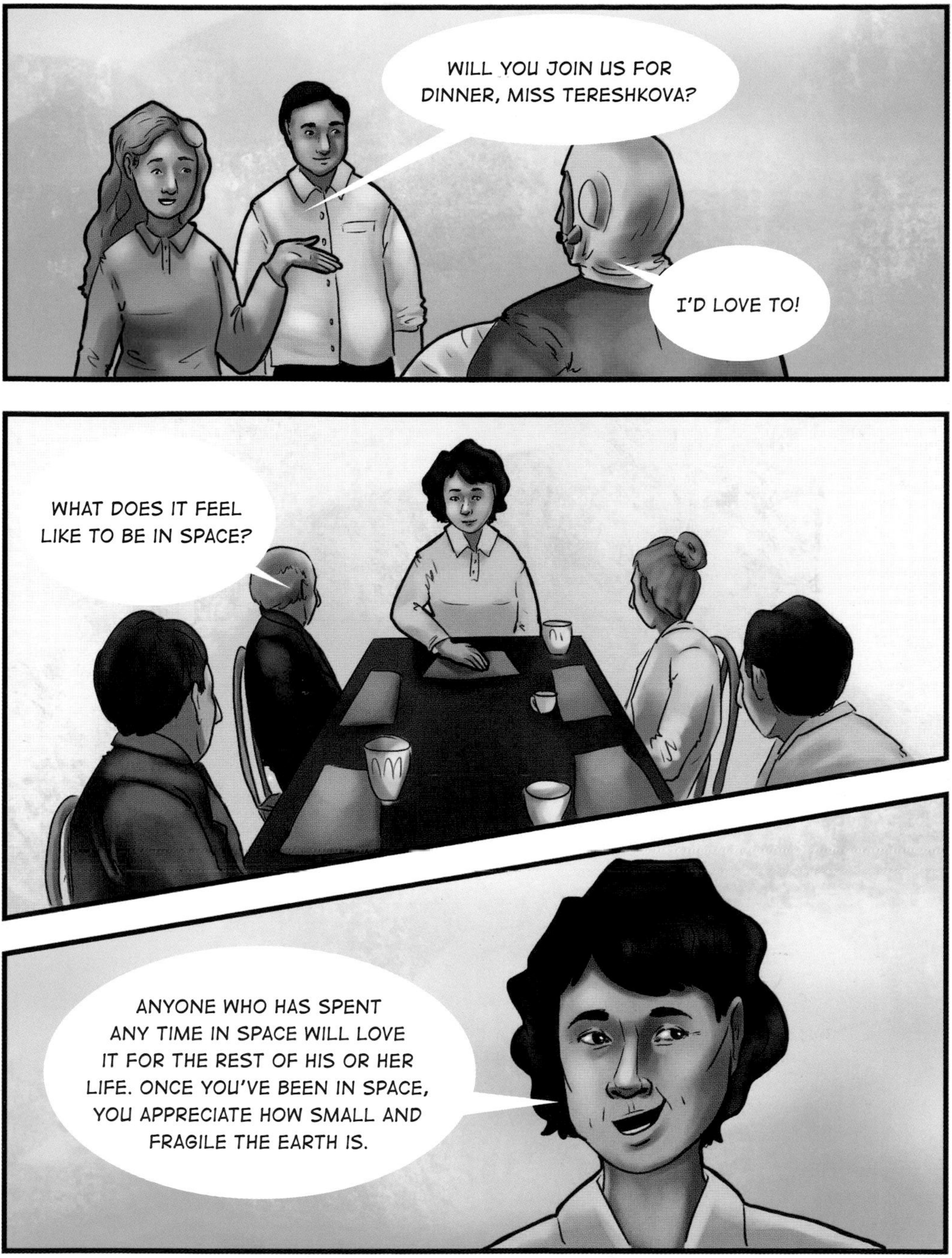
WILL YOU JOIN US FOR DINNER, MISS TERESHKOVA?
I'D LOVE TO!
WHAT DOES IT FEEL LIKE TO BE IN SPACE?
ANYONE WHO HAS SPENT ANY TIME IN SPACE WILL LOVE IT FOR THE REST OF HIS OR HER LIFE. ONCE YOU'VE BEEN IN SPACE, YOU APPRECIATE HOW SMALL AND FRAGILE THE EARTH IS.

VALENTINA CONTINUES TO BE ADMIRED FOR RISING FROM AN IMPOVERISHED CHILDHOOD TO BECOME THE FIRST WOMAN IN SPACE. IN HER OLD AGE, SHE HAS EVEN SPOKEN OF HER DESIRE TO TRAVEL TO MARS, SHOULD THE OPPORTUNITY ARISE.

THE APOLLO 11 CREW

NEIL ARMSTRONG, BUZZ ALDRIN & MICHAEL COLLINS

(1930–2012; 1930–present; 1930–present)

ONE GIANT LEAP

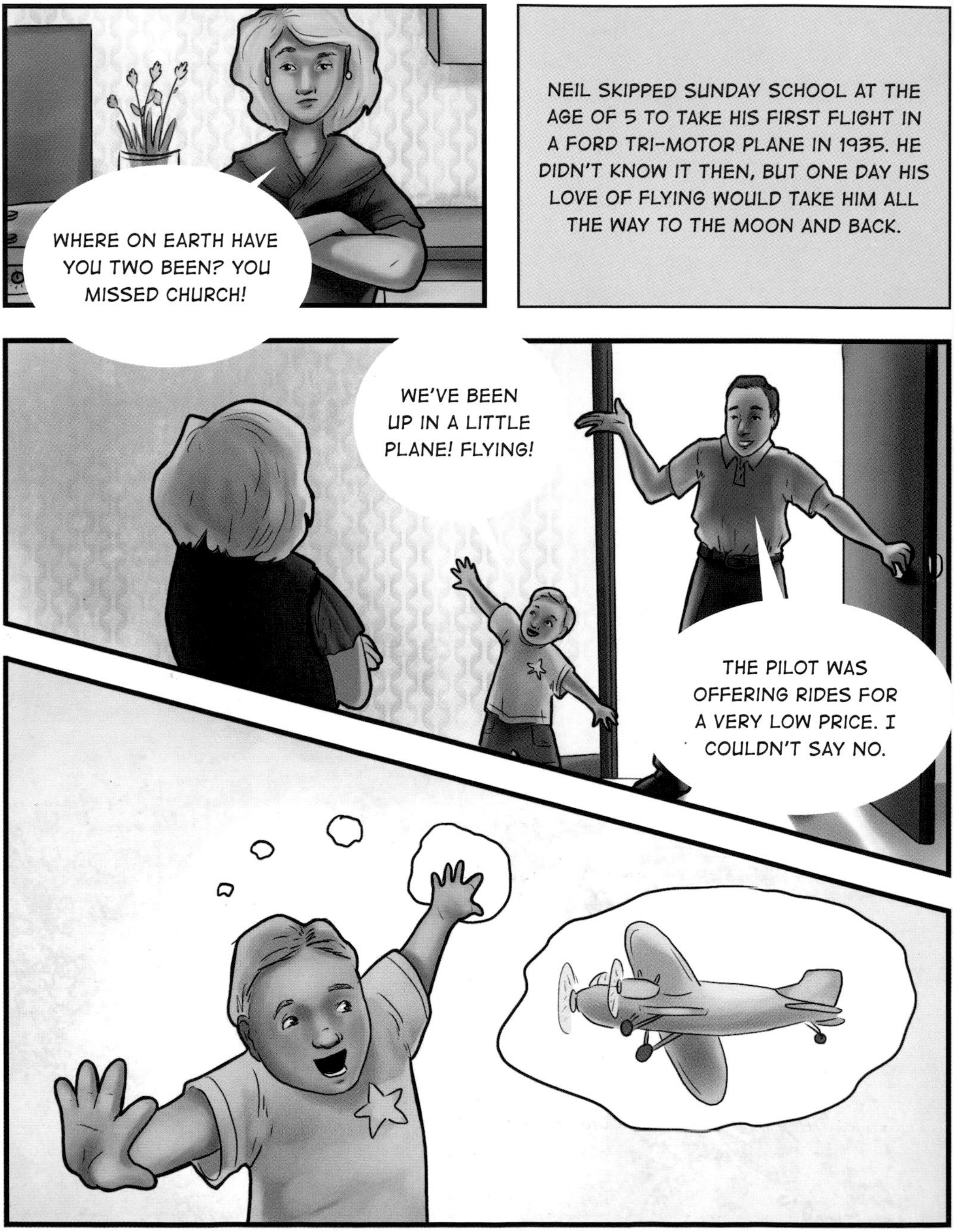
WHERE ON EARTH HAVE YOU TWO BEEN? YOU MISSED CHURCH!
NEIL SKIPPED SUNDAY SCHOOL AT THE AGE OF 5 TO TAKE HIS FIRST FLIGHT IN A FORD TRI-MOTOR PLANE IN 1935. HE DIDN'T KNOW IT THEN, BUT ONE DAY HIS LOVE OF FLYING WOULD TAKE HIM ALL THE WAY TO THE MOON AND BACK.
WE'VE BEEN UP IN A LITTLE PLANE! FLYING!
THE PILOT WAS OFFERING RIDES FOR A VERY LOW PRICE. I COULDN'T SAY NO.

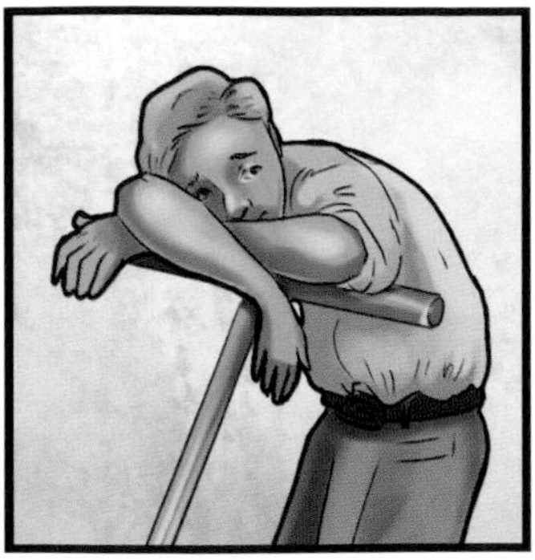

AS A TEENAGER, NEIL WORKED SEVERAL JOBS TO PAY FOR FLYING LESSONS AT THE LOCAL AIRPORT. HE EARNED HIS PILOT'S LICENSE ON HIS 16TH BIRTHDAY.

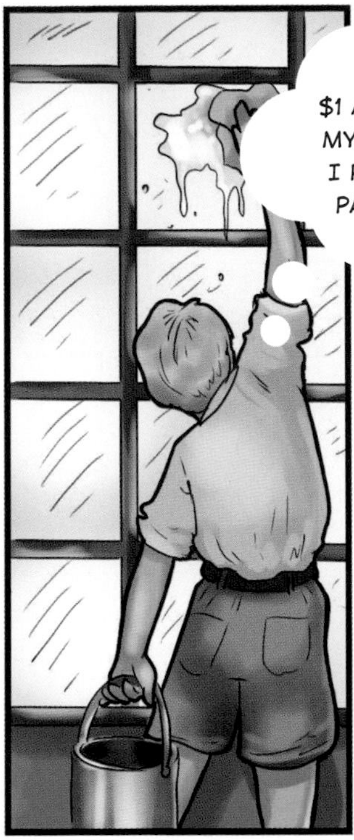
$1 A TIME FOR THIS, PLUS MY JOB AT THE BAKERY... I RECKON THAT SHOULD PAY FOR MY LESSONS.

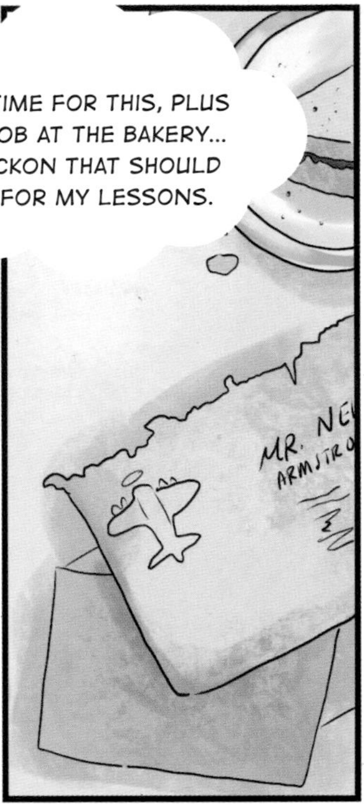

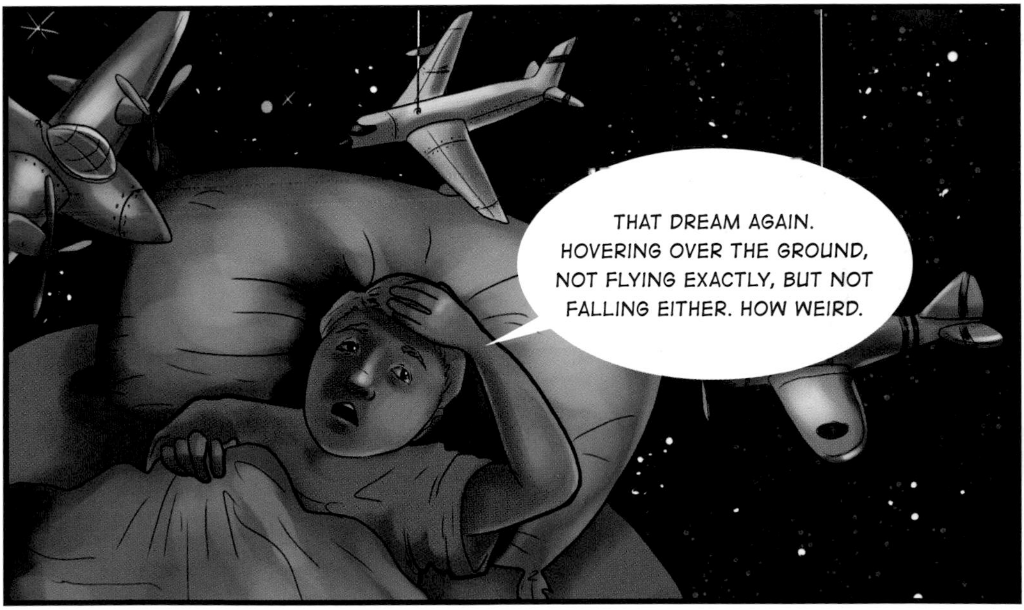
THAT DREAM AGAIN. HOVERING OVER THE GROUND, NOT FLYING EXACTLY, BUT NOT FALLING EITHER. HOW WEIRD.

NEIL WENT ON TO SERVE AS A PILOT IN THE NAVY, STUDY AERONAUTICAL ENGINEERING AT UNIVERSITY, AND LATER BECAME A TEST PILOT. IN 1962, AT THE AGE OF 32, HE WAS SELECTED BY NASA TO TRAIN AS AN ASTRONAUT.

WITH A FATHER IN THE ARMY, MICHAEL COLLINS SPENT HIS CHILDHOOD MOVING A LOT, ALL OVER THE WORLD. AFTER TAKING A FLIGHT AS A YOUNG TEENAGER, HE DREAMED OF JOINING THE AIR FORCE.

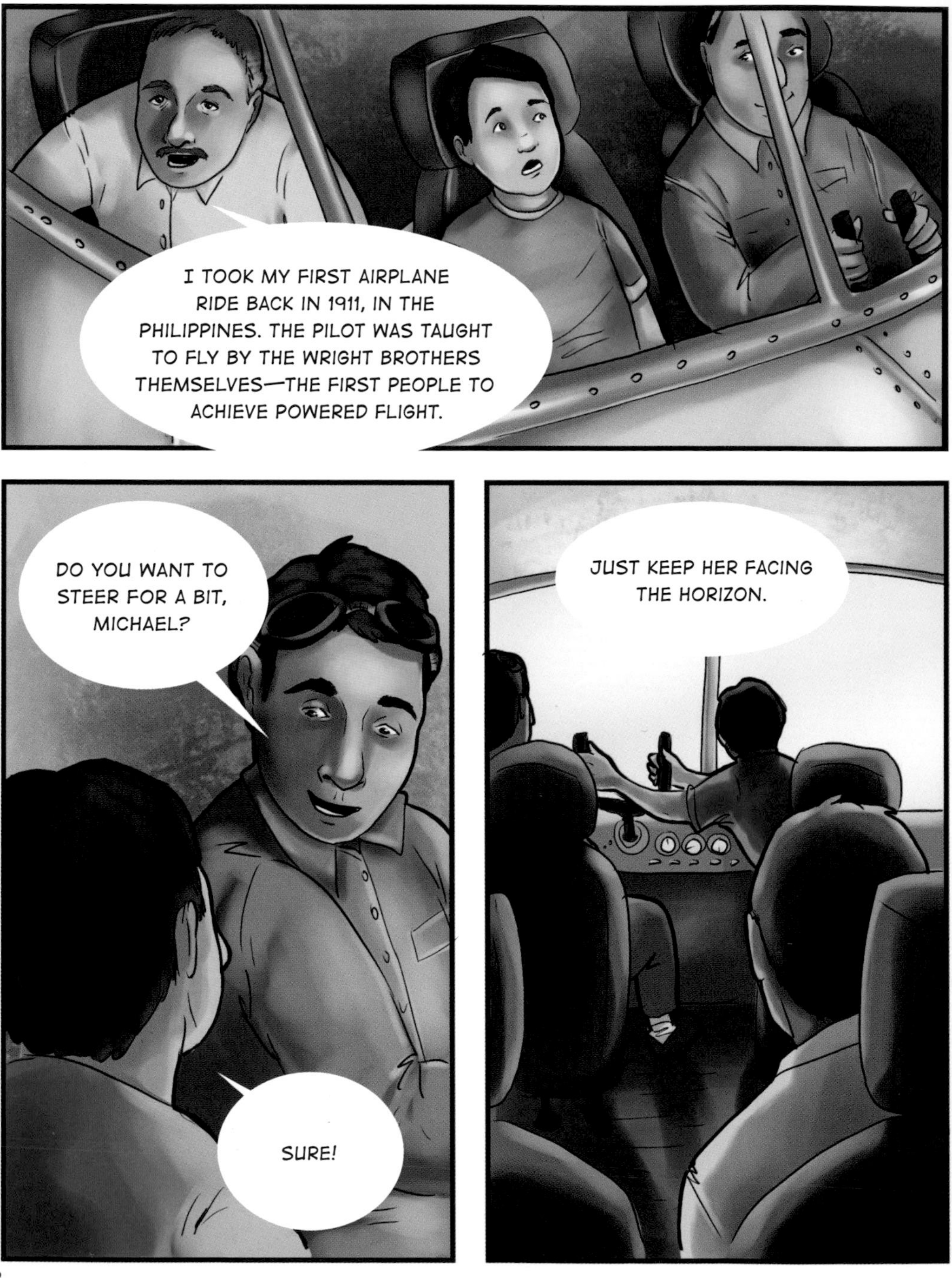
I TOOK MY FIRST AIRPLANE RIDE BACK IN 1911, IN THE PHILIPPINES. THE PILOT WAS TAUGHT TO FLY BY THE WRIGHT BROTHERS THEMSELVES—THE FIRST PEOPLE TO ACHIEVE POWERED FLIGHT.
DO YOU WANT TO STEER FOR A BIT, MICHAEL?
SURE!
JUST KEEP HER FACING THE HORIZON.

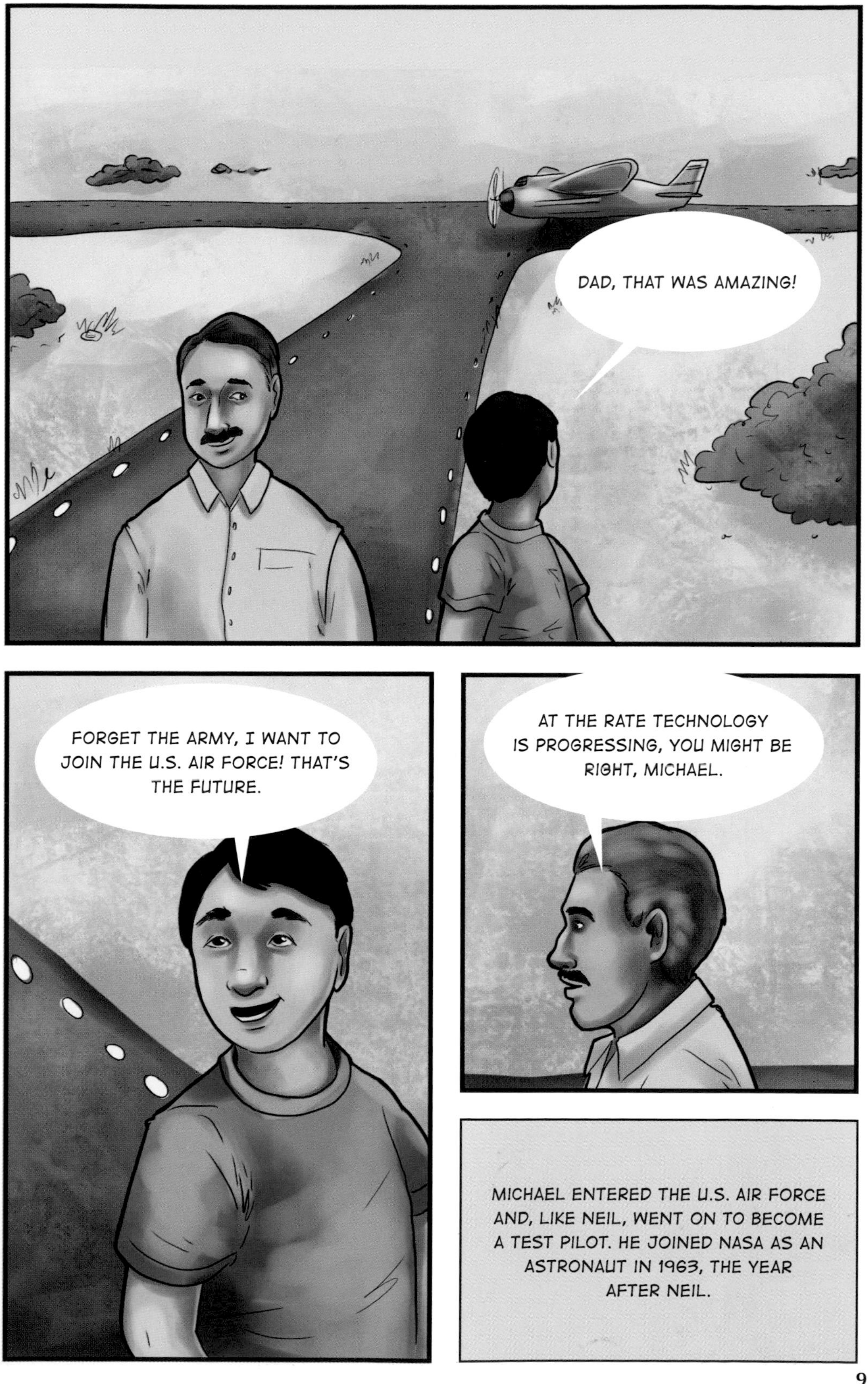
DAD, THAT WAS AMAZING!
FORGET THE ARMY, I WANT TO JOIN THE U.S. AIR FORCE! THAT'S THE FUTURE.
AT THE RATE TECHNOLOGY IS PROGRESSING, YOU MIGHT BE RIGHT, MICHAEL.
MICHAEL ENTERED THE U.S. AIR FORCE AND, LIKE NEIL, WENT ON TO BECOME A TEST PILOT. HE JOINED NASA AS AN ASTRONAUT IN 1963, THE YEAR AFTER NEIL.

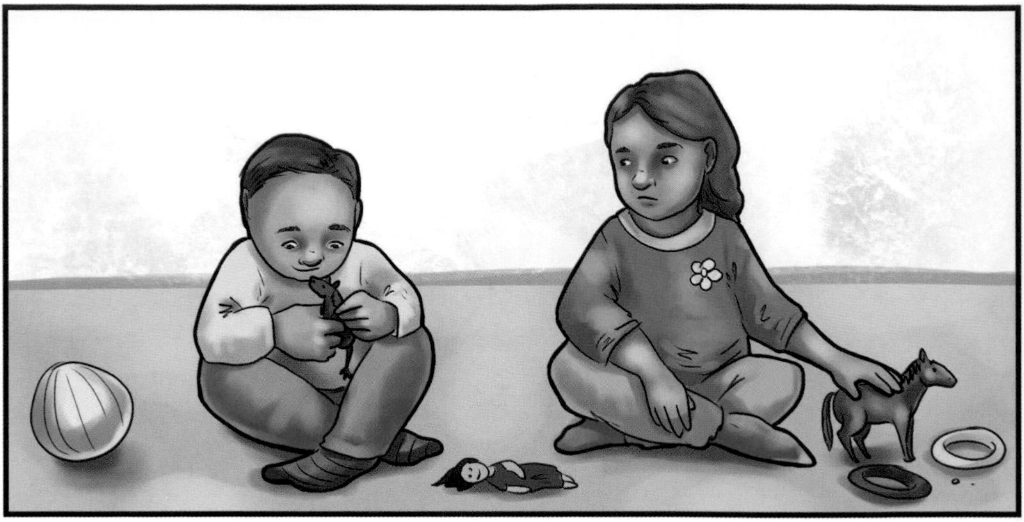

FROM A YOUNG AGE, EDWIN ALDRIN WANTED TO BE A FIGHTER PILOT. IN 1951, HE JOINED THE AIR FORCE. HIS SISTER FAY ANN GAVE HIM THE NICKNAME BUZZ.

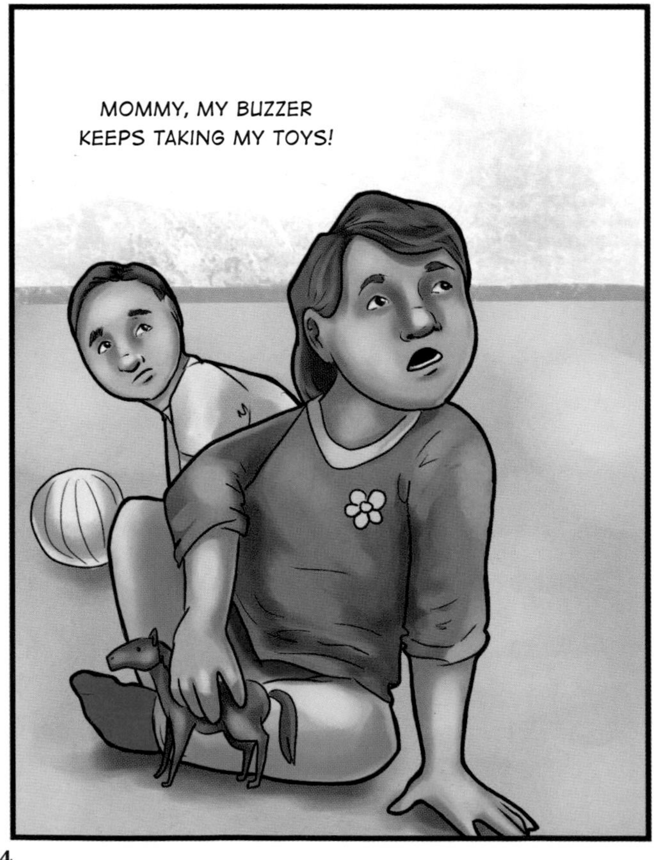
MOMMY, MY BUZZER KEEPS TAKING MY TOYS!

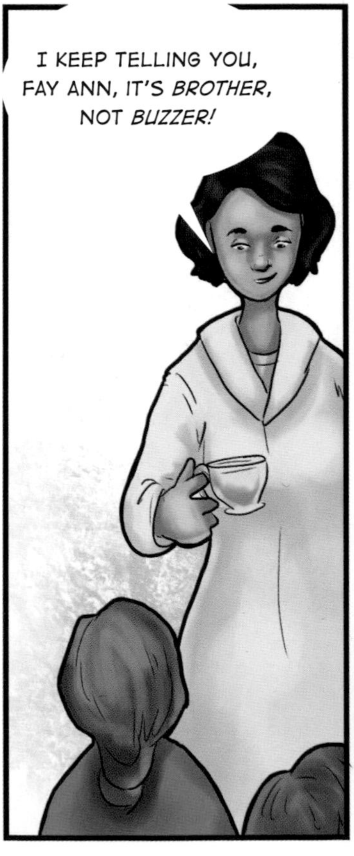
I KEEP TELLING YOU, FAY ANN, IT'S *BROTHER*, NOT *BUZZER*!

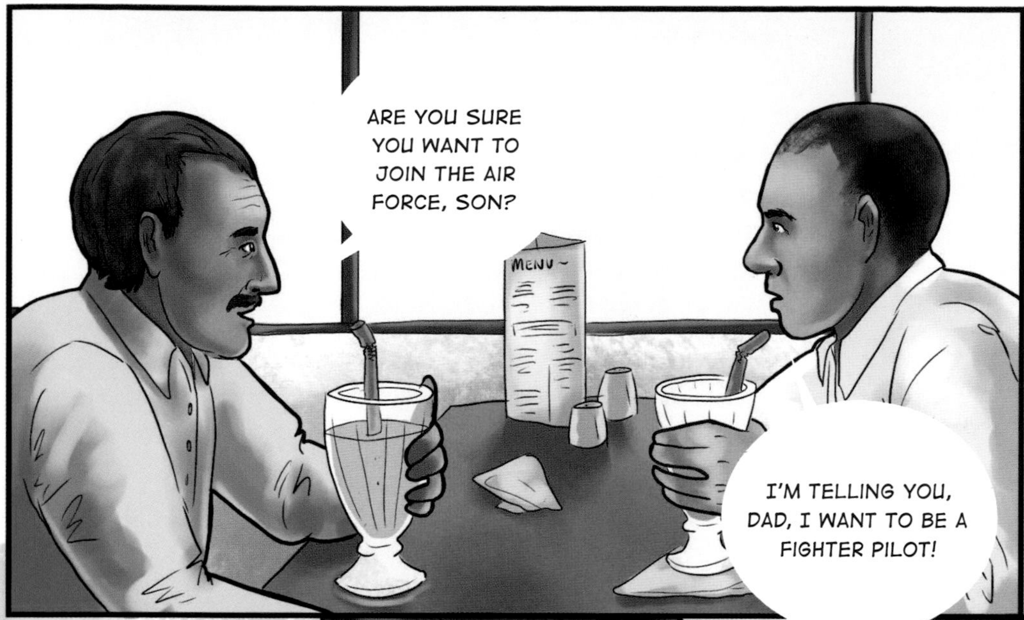
ARE YOU SURE YOU WANT TO JOIN THE AIR FORCE, SON?
MENU
I'M TELLING YOU, DAD, I WANT TO BE A FIGHTER PILOT!

BUZZ OFFICIALLY ENTERED THE U.S. AIR FORCE IN 1951. DURING HIS TIME IN THE MILITARY, ALDRIN JOINED THE 51ST FIGHTER WING, WHERE HE FLEW F-86 SABRE JETS IN 66 COMBAT MISSIONS IN KOREA.

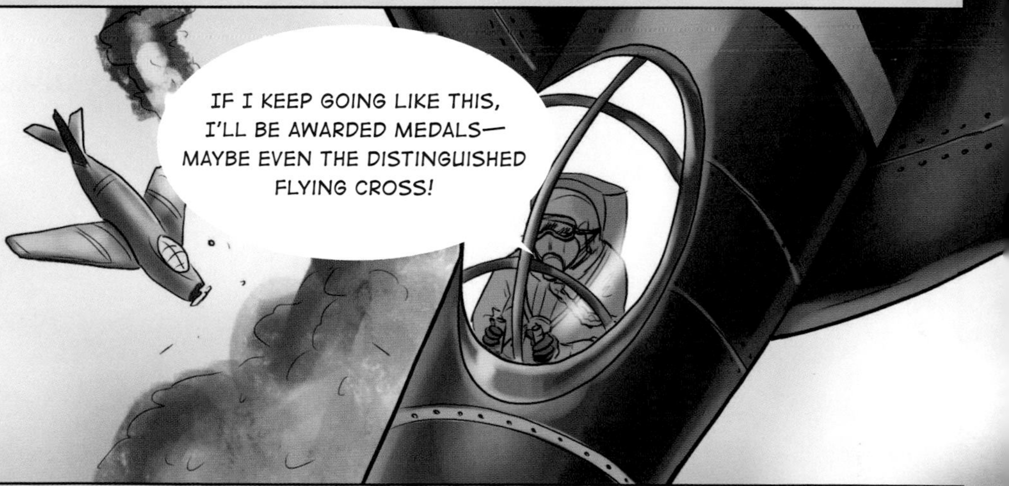
IF I KEEP GOING LIKE THIS, I'LL BE AWARDED MEDALS—MAYBE EVEN THE DISTINGUISHED FLYING CROSS!

BUZZ'S FIRST APPLICATION TO BECOME AN ASTRONAUT WAS REJECTED BECAUSE UNLIKE NEIL AND MICHAEL, HE'D NEVER BEEN A TEST PILOT. BUT IN 1963, NASA CHANGED THE REQUIREMENTS, AND BUZZ JOINED THE THIRD GROUP OF ASTRONAUTS-IN-TRAINING ALONGSIDE MICHAEL.

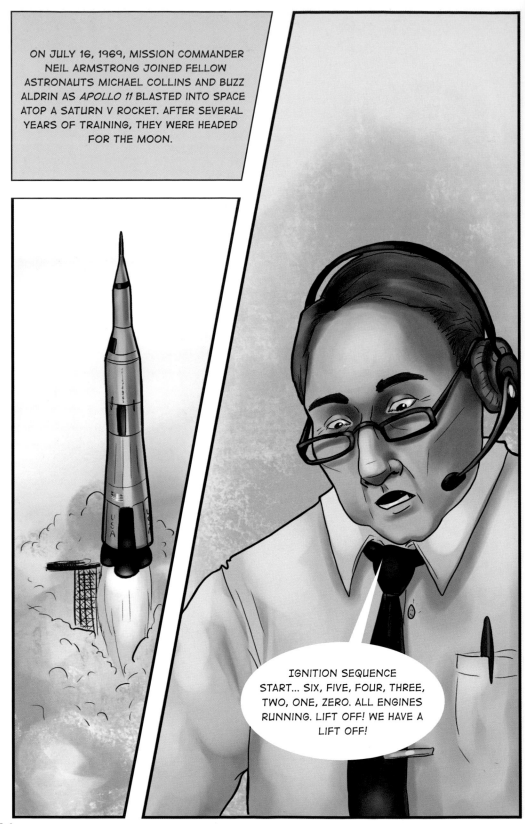

ON JULY 16, 1969, MISSION COMMANDER NEIL ARMSTRONG JOINED FELLOW ASTRONAUTS MICHAEL COLLINS AND BUZZ ALDRIN AS *APOLLO 11* BLASTED INTO SPACE ATOP A SATURN V ROCKET. AFTER SEVERAL YEARS OF TRAINING, THEY WERE HEADED FOR THE MOON.

IGNITION SEQUENCE START... SIX, FIVE, FOUR, THREE, TWO, ONE, ZERO. ALL ENGINES RUNNING. LIFT OFF! WE HAVE A LIFT OFF!

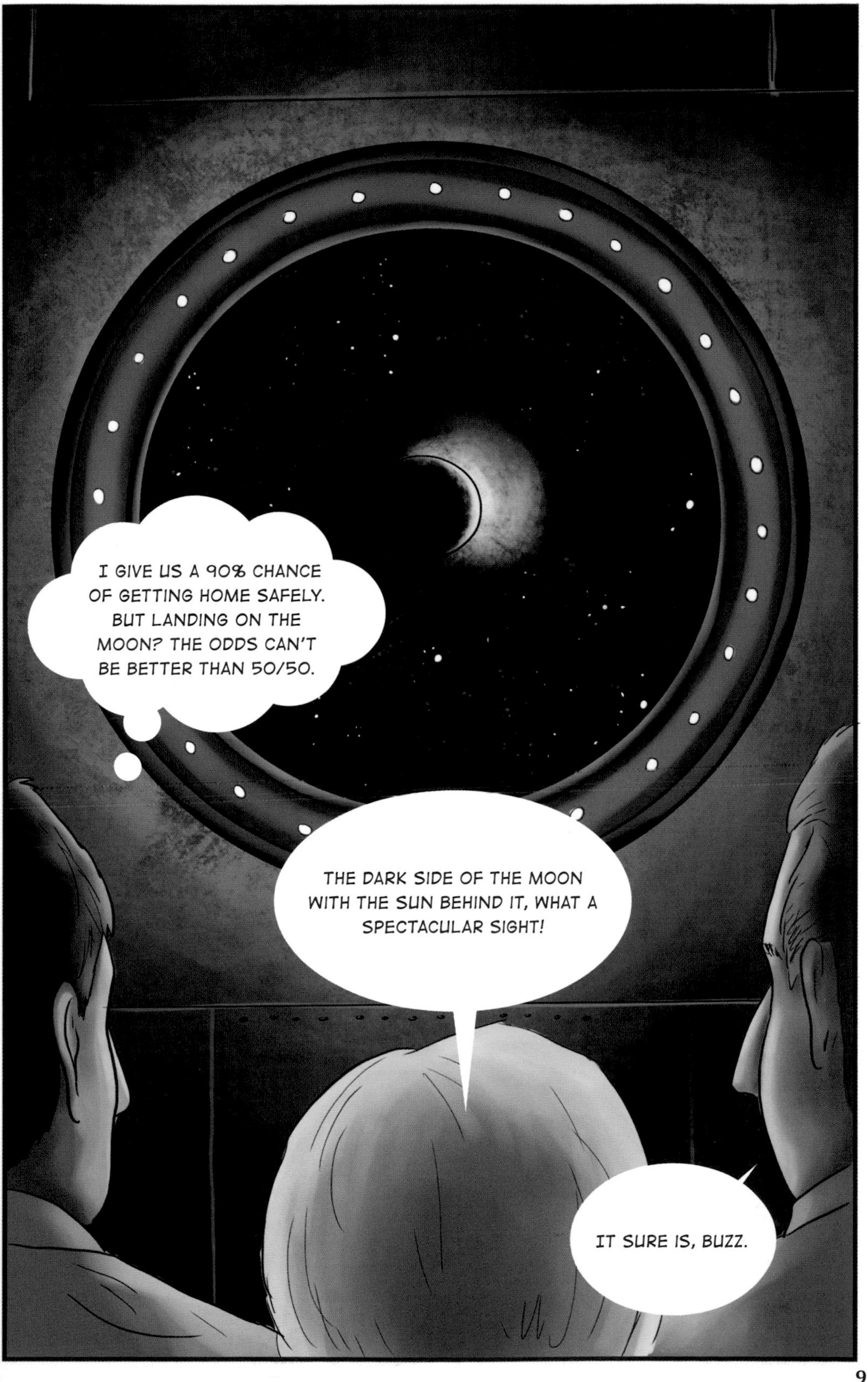
I GIVE US A 90% CHANCE OF GETTING HOME SAFELY. BUT LANDING ON THE MOON? THE ODDS CAN'T BE BETTER THAN 50/50.
THE DARK SIDE OF THE MOON WITH THE SUN BEHIND IT, WHAT A SPECTACULAR SIGHT!
IT SURE IS, BUZZ.

WHILE NEIL AND BUZZ HEADED OFF TO EXPLORE THE SURFACE OF THE MOON ABOARD THE LUNAR MODULE *EAGLE*, MICHAEL REMAINED ORBITING THE MOON ABOARD THE MAIN SPACECRAFT, *COLUMBIA*. ALONE AND COMPLETELY CUT OFF FROM RADIO CONTACT WITH EARTH, IT WAS A SOUL-SEARCHING TIME FOR HIM.

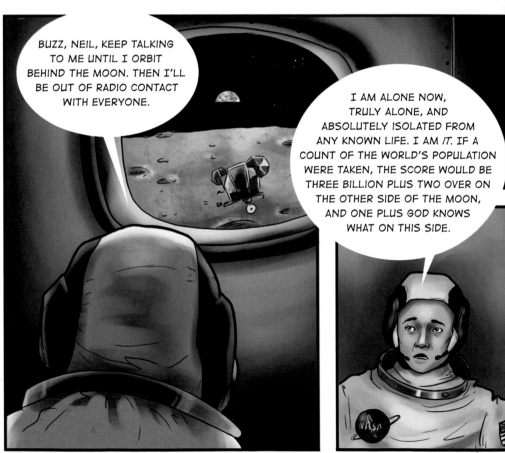

BUZZ, NEIL, KEEP TALKING TO ME UNTIL I ORBIT BEHIND THE MOON. THEN I'LL BE OUT OF RADIO CONTACT WITH EVERYONE.

I AM ALONE NOW, TRULY ALONE, AND ABSOLUTELY ISOLATED FROM ANY KNOWN LIFE. I AM *IT*. IF A COUNT OF THE WORLD'S POPULATION WERE TAKEN, THE SCORE WOULD BE THREE BILLION PLUS TWO OVER ON THE OTHER SIDE OF THE MOON, AND ONE PLUS GOD KNOWS WHAT ON THIS SIDE.

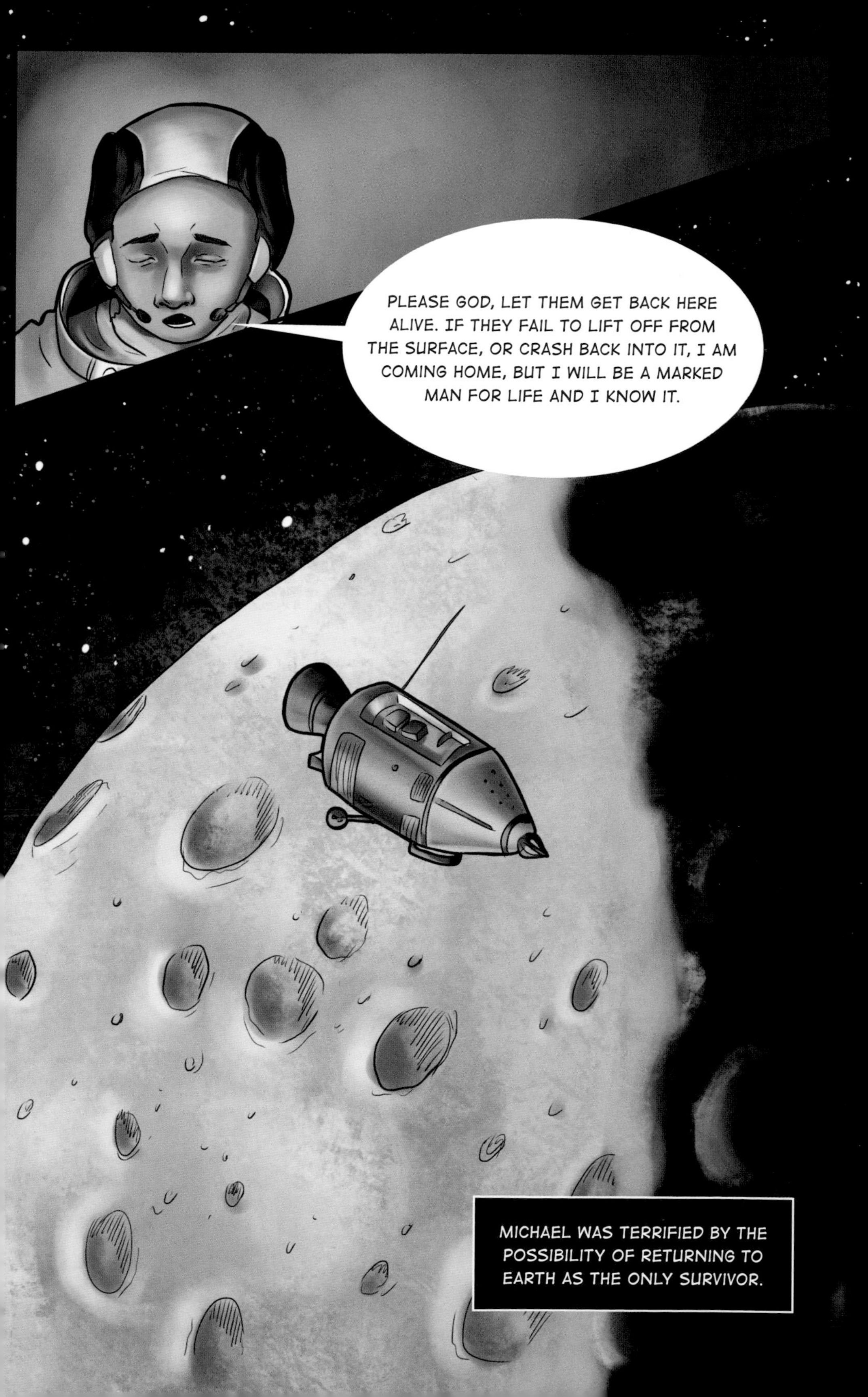
PLEASE GOD, LET THEM GET BACK HERE ALIVE. IF THEY FAIL TO LIFT OFF FROM THE SURFACE, OR CRASH BACK INTO IT, I AM COMING HOME, BUT I WILL BE A MARKED MAN FOR LIFE AND I KNOW IT.
MICHAEL WAS TERRIFIED BY THE POSSIBILITY OF RETURNING TO EARTH AS THE ONLY SURVIVOR.

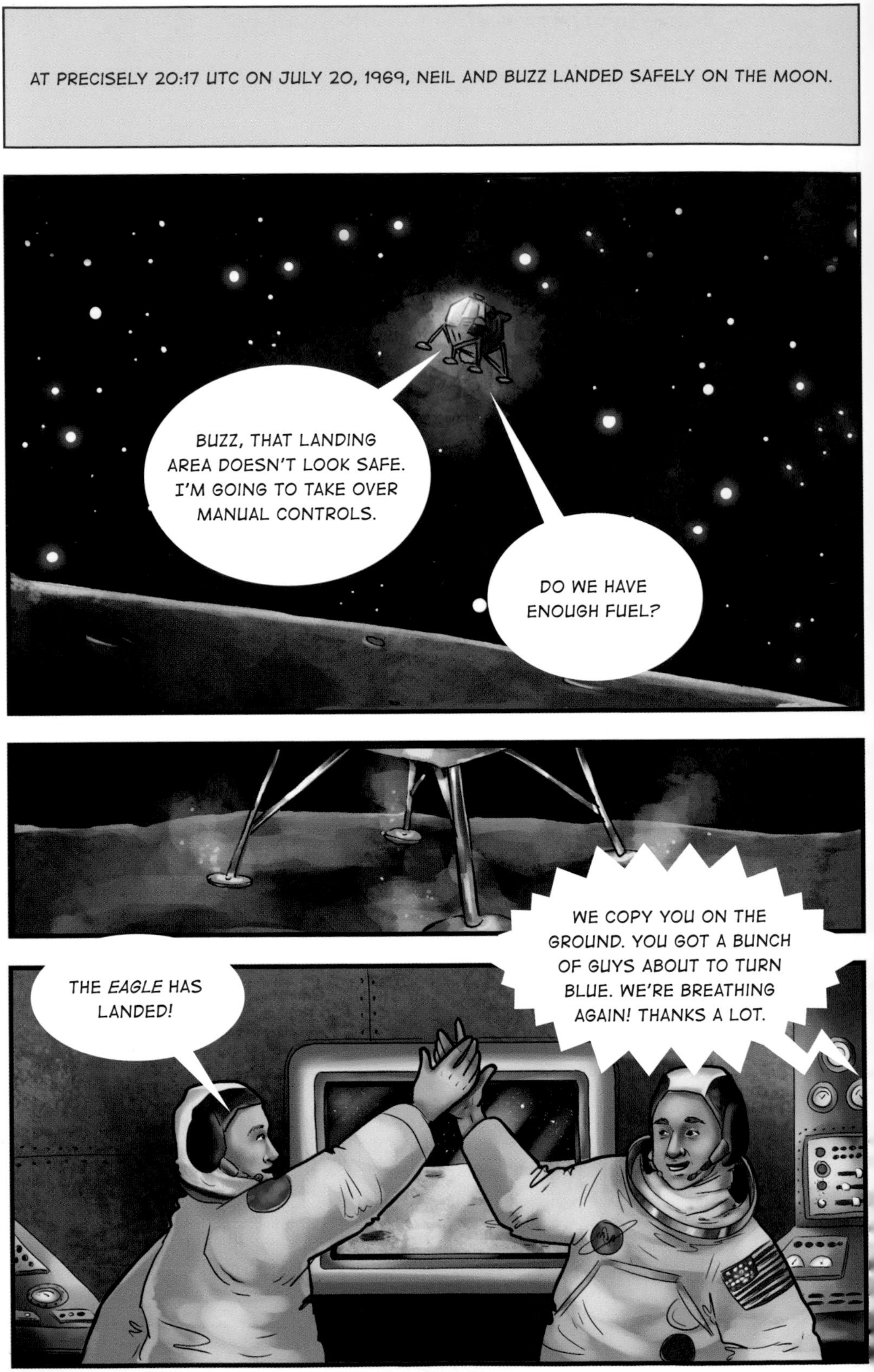
AT PRECISELY 20:17 UTC ON JULY 20, 1969, NEIL AND BUZZ LANDED SAFELY ON THE MOON.
BUZZ, THAT LANDING AREA DOESN'T LOOK SAFE. I'M GOING TO TAKE OVER MANUAL CONTROLS.
DO WE HAVE ENOUGH FUEL?
THE *EAGLE* HAS LANDED!
WE COPY YOU ON THE GROUND. YOU GOT A BUNCH OF GUYS ABOUT TO TURN BLUE. WE'RE BREATHING AGAIN! THANKS A LOT.

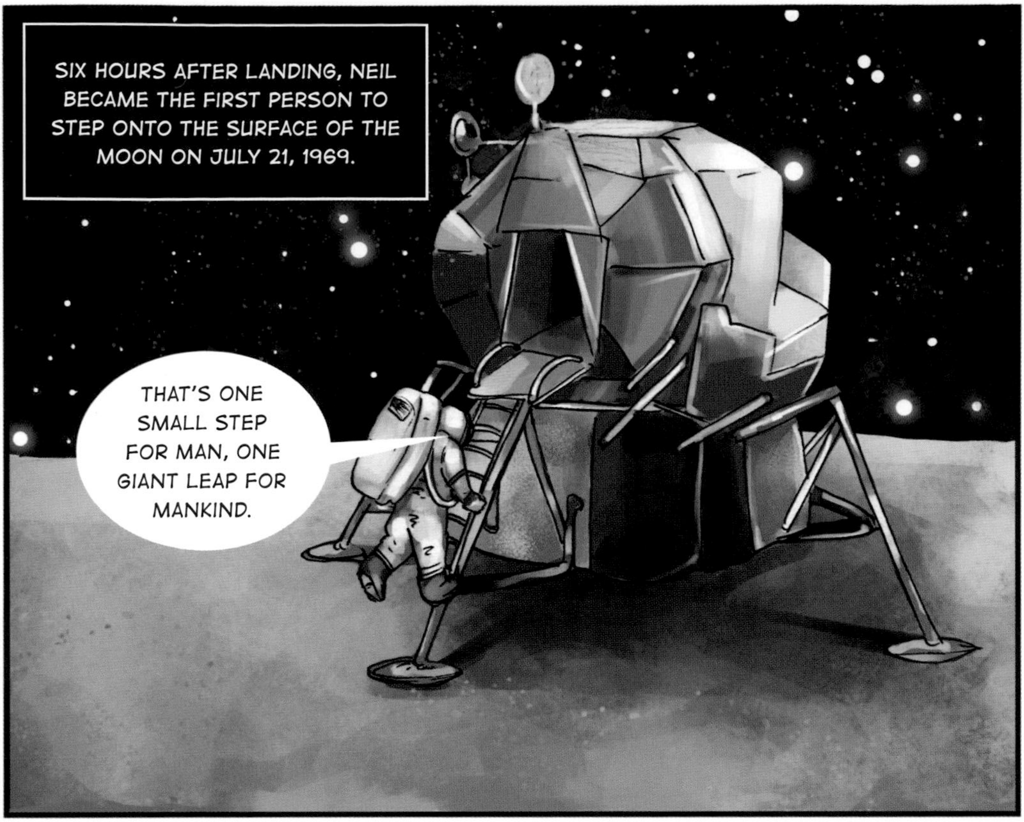
SIX HOURS AFTER LANDING, NEIL BECAME THE FIRST PERSON TO STEP ONTO THE SURFACE OF THE MOON ON JULY 21, 1969.
THAT'S ONE SMALL STEP FOR MAN, ONE GIANT LEAP FOR MANKIND.

OVER 236,000 MILES AWAY ON EARTH, SOME 600 MILLION PEOPLE WERE GLUED TO THEIR TELEVISION SETS, WATCHING THE MOON WALK LIVE.

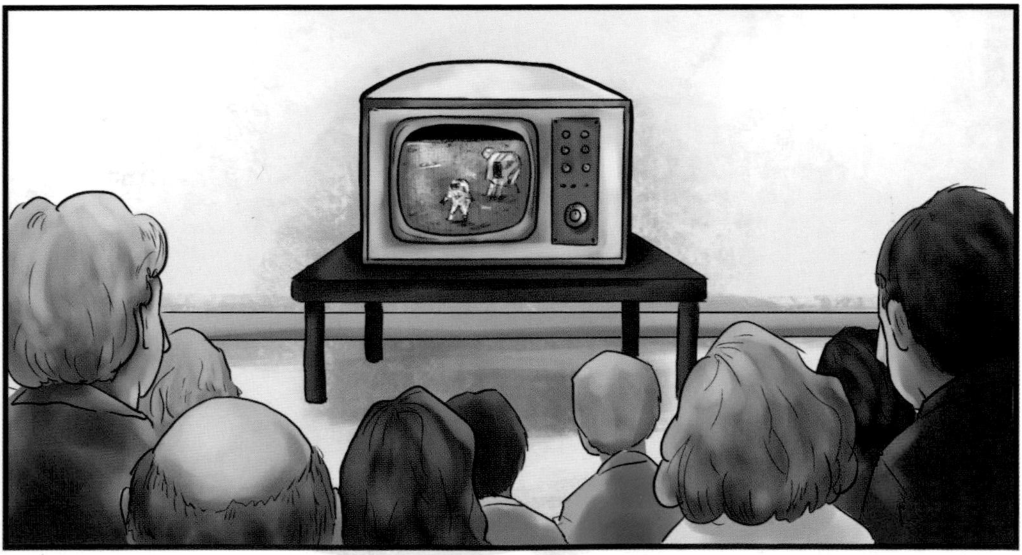

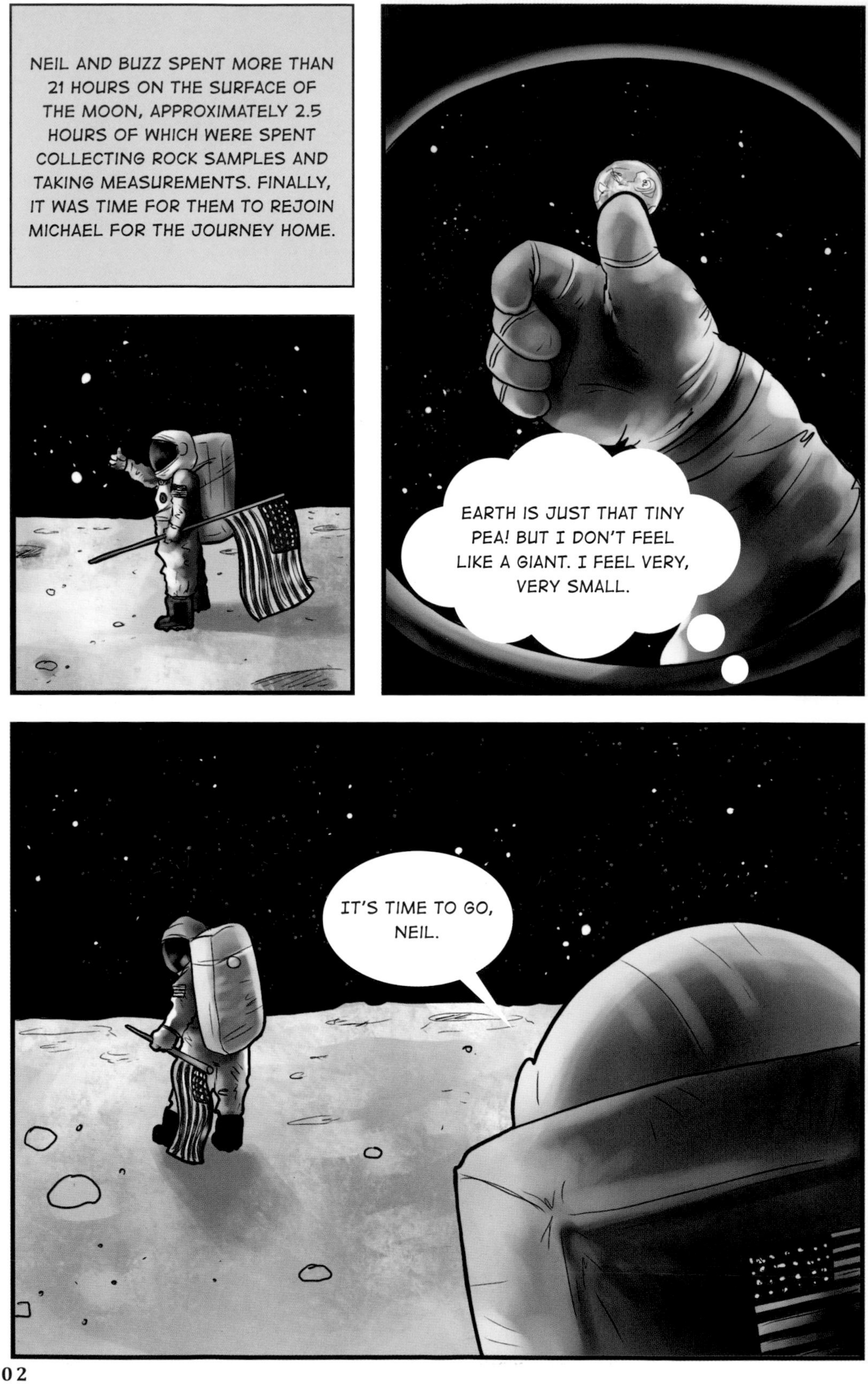
NEIL AND BUZZ SPENT MORE THAN 21 HOURS ON THE SURFACE OF THE MOON, APPROXIMATELY 2.5 HOURS OF WHICH WERE SPENT COLLECTING ROCK SAMPLES AND TAKING MEASUREMENTS. FINALLY, IT WAS TIME FOR THEM TO REJOIN MICHAEL FOR THE JOURNEY HOME.
EARTH IS JUST THAT TINY PEA! BUT I DON'T FEEL LIKE A GIANT. I FEEL VERY, VERY SMALL.
IT'S TIME TO GO, NEIL.

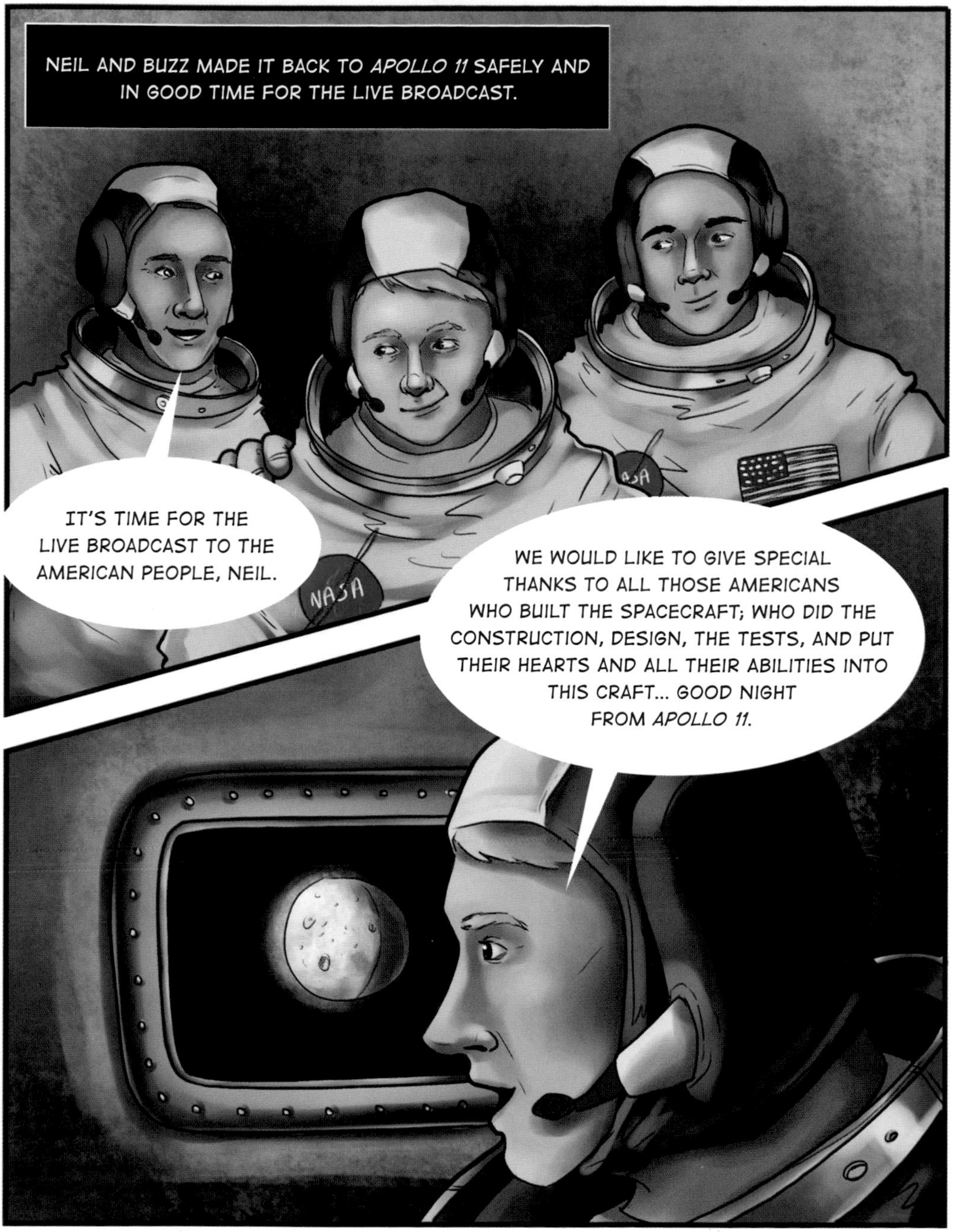
NEIL AND BUZZ MADE IT BACK TO *APOLLO 11* SAFELY AND IN GOOD TIME FOR THE LIVE BROADCAST.
IT'S TIME FOR THE LIVE BROADCAST TO THE AMERICAN PEOPLE, NEIL.
NASA
NASA
WE WOULD LIKE TO GIVE SPECIAL THANKS TO ALL THOSE AMERICANS WHO BUILT THE SPACECRAFT; WHO DID THE CONSTRUCTION, DESIGN, THE TESTS, AND PUT THEIR HEARTS AND ALL THEIR ABILITIES INTO THIS CRAFT... GOOD NIGHT FROM *APOLLO 11*.

THE MOON LANDING CONTINUES TO BE REGARDED AS ONE OF HUMANKIND'S GREATEST ACHIEVEMENTS. IT INSPIRED A NEW GENERATION OF SCIENTISTS AND EXPLORERS, AND OVER THE NEXT FEW YEARS, TEN MORE ASTRONAUTS WOULD FOLLOW IN BUZZ AND NEIL'S FOOTSTEPS TO WALK ON THE MOON.

JOHN W. YOUNG & ROBERT L. CRIPPEN
(1930–2018; 1937–present)
THE SPACE SHUTTLE IS A GO!

AFTER FLYING IN THE U.S. NAVY FOR TEN YEARS, JOHN YOUNG JOINED NASA IN 1962, WHEN HE WAS 32 YEARS OLD.

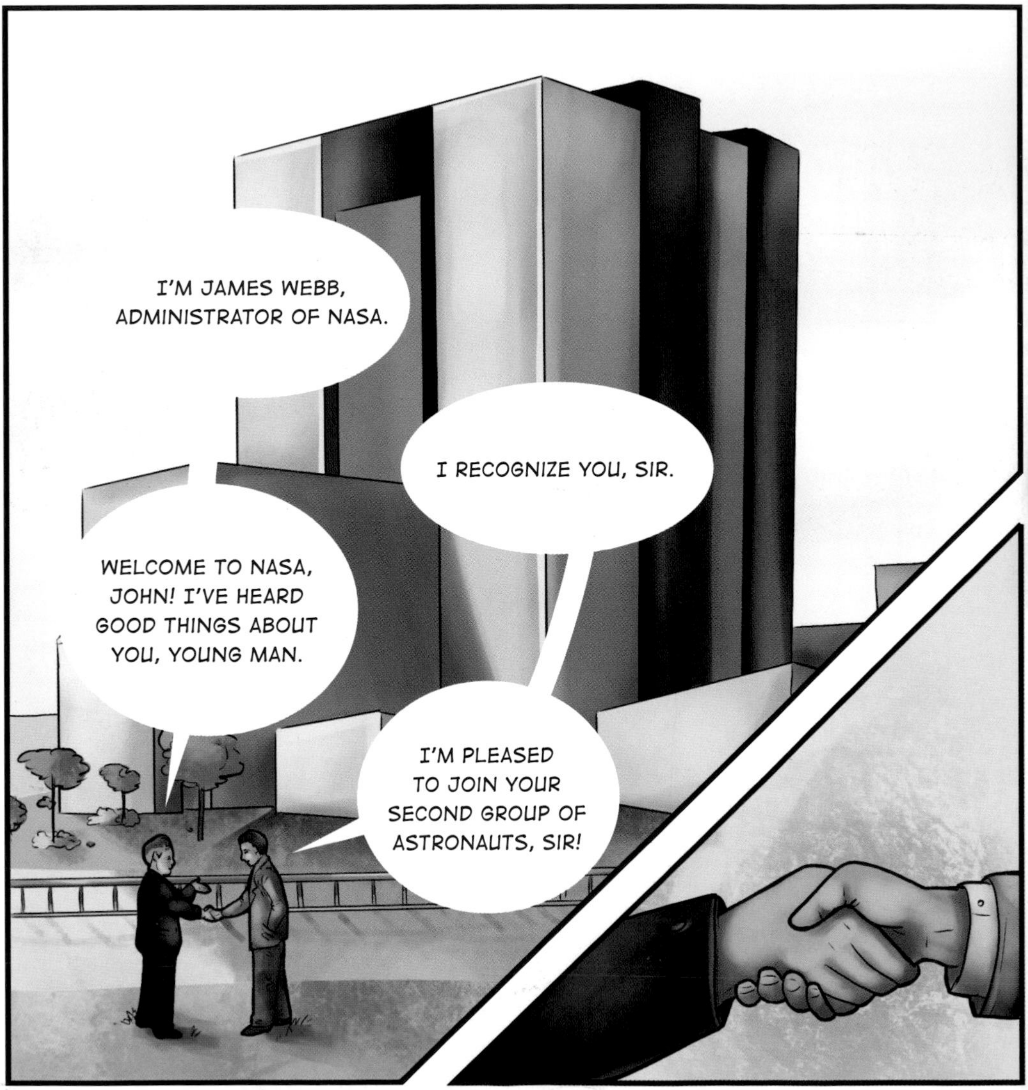
I'M JAMES WEBB, ADMINISTRATOR OF NASA.
WELCOME TO NASA, JOHN! I'VE HEARD GOOD THINGS ABOUT YOU, YOUNG MAN.
I RECOGNIZE YOU, SIR.
I'M PLEASED TO JOIN YOUR SECOND GROUP OF ASTRONAUTS, SIR!

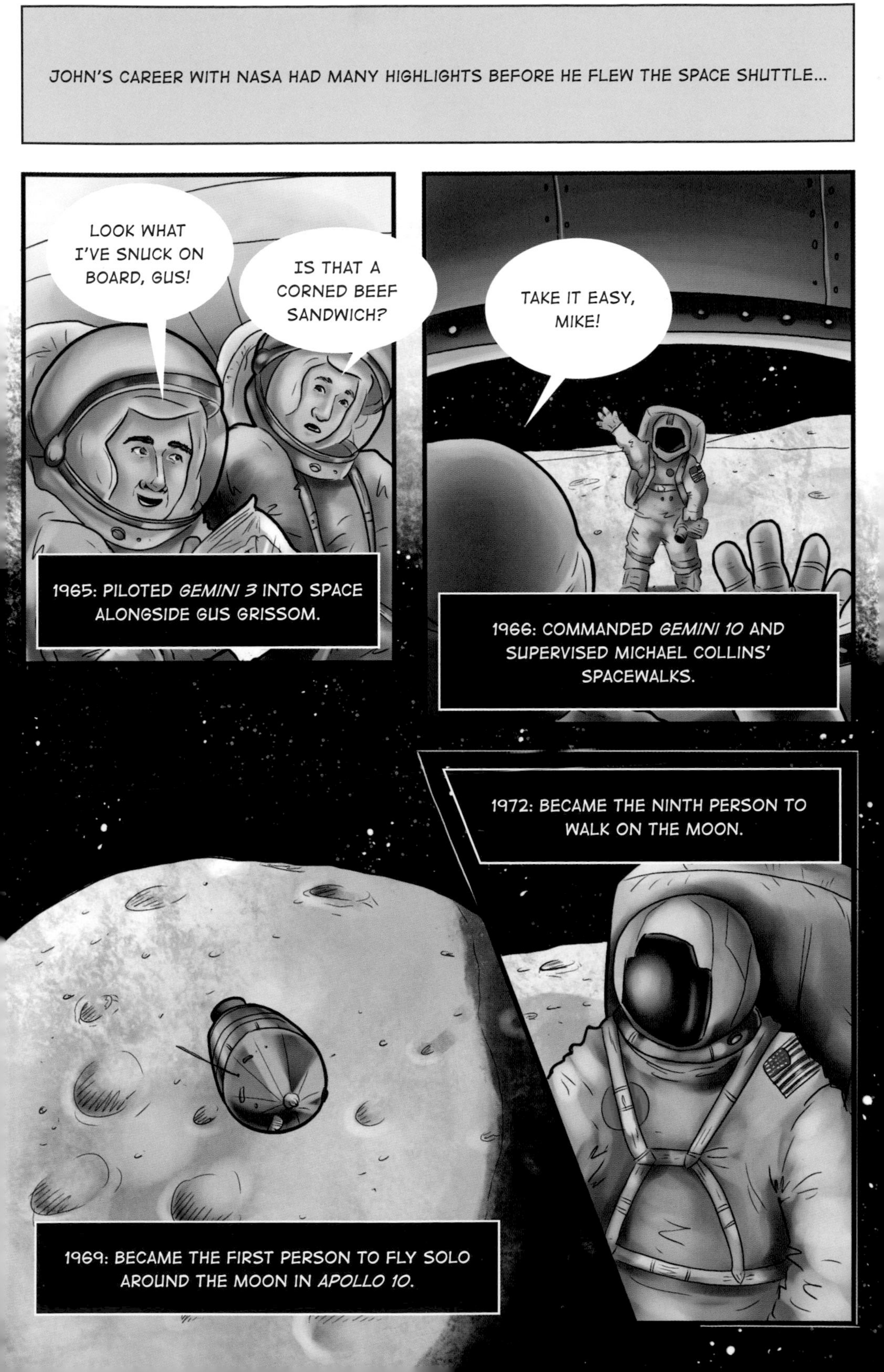
JOHN'S CAREER WITH NASA HAD MANY HIGHLIGHTS BEFORE HE FLEW THE SPACE SHUTTLE...
LOOK WHAT I'VE SNUCK ON BOARD, GUS!
IS THAT A CORNED BEEF SANDWICH?
1965: PILOTED *GEMINI 3* INTO SPACE ALONGSIDE GUS GRISSOM.
TAKE IT EASY, MIKE!
1966: COMMANDED *GEMINI 10* AND SUPERVISED MICHAEL COLLINS' SPACEWALKS.
1969: BECAME THE FIRST PERSON TO FLY SOLO AROUND THE MOON IN *APOLLO 10*.
1972: BECAME THE NINTH PERSON TO WALK ON THE MOON.

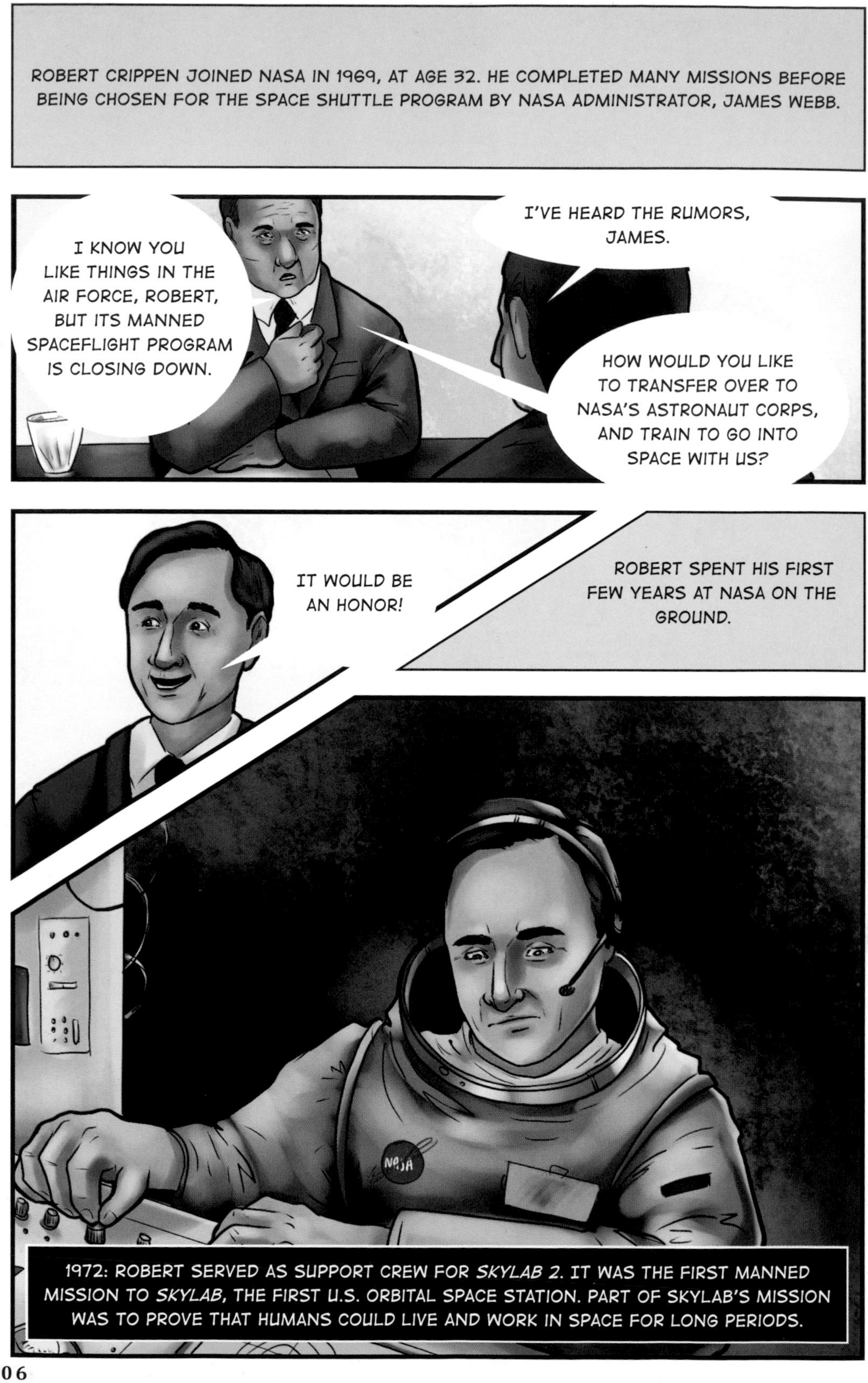
ROBERT CRIPPEN JOINED NASA IN 1969, AT AGE 32. HE COMPLETED MANY MISSIONS BEFORE BEING CHOSEN FOR THE SPACE SHUTTLE PROGRAM BY NASA ADMINISTRATOR, JAMES WEBB.
I KNOW YOU LIKE THINGS IN THE AIR FORCE, ROBERT, BUT ITS MANNED SPACEFLIGHT PROGRAM IS CLOSING DOWN.
I'VE HEARD THE RUMORS, JAMES.
HOW WOULD YOU LIKE TO TRANSFER OVER TO NASA'S ASTRONAUT CORPS, AND TRAIN TO GO INTO SPACE WITH US?
IT WOULD BE AN HONOR!
ROBERT SPENT HIS FIRST FEW YEARS AT NASA ON THE GROUND.
NASA
1972: ROBERT SERVED AS SUPPORT CREW FOR *SKYLAB 2*. IT WAS THE FIRST MANNED MISSION TO *SKYLAB*, THE FIRST U.S. ORBITAL SPACE STATION. PART OF SKYLAB'S MISSION WAS TO PROVE THAT HUMANS COULD LIVE AND WORK IN SPACE FOR LONG PERIODS.

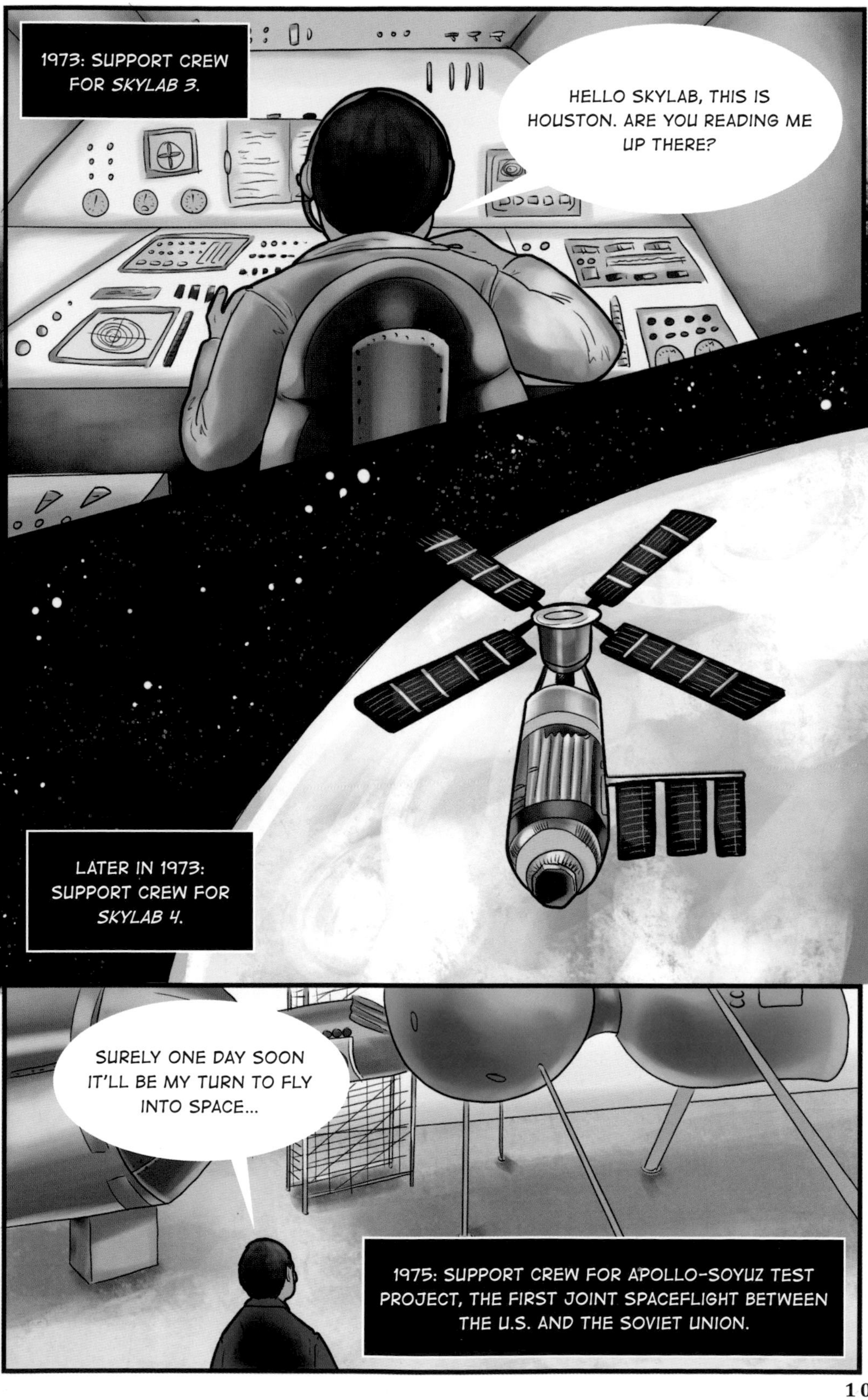
1973: SUPPORT CREW FOR *SKYLAB 3*.
HELLO SKYLAB, THIS IS HOUSTON. ARE YOU READING ME UP THERE?
LATER IN 1973: SUPPORT CREW FOR *SKYLAB 4*.
SURELY ONE DAY SOON IT'LL BE MY TURN TO FLY INTO SPACE...
1975: SUPPORT CREW FOR APOLLO-SOYUZ TEST PROJECT, THE FIRST JOINT SPACEFLIGHT BETWEEN THE U.S. AND THE SOVIET UNION.

IN 1978, GEORGE ABBEY, DIRECTOR OF FLIGHT OPERATIONS FOR THE APOLLO PROGRAM, HAD GOOD NEWS FOR JOHN AND ROBERT. HE TOLD THEM THAT THEY'D BEEN CHOSEN AS THE CREW FOR THE FIRST SPACE TRANSPORTATION SYSTEM 1 (STS-1) MISSION ABOARD THE SPACE SHUTTLE *COLUMBIA*.

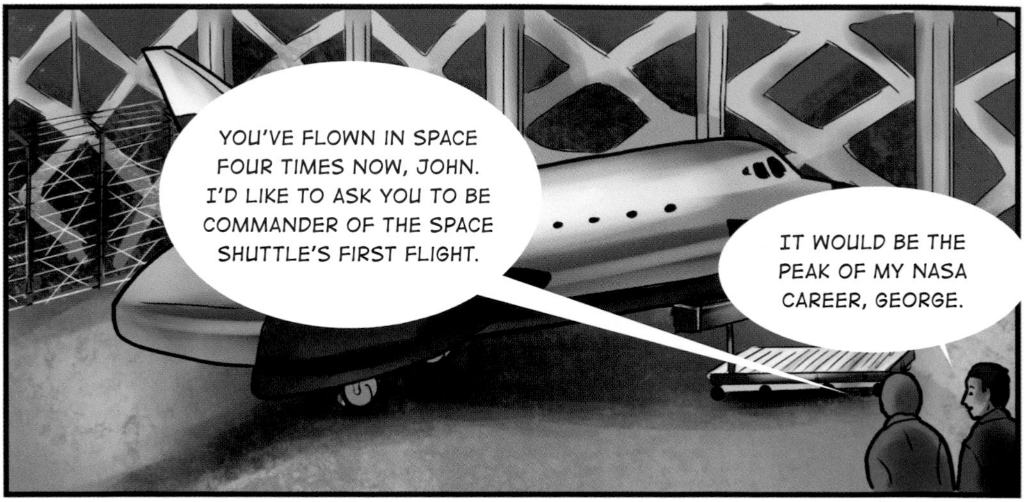
YOU'VE FLOWN IN SPACE FOUR TIMES NOW, JOHN. I'D LIKE TO ASK YOU TO BE COMMANDER OF THE SPACE SHUTTLE'S FIRST FLIGHT.
IT WOULD BE THE PEAK OF MY NASA CAREER, GEORGE.

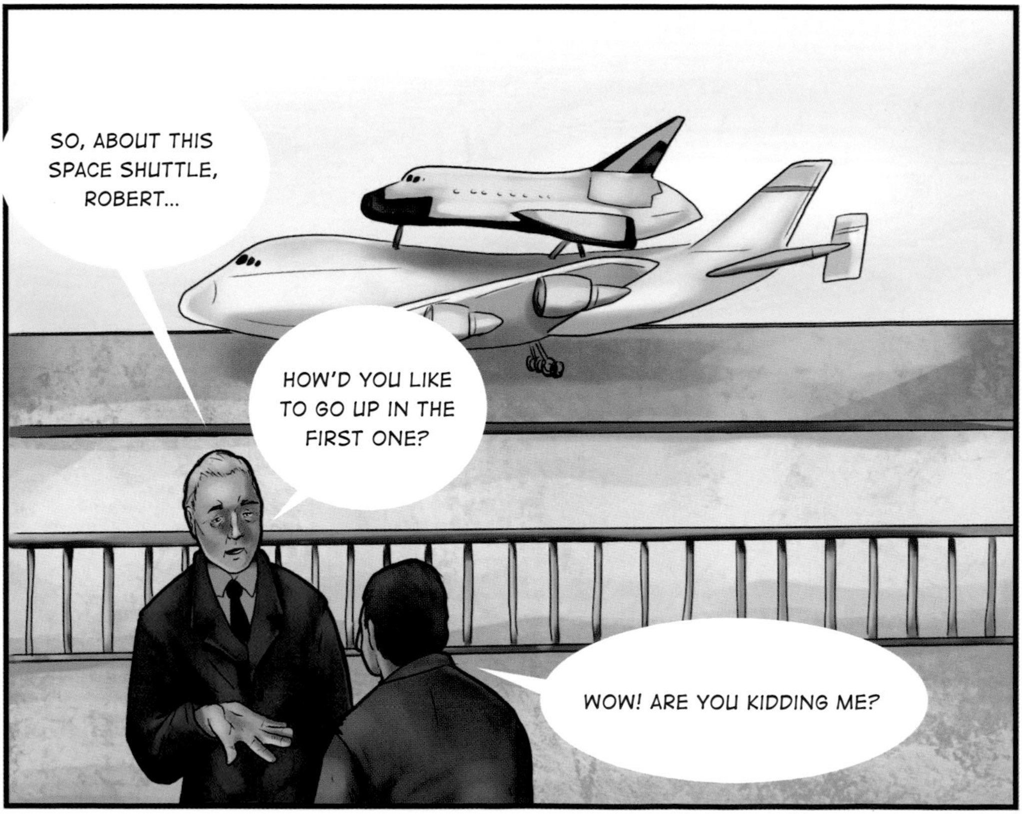
SO, ABOUT THIS SPACE SHUTTLE, ROBERT...
HOW'D YOU LIKE TO GO UP IN THE FIRST ONE?
WOW! ARE YOU KIDDING ME?

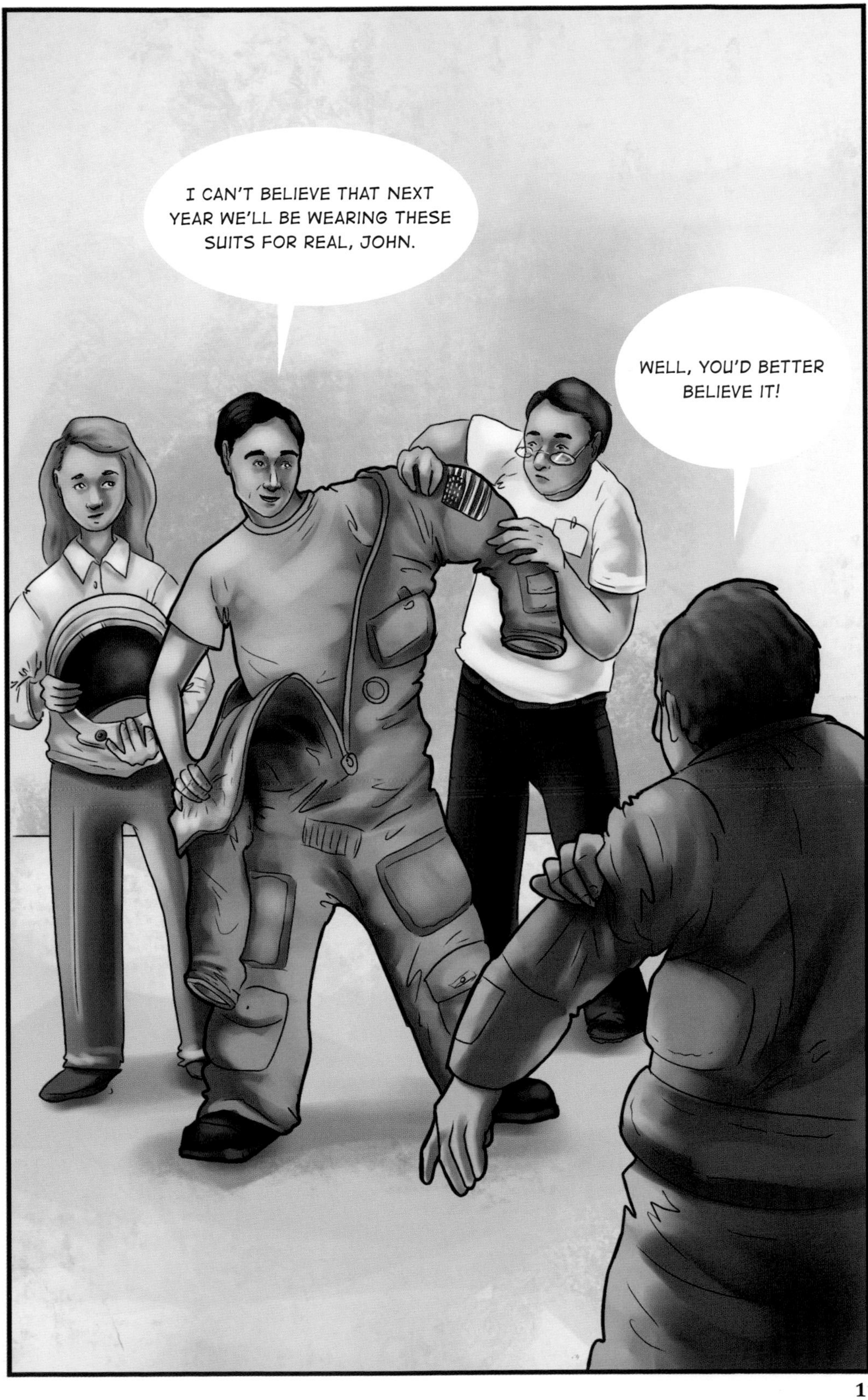
I CAN'T BELIEVE THAT NEXT YEAR WE'LL BE WEARING THESE SUITS FOR REAL, JOHN.
WELL, YOU'D BETTER BELIEVE IT!

PROBLEMS WITH THE ENGINES AND THE SYSTEM PROTECTING THE SHUTTLE FROM HEAT DAMAGE MEANT THAT JOHN AND ROBERT TRAINED TOGETHER FOR ALMOST FOUR YEARS BEFORE FINALLY FLYING TOGETHER.

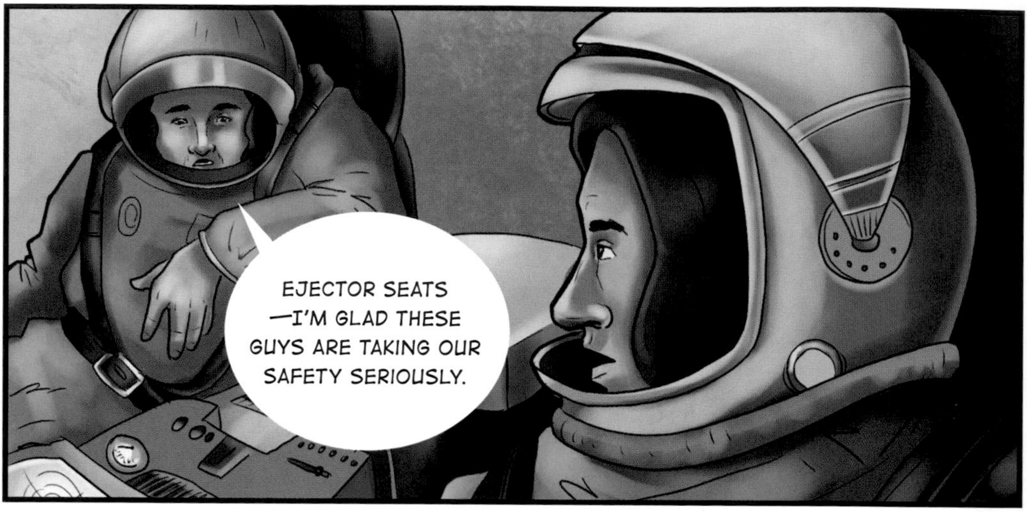
EJECTOR SEATS —I'M GLAD THESE GUYS ARE TAKING OUR SAFETY SERIOUSLY.

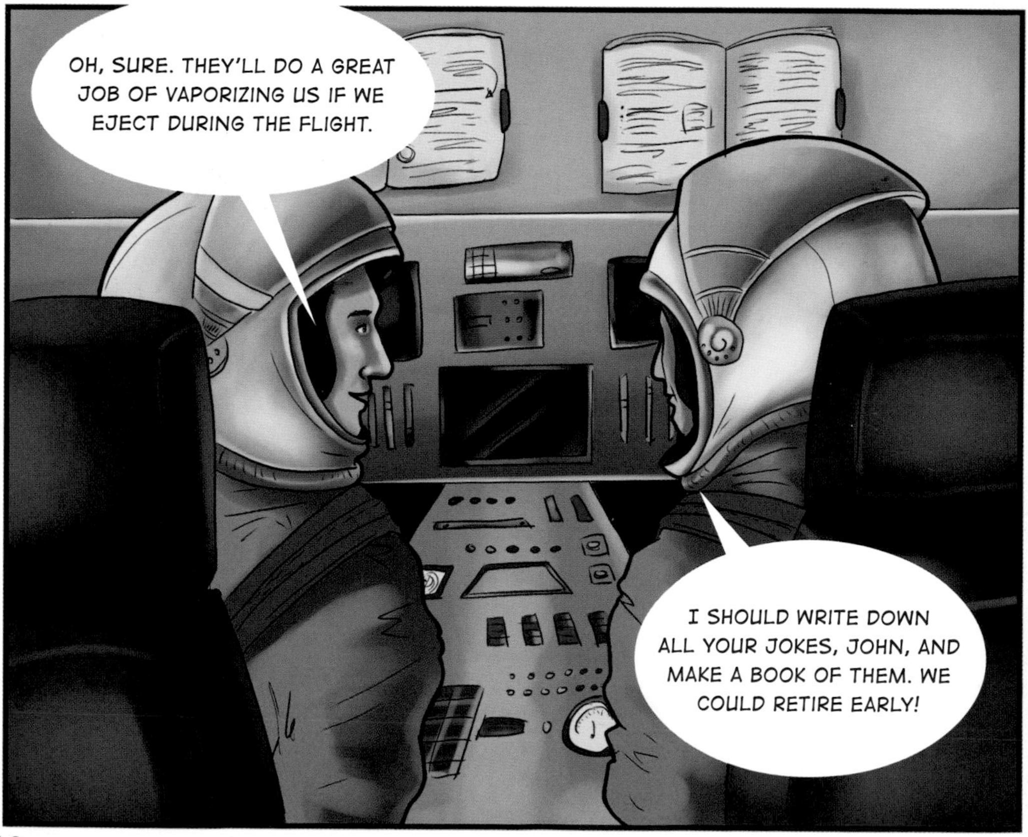
OH, SURE. THEY'LL DO A GREAT JOB OF VAPORIZING US IF WE EJECT DURING THE FLIGHT.
I SHOULD WRITE DOWN ALL YOUR JOKES, JOHN, AND MAKE A BOOK OF THEM. WE COULD RETIRE EARLY!

OVER LUNCH ONE DAY, IN THE KENNEDY SPACE CENTER CAFETERIA, FELLOW ASTRONAUT JOE ALLEN PAID THE BILL. FEELING NERVOUS ABOUT WHETHER OR NOT HE WOULD SURVIVE THE MISSION, ROBERT INSISTED ON PAYING HIM BACK.

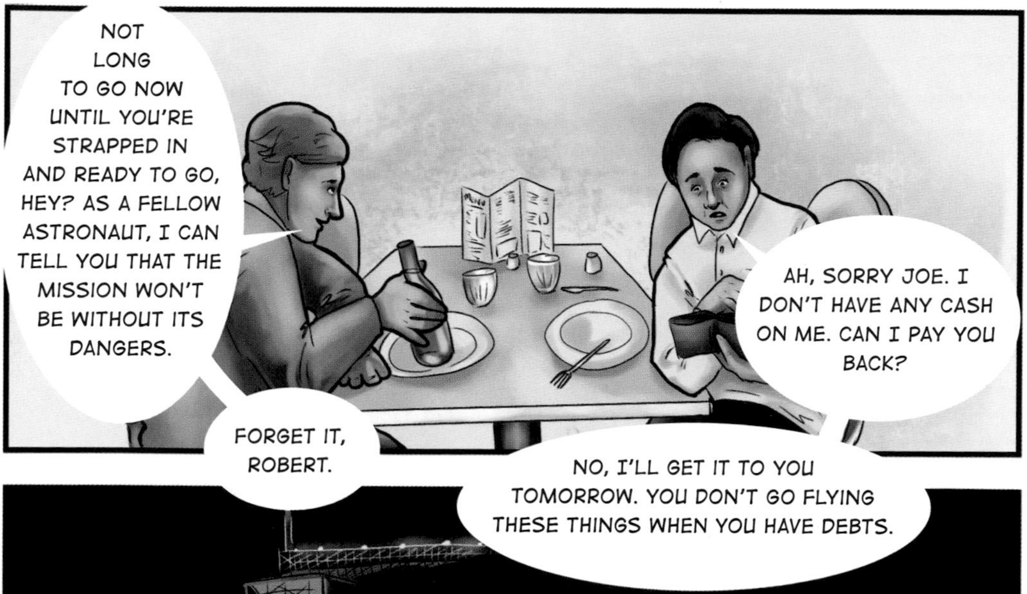

NOT LONG TO GO NOW UNTIL YOU'RE STRAPPED IN AND READY TO GO, HEY? AS A FELLOW ASTRONAUT, I CAN TELL YOU THAT THE MISSION WON'T BE WITHOUT ITS DANGERS.
AH, SORRY JOE. I DON'T HAVE ANY CASH ON ME. CAN I PAY YOU BACK?
FORGET IT, ROBERT.
NO, I'LL GET IT TO YOU TOMORROW. YOU DON'T GO FLYING THESE THINGS WHEN YOU HAVE DEBTS.

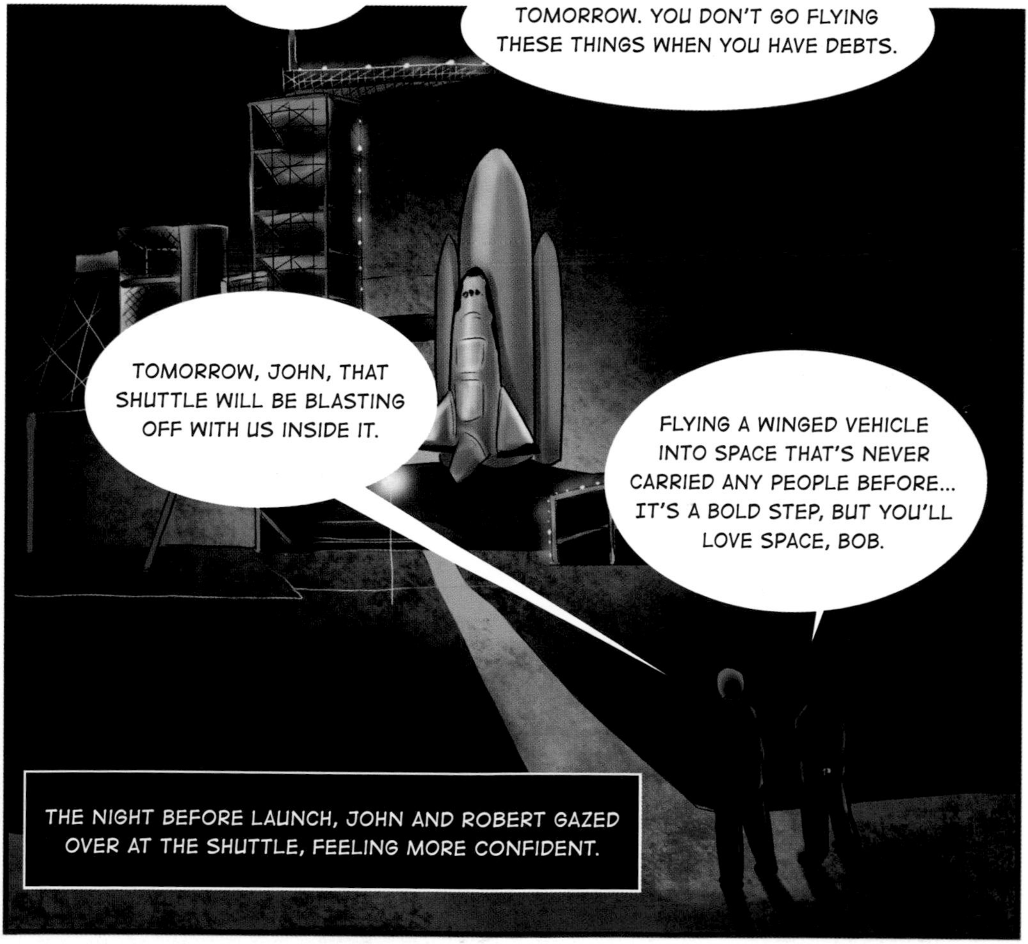

TOMORROW, JOHN, THAT SHUTTLE WILL BE BLASTING OFF WITH US INSIDE IT.
FLYING A WINGED VEHICLE INTO SPACE THAT'S NEVER CARRIED ANY PEOPLE BEFORE... IT'S A BOLD STEP, BUT YOU'LL LOVE SPACE, BOB.
THE NIGHT BEFORE LAUNCH, JOHN AND ROBERT GAZED OVER AT THE SHUTTLE, FEELING MORE CONFIDENT.

On April 12, 1981—the twentieth anniversary of Yuri Gagarin entering orbit—Space Shuttle *Columbia* launched into space for the very first time, piloted by John and Robert. It was the first winged, manned vehicle to launch with solid rocket boosters, and the most complex spacecraft ever built.

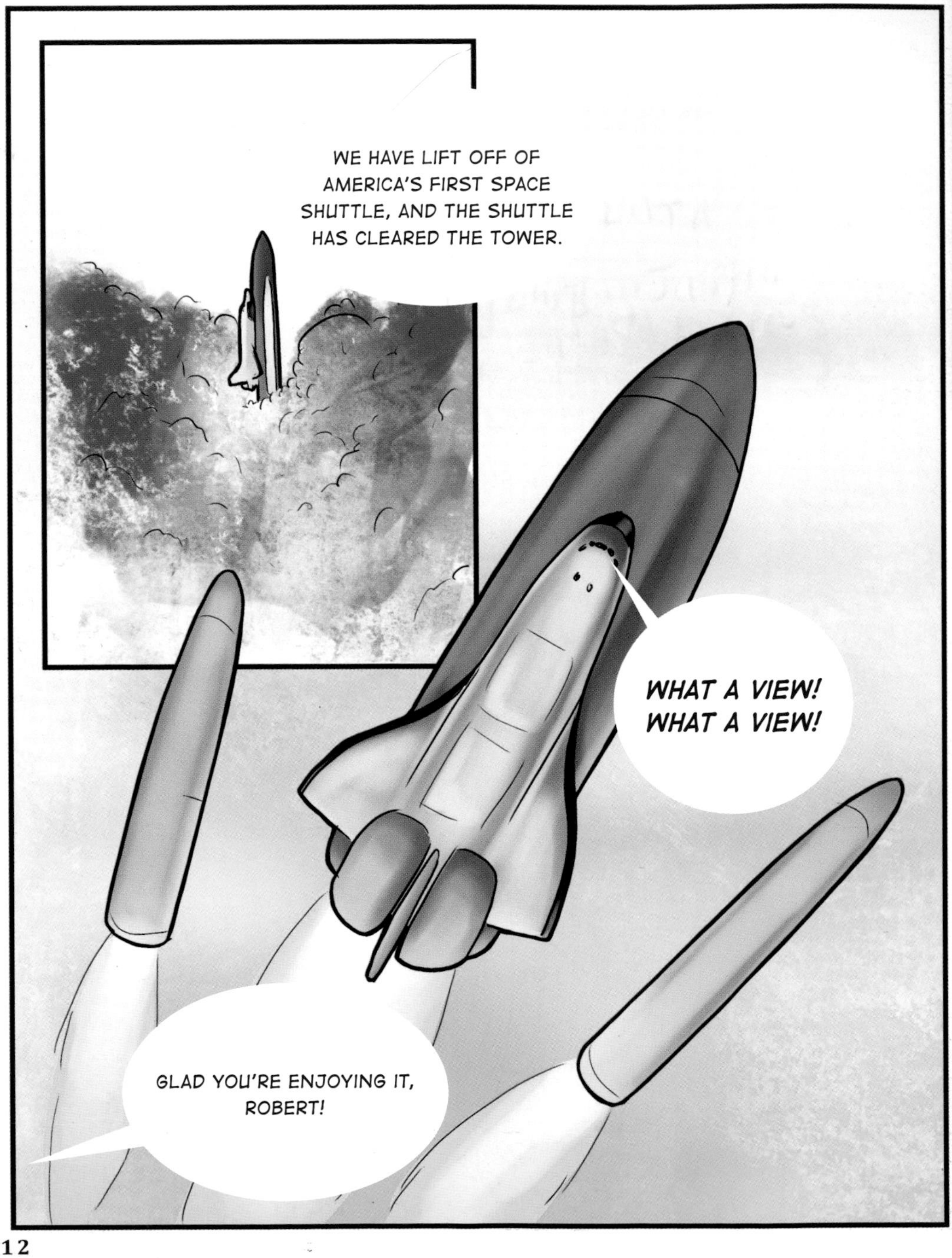
WE HAVE LIFT OFF OF AMERICA'S FIRST SPACE SHUTTLE, AND THE SHUTTLE HAS CLEARED THE TOWER.
WHAT A VIEW! WHAT A VIEW!
GLAD YOU'RE ENJOYING IT, ROBERT!

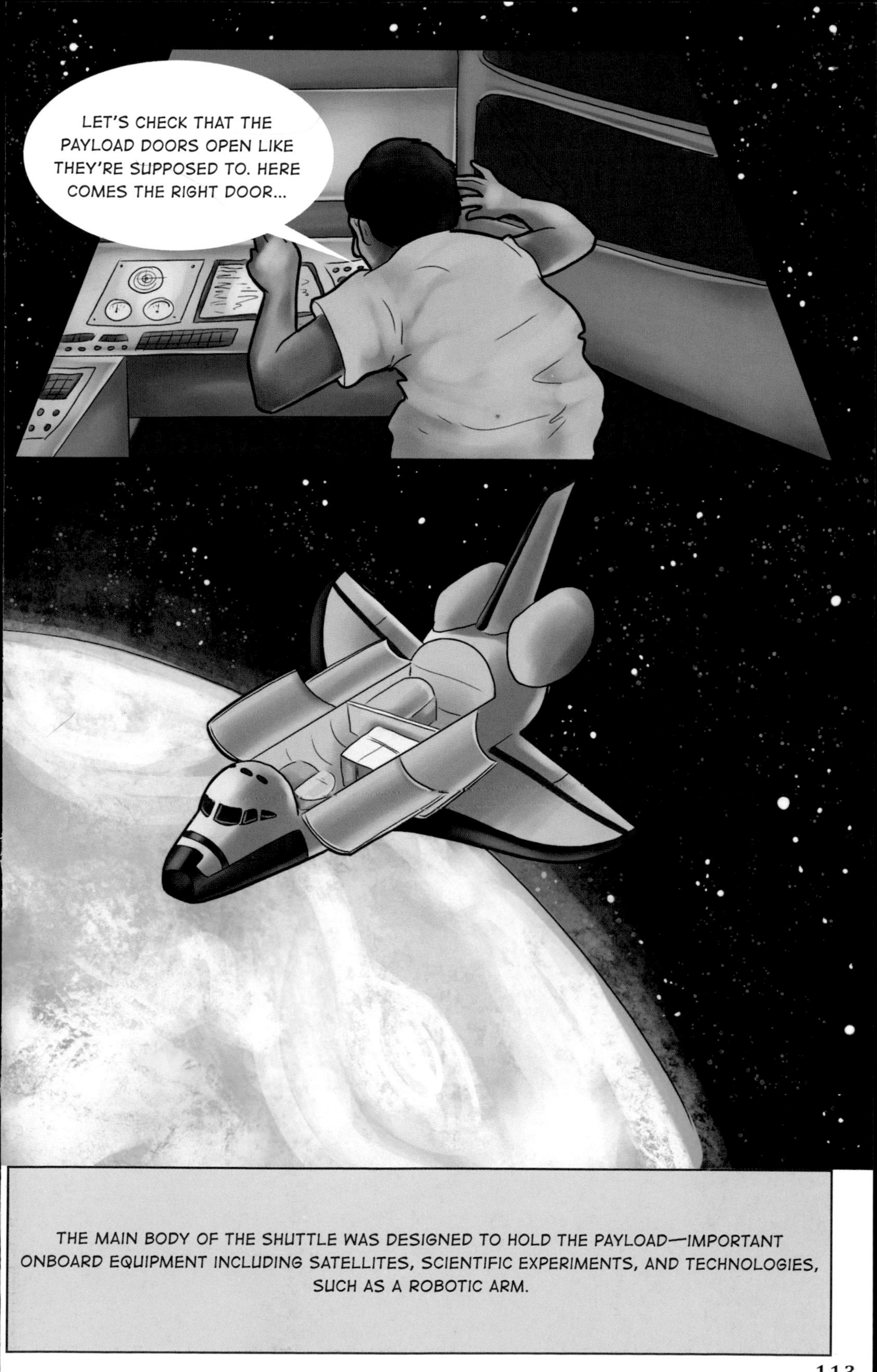
LET'S CHECK THAT THE PAYLOAD DOORS OPEN LIKE THEY'RE SUPPOSED TO. HERE COMES THE RIGHT DOOR...
THE MAIN BODY OF THE SHUTTLE WAS DESIGNED TO HOLD THE PAYLOAD—IMPORTANT ONBOARD EQUIPMENT INCLUDING SATELLITES, SCIENTIFIC EXPERIMENTS, AND TECHNOLOGIES, SUCH AS A ROBOTIC ARM.

NEARLY 55 HOURS AFTER LAUNCH, JOHN AND ROBERT LANDED SAFELY, HAVING ORBITED EARTH 37 TIMES. THE SHUTTLE BECAME THE FIRST WINGED REENTRY VEHICLE TO LAND ON A CONVENTIONAL RUNWAY. IT WOULD GO ON TO HELP BUILD THE INTERNATIONAL SPACE STATION AND LAUNCH THE HUBBLE SPACE TELESCOPE.

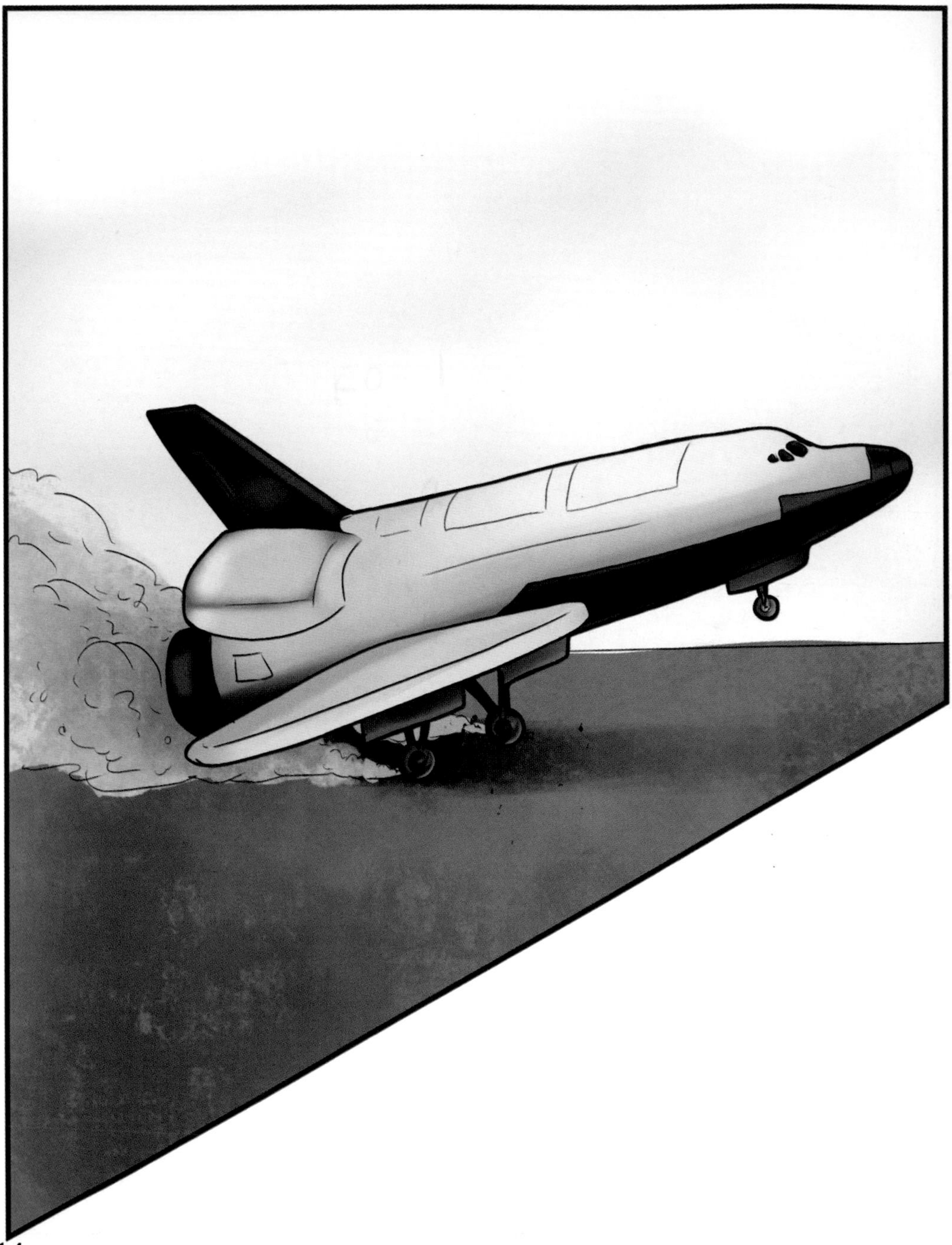

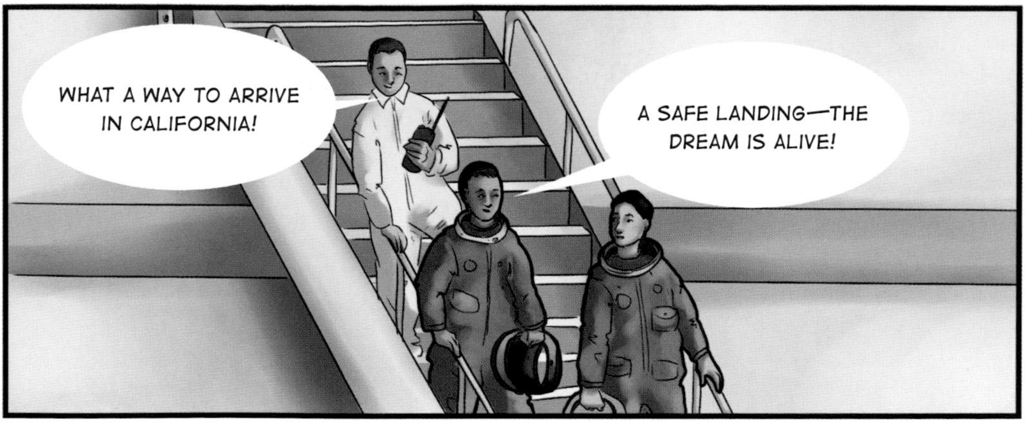
WHAT A WAY TO ARRIVE IN CALIFORNIA!
A SAFE LANDING—THE DREAM IS ALIVE!

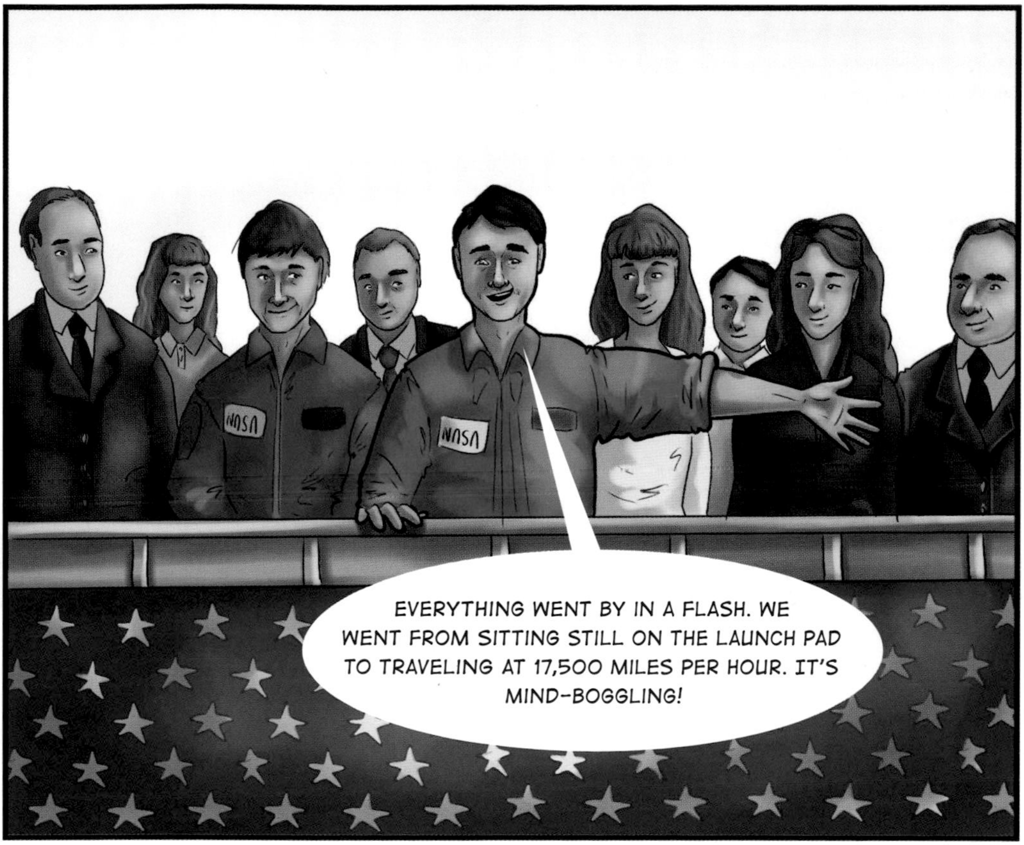
NASA
NASA
EVERYTHING WENT BY IN A FLASH. WE WENT FROM SITTING STILL ON THE LAUNCH PAD TO TRAVELING AT 17,500 MILES PER HOUR. IT'S MIND-BOGGLING!

THE SPACE SHUTTLE PROGRAM CARRIED ASTRONAUTS INTO SPACE FOR 30 YEARS. BEFORE THE FINAL TOUCHDOWN IN 2011, THE FLEET—*COLUMBIA*, *CHALLENGER*, *DISCOVERY*, *ATLANTIS*, AND *ENDEAVOUR*—FLEW 135 MISSIONS, LAUNCHED AND REPAIRED SATELLITES, CONDUCTED CUTTING-EDGE RESEARCH, AND HELPED CONSTRUCT THE INTERNATIONAL SPACE STATION.

KOICHI WAKATA
(1963–present)
SPACE STATION VETERAN

AS A YOUNG CHILD IN JAPAN, KOICHI WAKATA DREAMED OF BECOMING AN ASTRONAUT. HE WAS 5 YEARS OLD WHEN NEIL ARMSTRONG BECAME THE FIRST PERSON TO WALK ON THE MOON.

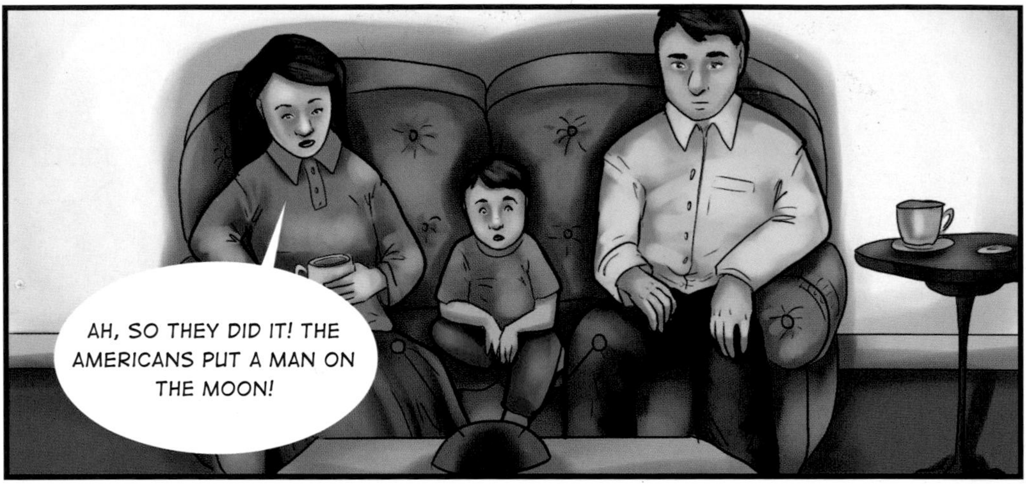
AH, SO THEY DID IT! THE AMERICANS PUT A MAN ON THE MOON!

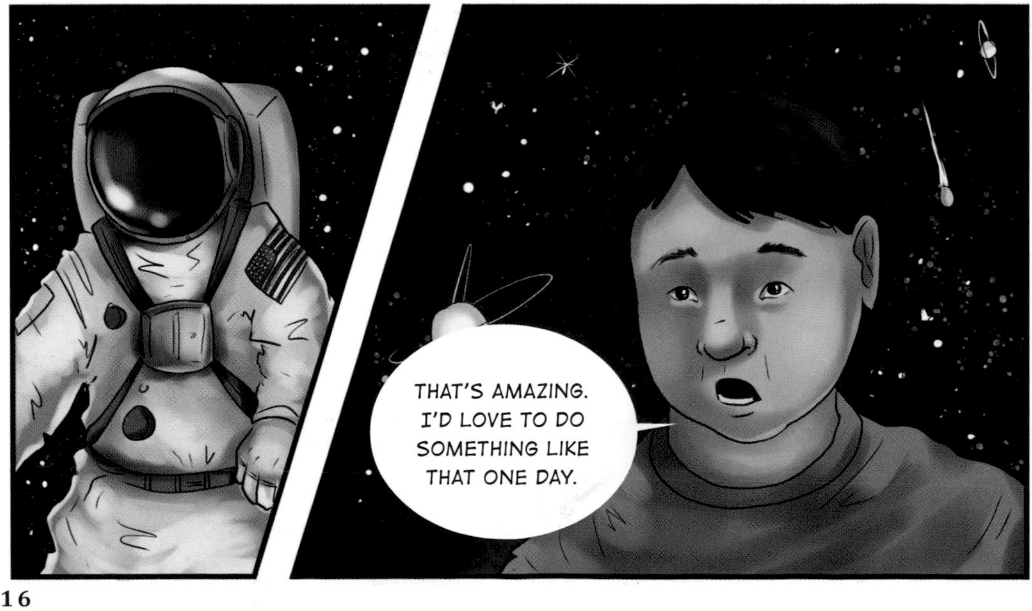
THAT'S AMAZING. I'D LOVE TO DO SOMETHING LIKE THAT ONE DAY.

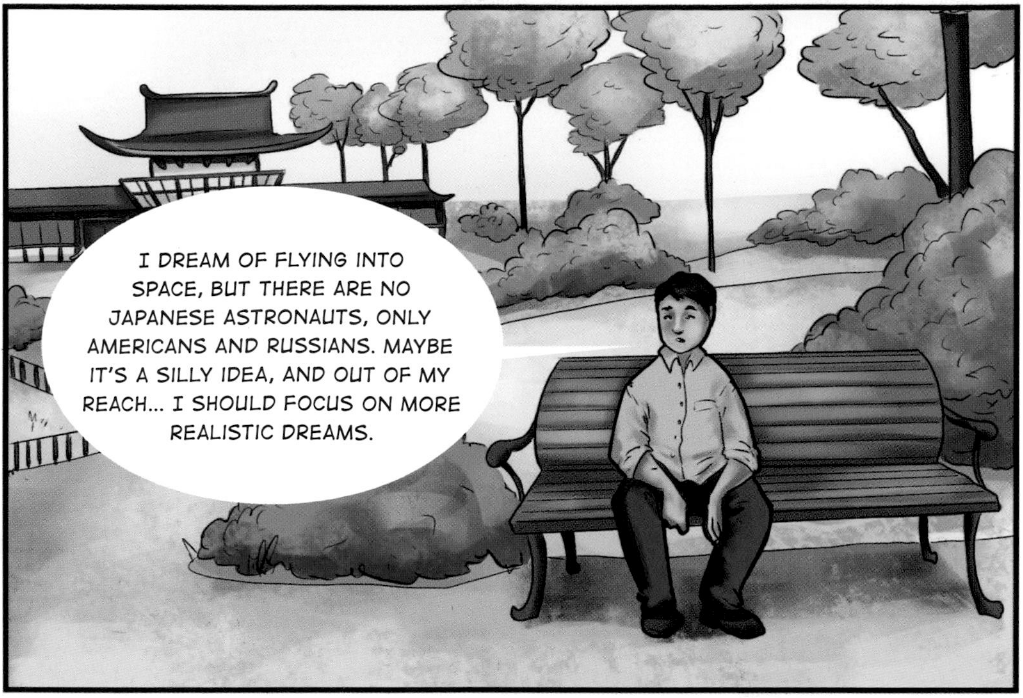
I DREAM OF FLYING INTO SPACE, BUT THERE ARE NO JAPANESE ASTRONAUTS, ONLY AMERICANS AND RUSSIANS. MAYBE IT'S A SILLY IDEA, AND OUT OF MY REACH... I SHOULD FOCUS ON MORE REALISTIC DREAMS.

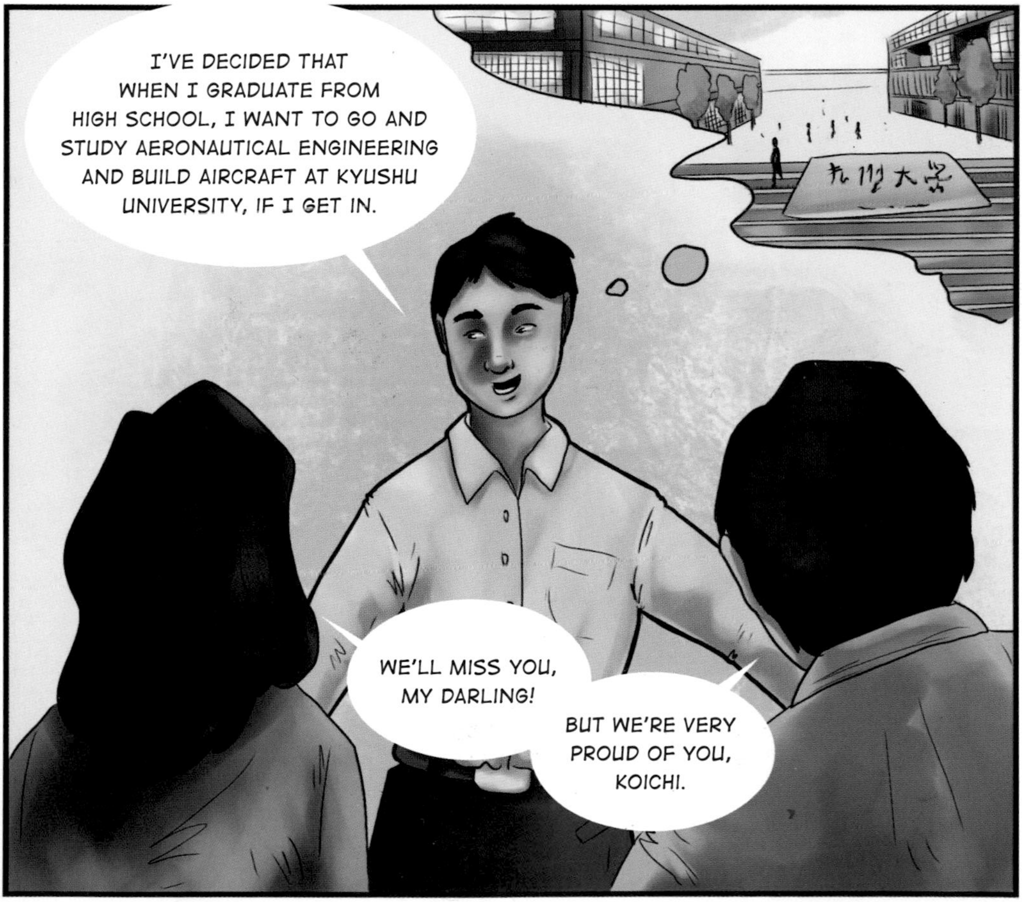
I'VE DECIDED THAT WHEN I GRADUATE FROM HIGH SCHOOL, I WANT TO GO AND STUDY AERONAUTICAL ENGINEERING AND BUILD AIRCRAFT AT KYUSHU UNIVERSITY, IF I GET IN.
WE'LL MISS YOU, MY DARLING!
BUT WE'RE VERY PROUD OF YOU, KOICHI.

FASCINATED BY PLANES, KOICHI STUDIED AERONAUTICS AND BECAME AN ENGINEER WITH JAPAN AIRLINES. IN 1991, THE JAPANESE SPACE AGENCY STARTED LOOKING FOR ASTRONAUTS AND KOICHI APPLIED.

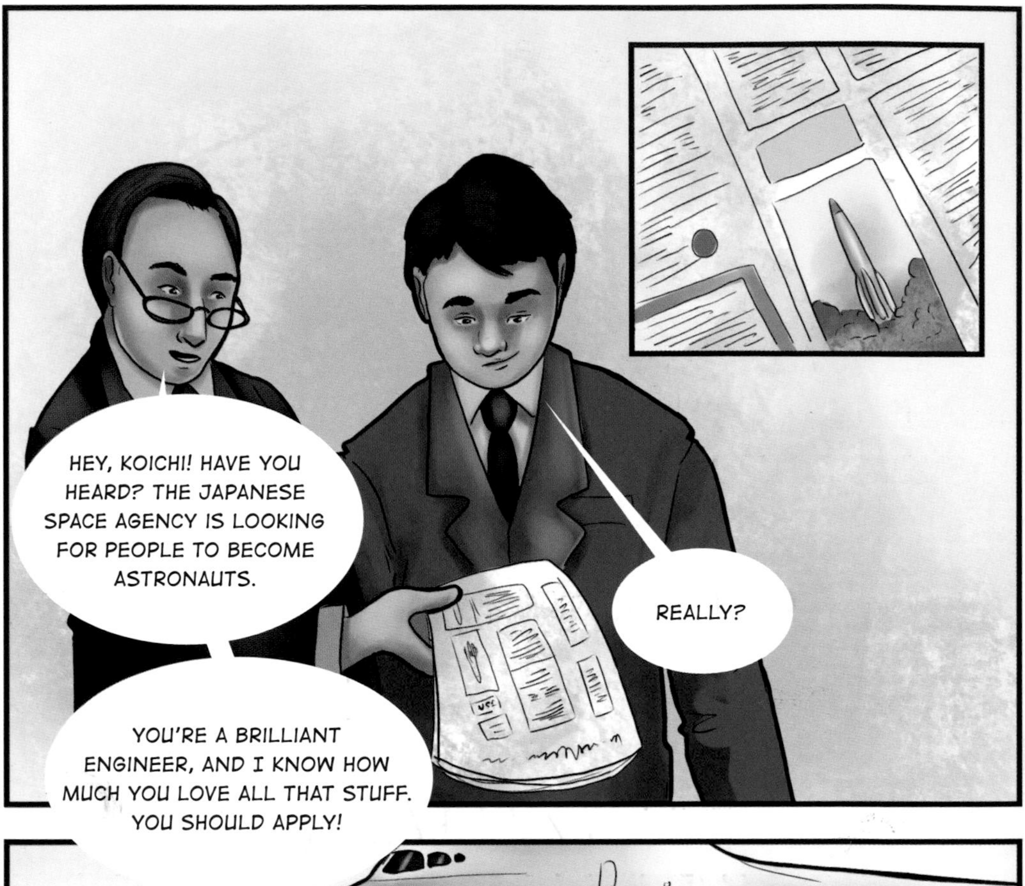
HEY, KOICHI! HAVE YOU HEARD? THE JAPANESE SPACE AGENCY IS LOOKING FOR PEOPLE TO BECOME ASTRONAUTS.
REALLY?
YOU'RE A BRILLIANT ENGINEER, AND I KNOW HOW MUCH YOU LOVE ALL THAT STUFF. YOU SHOULD APPLY!

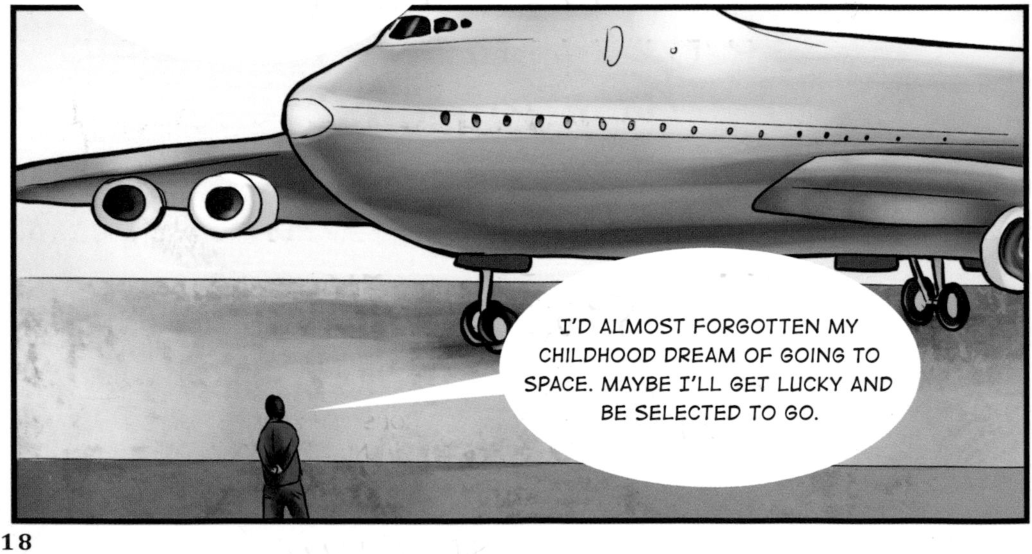
I'D ALMOST FORGOTTEN MY CHILDHOOD DREAM OF GOING TO SPACE. MAYBE I'LL GET LUCKY AND BE SELECTED TO GO.

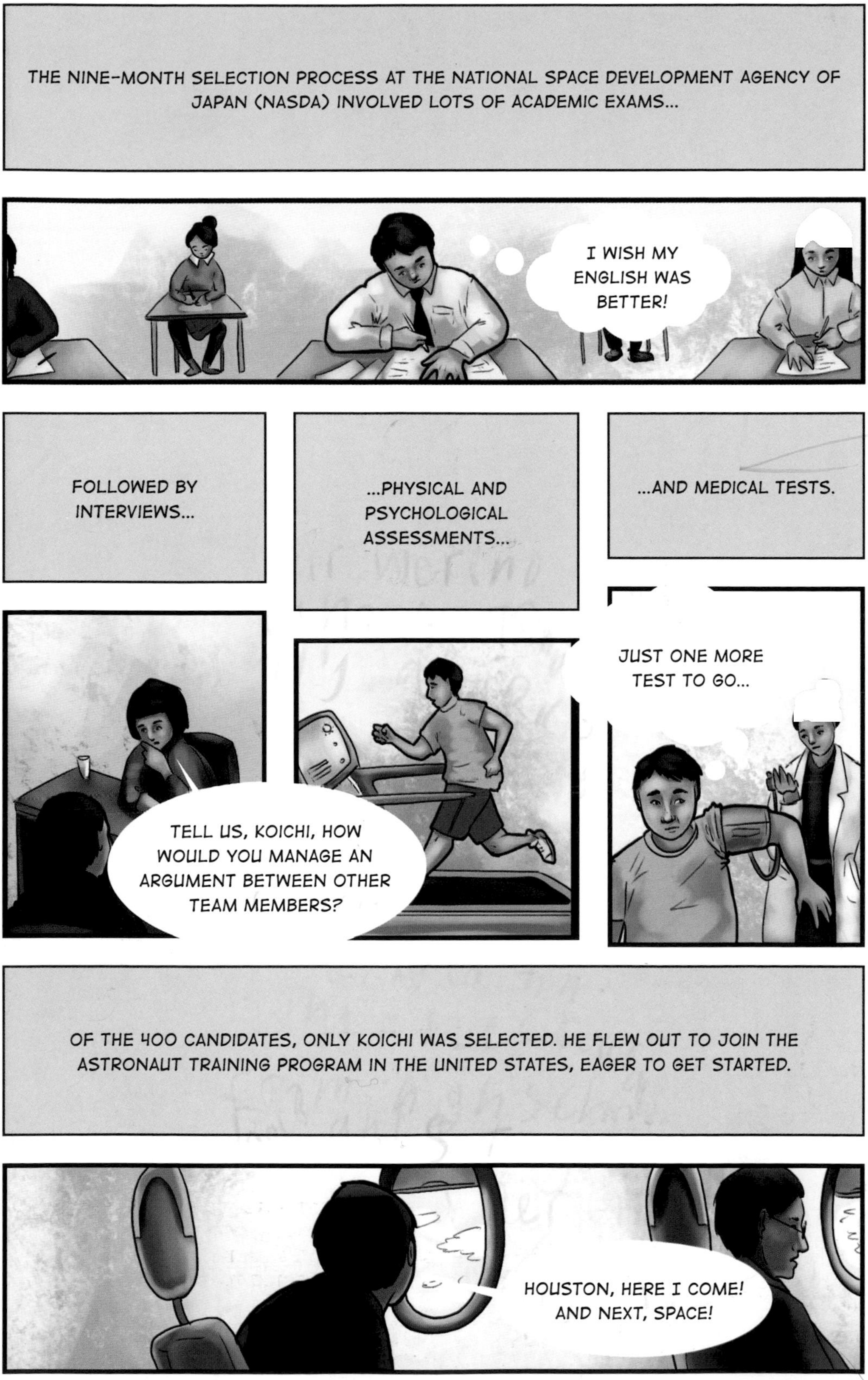
THE NINE-MONTH SELECTION PROCESS AT THE NATIONAL SPACE DEVELOPMENT AGENCY OF JAPAN (NASDA) INVOLVED LOTS OF ACADEMIC EXAMS...
I WISH MY ENGLISH WAS BETTER!
FOLLOWED BY INTERVIEWS...
...PHYSICAL AND PSYCHOLOGICAL ASSESSMENTS...
...AND MEDICAL TESTS.
TELL US, KOICHI, HOW WOULD YOU MANAGE AN ARGUMENT BETWEEN OTHER TEAM MEMBERS?
JUST ONE MORE TEST TO GO...
OF THE 400 CANDIDATES, ONLY KOICHI WAS SELECTED. HE FLEW OUT TO JOIN THE ASTRONAUT TRAINING PROGRAM IN THE UNITED STATES, EAGER TO GET STARTED.
HOUSTON, HERE I COME! AND NEXT, SPACE!

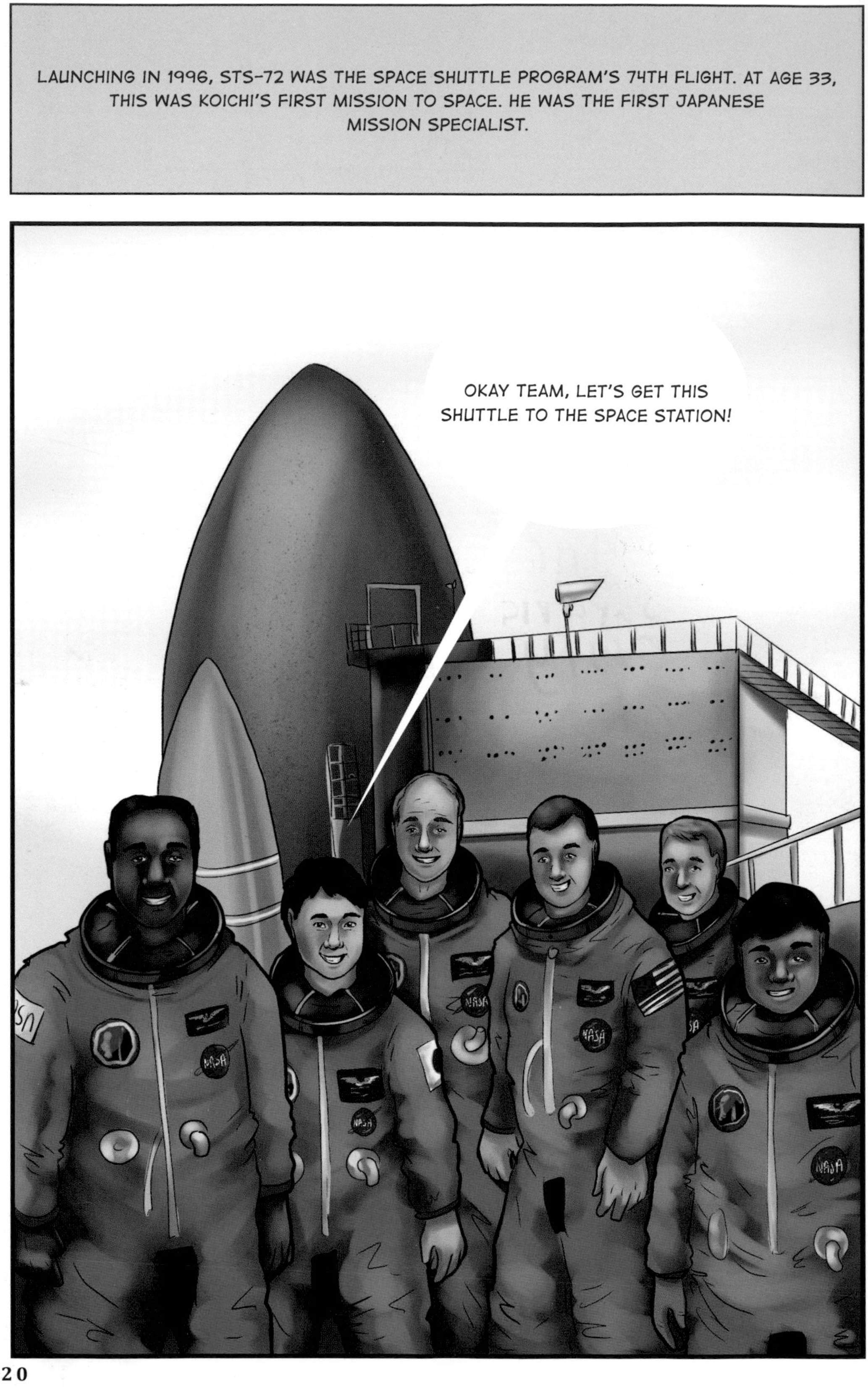
LAUNCHING IN 1996, STS-72 WAS THE SPACE SHUTTLE PROGRAM'S 74TH FLIGHT. AT AGE 33, THIS WAS KOICHI'S FIRST MISSION TO SPACE. HE WAS THE FIRST JAPANESE MISSION SPECIALIST.
OKAY TEAM, LET'S GET THIS SHUTTLE TO THE SPACE STATION!

ON THE THIRD DAY OF THE FLIGHT ABOARD *ENDEAVOUR*, KOICHI HAD THE IMPORTANT JOB OF CAPTURING A JAPANESE RESEARCH SPACECRAFT FROM SPACE. HE WAS WATCHED BY FELLOW ASTRONAUT, LEROY CHIAO.

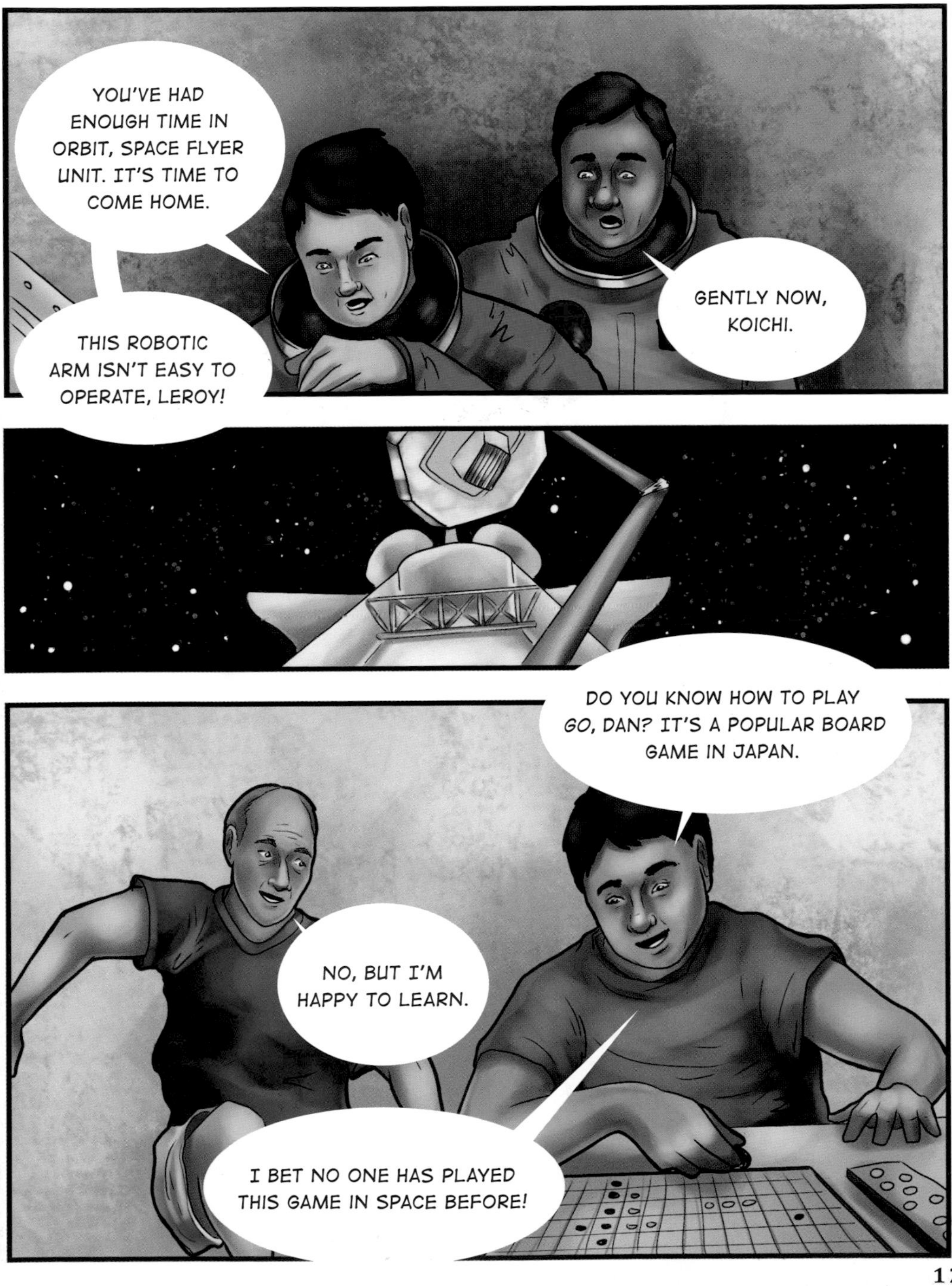

YOU'VE HAD ENOUGH TIME IN ORBIT, SPACE FLYER UNIT. IT'S TIME TO COME HOME.
THIS ROBOTIC ARM ISN'T EASY TO OPERATE, LEROY!
GENTLY NOW, KOICHI.
DO YOU KNOW HOW TO PLAY *GO*, DAN? IT'S A POPULAR BOARD GAME IN JAPAN.
NO, BUT I'M HAPPY TO LEARN.
I BET NO ONE HAS PLAYED THIS GAME IN SPACE BEFORE!

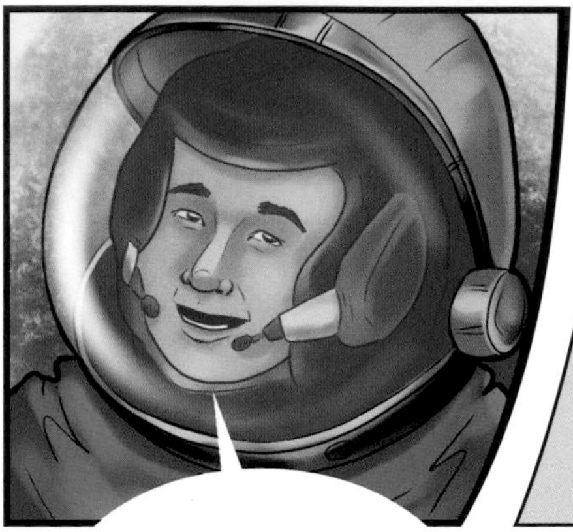
I'M SO EXCITED, BUT THERE'S A LOT OF HARD WORK AHEAD!

IN 2000, KOICHI BECAME THE FIRST JAPANESE ASTRONAUT TO HELP ASSEMBLE THE INTERNATIONAL SPACE STATION (ISS), AS PART OF THE STS-92 MISSION ABOARD SPACE SHUTTLE *DISCOVERY*. IT WAS THE 100TH LAUNCH IN THE HISTORY OF THE SPACE SHUTTLE PROGRAM. THE ISS WOULD BECOME A LONG-TERM HOME FOR HUMANS IN SPACE AND SERVE AS AN IMPORTANT SCIENCE LAB.

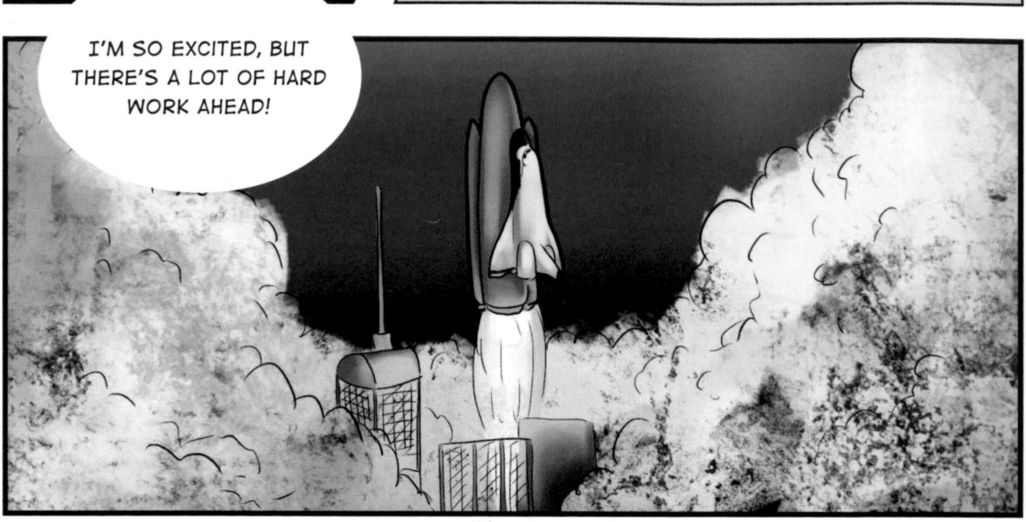

ON THE SECOND DAY OF THE MISSION, *DISCOVERY* SUCCESSFULLY DOCKED WITH THE ISS, READY FOR SIX DAYS OF CONSTRUCTION.

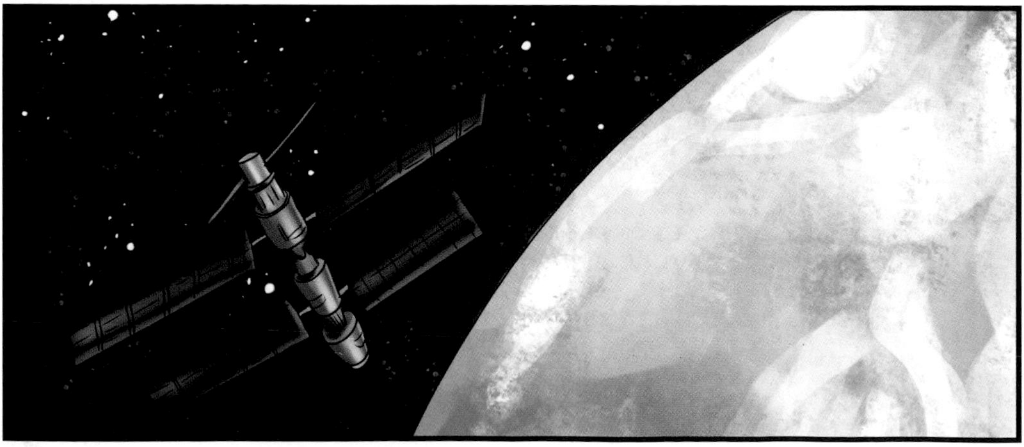

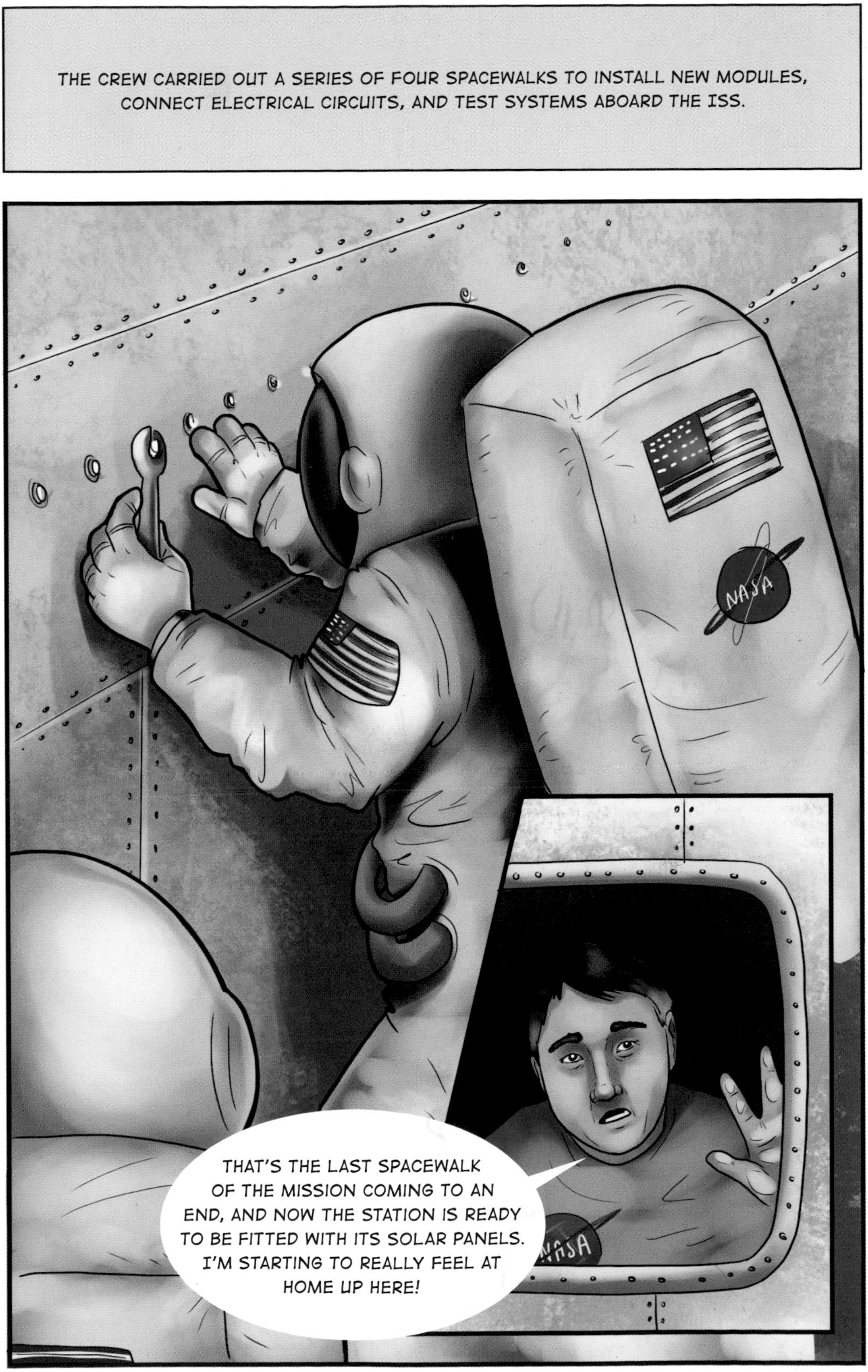
THE CREW CARRIED OUT A SERIES OF FOUR SPACEWALKS TO INSTALL NEW MODULES, CONNECT ELECTRICAL CIRCUITS, AND TEST SYSTEMS ABOARD THE ISS.
NASA
THAT'S THE LAST SPACEWALK OF THE MISSION COMING TO AN END, AND NOW THE STATION IS READY TO BE FITTED WITH ITS SOLAR PANELS. I'M STARTING TO REALLY FEEL AT HOME UP HERE!

KOICHI JOINED THE ISS ON THE STS-119 MISSION AND BECAME THE FIRST RESIDENT STATION CREW MEMBER FROM THE JAPANESE AEROSPACE EXPLORATION AGENCY (JAXA). REMAINING ABOARD FOR A FURTHER TWO BACK-TO-BACK MISSIONS, KOICHI HELPED SET UP THE ISS TO SUPPORT A BIGGER CREW—OF UP TO SIX AT A TIME.

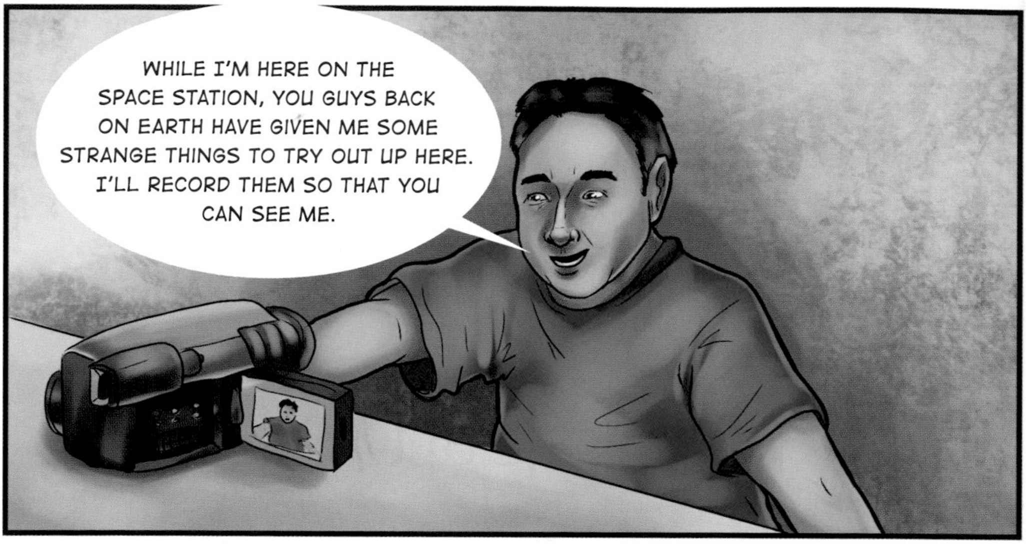
WHILE I'M HERE ON THE SPACE STATION, YOU GUYS BACK ON EARTH HAVE GIVEN ME SOME STRANGE THINGS TO TRY OUT UP HERE. I'LL RECORD THEM SO THAT YOU CAN SEE ME.

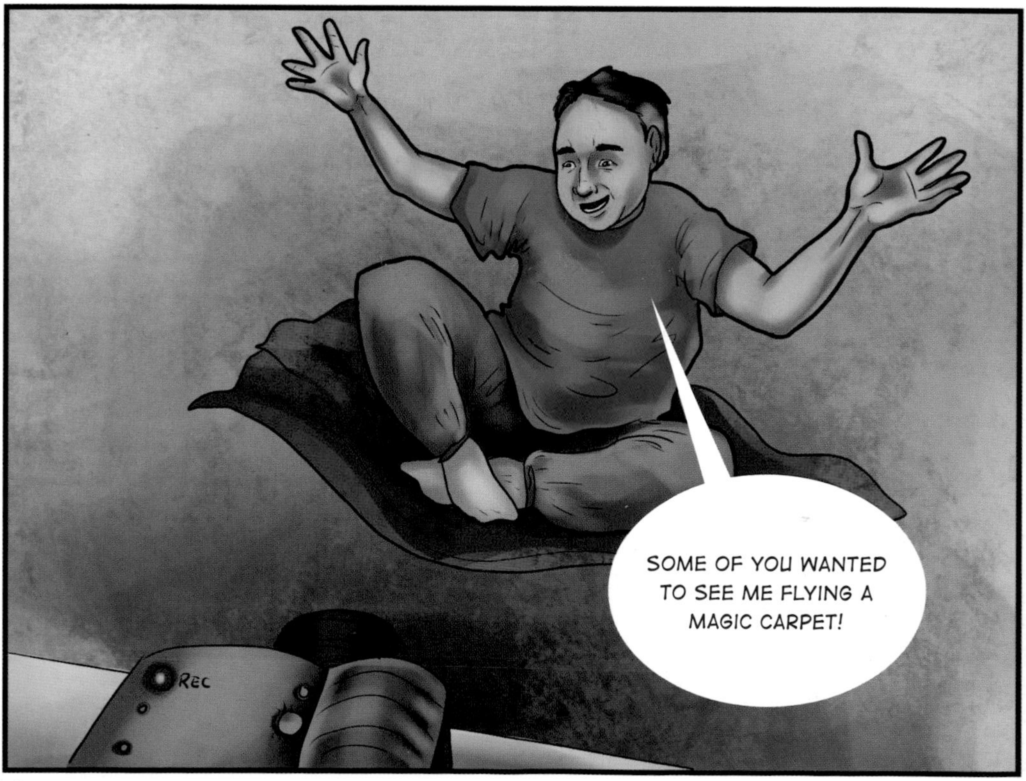
SOME OF YOU WANTED TO SEE ME FLYING A MAGIC CARPET!
REC

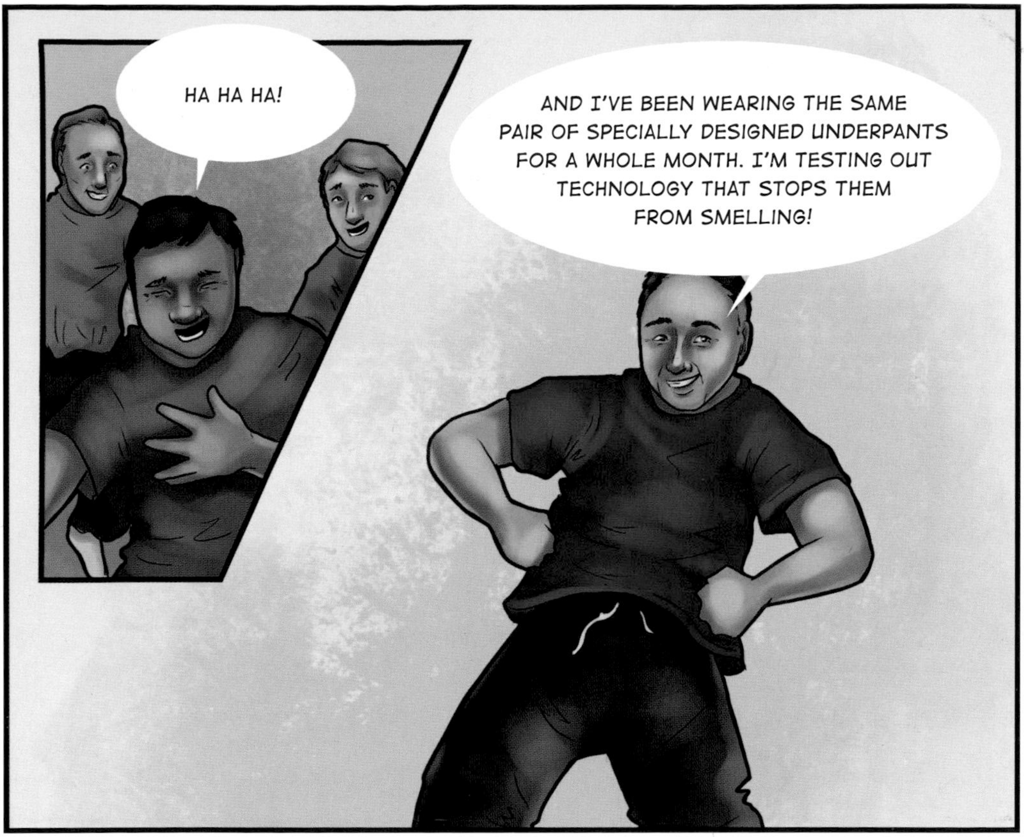
HA HA HA!
AND I'VE BEEN WEARING THE SAME PAIR OF SPECIALLY DESIGNED UNDERPANTS FOR A WHOLE MONTH. I'M TESTING OUT TECHNOLOGY THAT STOPS THEM FROM SMELLING!

KOICHI AND THE STS-127 CREW DISEMBARKED FROM THE ISS ABOARD *ENDEAVOUR* IN JULY 2009 AND HEADED BACK TO EARTH. KOICHI WAS PROUD THAT HE'D BEEN ABLE TO IMPROVE THE ISS AND PREPARE IT FOR FUTURE MISSIONS.

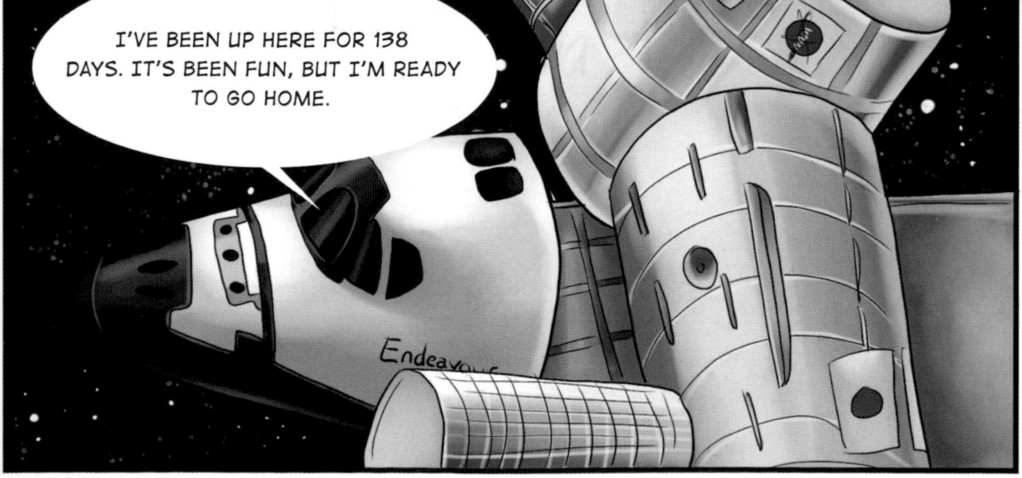
I'VE BEEN UP HERE FOR 138 DAYS. IT'S BEEN FUN, BUT I'M READY TO GO HOME.

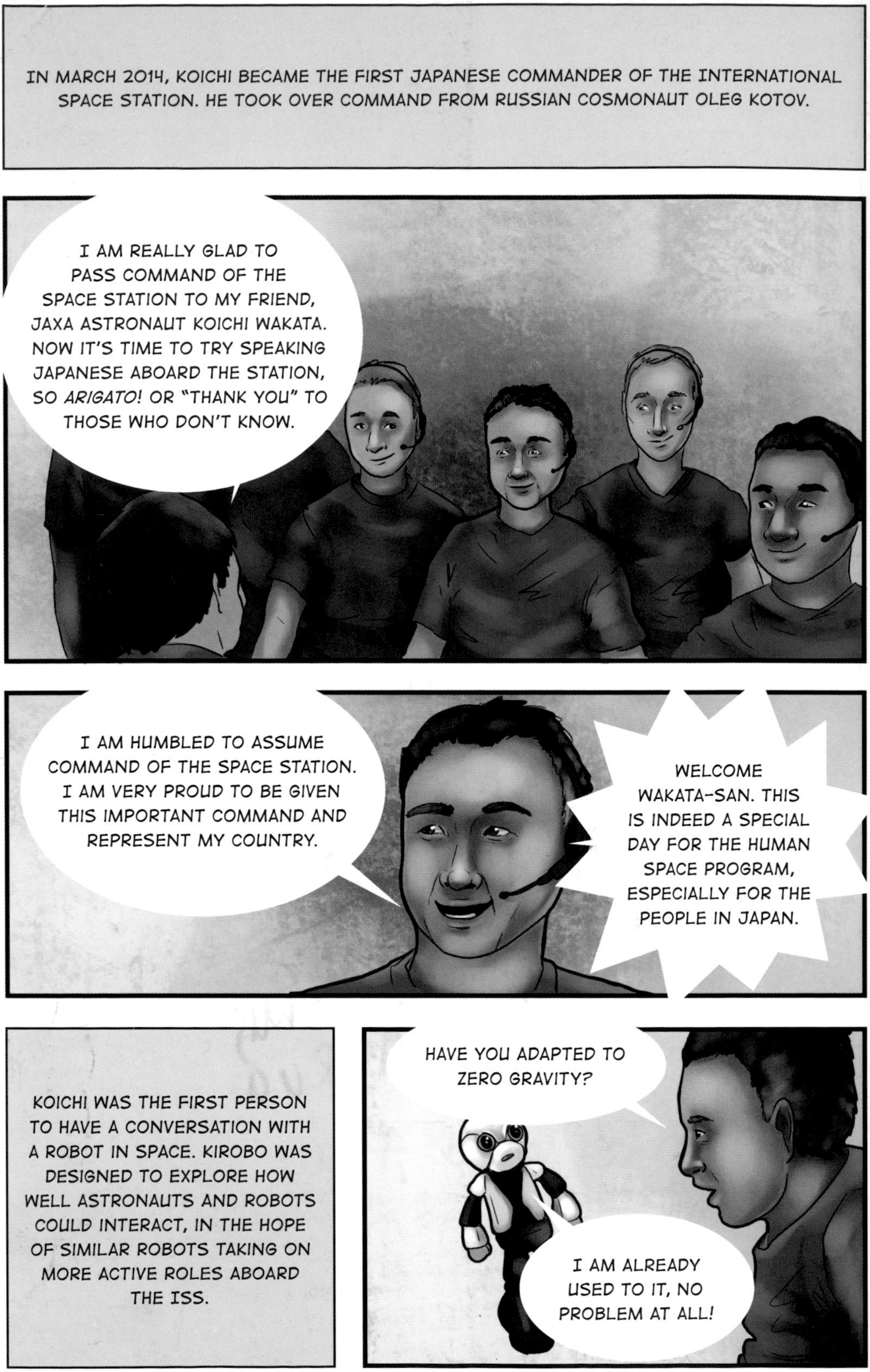
IN MARCH 2014, KOICHI BECAME THE FIRST JAPANESE COMMANDER OF THE INTERNATIONAL SPACE STATION. HE TOOK OVER COMMAND FROM RUSSIAN COSMONAUT OLEG KOTOV.
I AM REALLY GLAD TO PASS COMMAND OF THE SPACE STATION TO MY FRIEND, JAXA ASTRONAUT KOICHI WAKATA. NOW IT'S TIME TO TRY SPEAKING JAPANESE ABOARD THE STATION, SO *ARIGATO!* OR "THANK YOU" TO THOSE WHO DON'T KNOW.
I AM HUMBLED TO ASSUME COMMAND OF THE SPACE STATION. I AM VERY PROUD TO BE GIVEN THIS IMPORTANT COMMAND AND REPRESENT MY COUNTRY.
WELCOME WAKATA-SAN. THIS IS INDEED A SPECIAL DAY FOR THE HUMAN SPACE PROGRAM, ESPECIALLY FOR THE PEOPLE IN JAPAN.
KOICHI WAS THE FIRST PERSON TO HAVE A CONVERSATION WITH A ROBOT IN SPACE. KIROBO WAS DESIGNED TO EXPLORE HOW WELL ASTRONAUTS AND ROBOTS COULD INTERACT, IN THE HOPE OF SIMILAR ROBOTS TAKING ON MORE ACTIVE ROLES ABOARD THE ISS.
HAVE YOU ADAPTED TO ZERO GRAVITY?
I AM ALREADY USED TO IT, NO PROBLEM AT ALL!

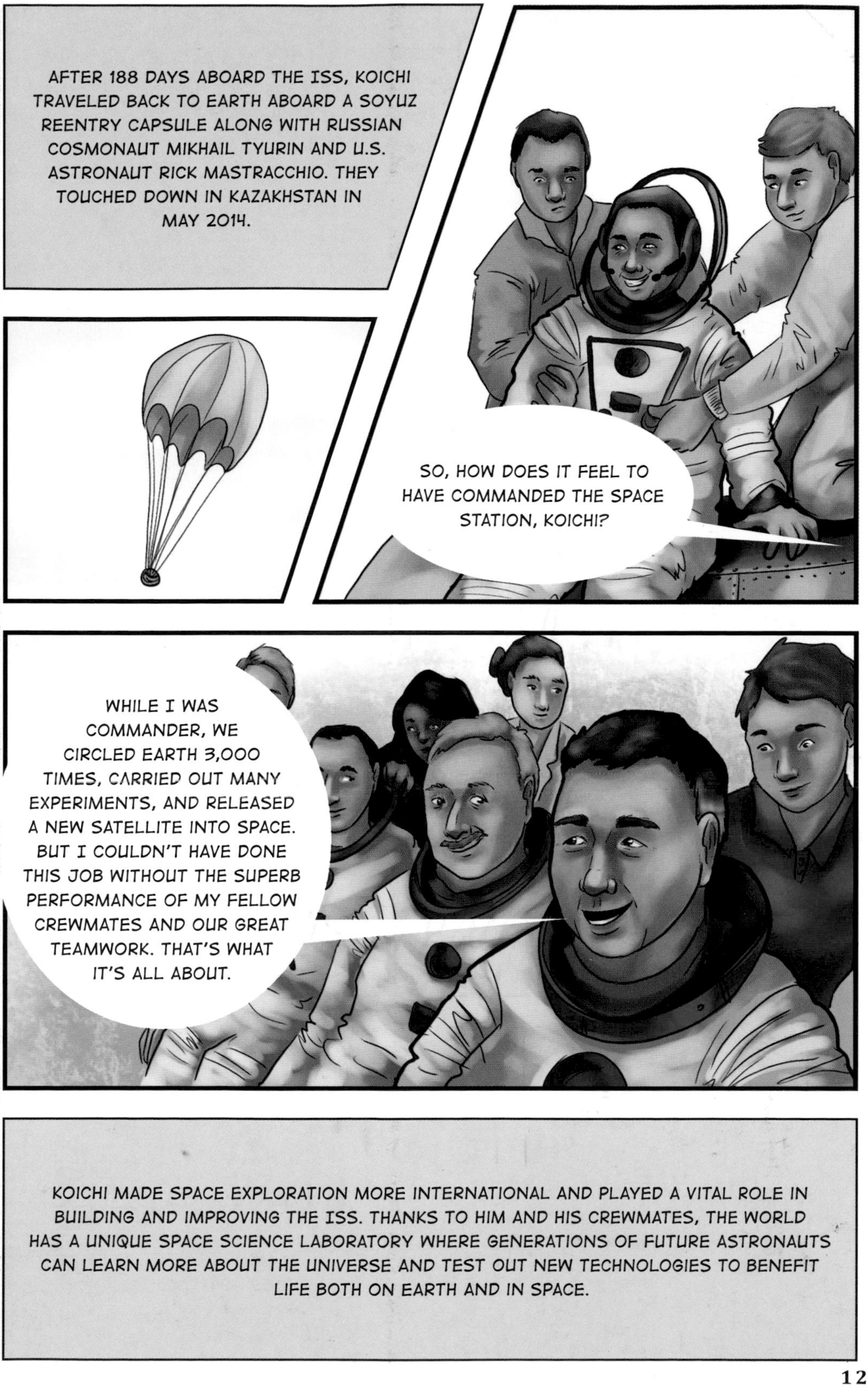
AFTER 188 DAYS ABOARD THE ISS, KOICHI TRAVELED BACK TO EARTH ABOARD A SOYUZ REENTRY CAPSULE ALONG WITH RUSSIAN COSMONAUT MIKHAIL TYURIN AND U.S. ASTRONAUT RICK MASTRACCHIO. THEY TOUCHED DOWN IN KAZAKHSTAN IN MAY 2014.
SO, HOW DOES IT FEEL TO HAVE COMMANDED THE SPACE STATION, KOICHI?
WHILE I WAS COMMANDER, WE CIRCLED EARTH 3,000 TIMES, CARRIED OUT MANY EXPERIMENTS, AND RELEASED A NEW SATELLITE INTO SPACE. BUT I COULDN'T HAVE DONE THIS JOB WITHOUT THE SUPERB PERFORMANCE OF MY FELLOW CREWMATES AND OUR GREAT TEAMWORK. THAT'S WHAT IT'S ALL ABOUT.
KOICHI MADE SPACE EXPLORATION MORE INTERNATIONAL AND PLAYED A VITAL ROLE IN BUILDING AND IMPROVING THE ISS. THANKS TO HIM AND HIS CREWMATES, THE WORLD HAS A UNIQUE SPACE SCIENCE LABORATORY WHERE GENERATIONS OF FUTURE ASTRONAUTS CAN LEARN MORE ABOUT THE UNIVERSE AND TEST OUT NEW TECHNOLOGIES TO BENEFIT LIFE BOTH ON EARTH AND IN SPACE.

INDEX